NOTES
ON
ARYAN AND DRAVIDIAN PHILOLOGY

NOTES
ON
ARYAN AND DRAVIDIAN PHILOLOGY

BY

M. SESHAGIRI SASTRI, M.A.,
SUPERINTENDENT OF VERNACULAR STUDIES,
PRESIDENCY COLLEGE, MADRAS.

GYAN

Published by

GYAN

Gyan Publishing House
5, Ansari Road
Daryaganj, New Delhi-110002
Phone: 011-47034999, 9811692060
E-mail: books@gyanbooks.com

Distribution Network
gyanbooks.com
India, USA, Canada, UK, Australia, France

ISBN : 978-81-212-3831-1 (PB)
First Published, 1884

2nd Impression 2020

Printed at: Gyan Press, Delhi.

TO

THE HON. D. F. CARMICHAEL

IN

ACKNOWLEDGMENT OF THE INTEREST HE TOOK IN THE STUDY AND PROGRESS OF THE LANGUAGES AND LITERATURES OF THE COUNTRY AND IN TOKEN OF RESPECT AND ADMIRATION

THIS VOLUME IS DEDICATED

BY

THE AUTHOR

Madras, Sept. 1884.

PREFACE.

I STUDIED while young Mahrathi, Tamil, Telugu and Sanskrit for many years, and, after finishing my collegiate course of studies, learnt Kanarese, Malayalam, Hindustani, Bengali and Uriya. Having seen my taste for linguistic study, my teacher, Mr. E. Thompson, the late Principal of the Presidency College, recommended to me a comparative study of the languages, and I carried out the advice. This comparative method gave a fresh impetus to my study of languages and made the otherwise uninteresting and barren investigation of words and grammatical forms of languages very pleasant and fruitful. He recommended me also to learn Latin and Greek, and in my study of those languages he rendered me much assistance for which I have to thank him for ever. By means of this peculiar study I was able to discover many facts concerning the languages, I studied, which had remained in deep obscurity, to assign proper derivations to difficult words, and to explain grammatical formations by sound philological laws. I have thus gathered materials for an etymological dictionary of each of the languages I studied, and a comparative grammar of each family of those languages; and all these works are in preparation. Before publishing them I wished to communicate to the reading public the new laws and rules which I have discovered in the Aryan and Dravidian languages and be benefited by the criticism of competent scholars. With this view I have written a series of volumes which treat of the Aryan and Dravidian languages alternately and of which this is the first.

The method I have followed in treating of the subject is my own and is in keeping with the analytical scheme of my investigations.

Each word mentioned in a Group must be traced directly to the word from which it is derived, and ultimately connected with the principal word which heads the Group. But, in some cases, I have provisionally included words in one Group, and they may be referred to another with equal propriety.

The different Groups which are headed by different words may be blended into one on account of the alliance of the representative words which may be proved hereafter. In the same way one Group may be separated into more Groups owing to the errors I may have committed in putting some words in a particular Group.

In deriving words from a primitive source I have conceived forms which do not now exist, though they might have been in use formerly; but I have not marked them and have left the readers to know them and treat them as such. Those who cannot make the distinction may bear the fact in mind that such forms will not be mentioned in the Index which will appear at the end of this volume.

The results of my investigations may be imperfect, and, in some cases, erroneous, owing to the incomprehensiveness of my knowledge of the Aryan languages, which is confined to Sanskrit, Greek, Latin and Anglo-Saxon. But I have been emboldened to put them before the public by a conviction which I have myself derived and which was strengthened by the agreement of some of my learned friends in my views and theories notwithstanding their novelty.

With regard to the languages treated in this book, it is to be remarked that Sanskrit being the oldest of the Aryan languages occupies a prominent position and next come Greek and Latin and other languages. In Sanskrit too we must recognize a threefold division according to the three stages of the language. The first stage may be called primitive, the second, derivative, and the third, corruptive. The Vedic Sanskrit occupies the first stage and has passed the agglutinative character and assumed the inflexional. We have no record of the language in its agglutinative character. The second stage is occupied by the Classical Sanskrit in which there is a greater change than seen in the Vedic Sanskrit. The last stage is to be assigned to Prakrit which has undergone a greater modification than the previous two have done. But the present classification of Sanskrit into the three kinds is not coterminous with the above three stages, but arbitrarily created by Pāṇini and his predecessors who separated the Classical from the Vedic, and by Vararuci, Hemacandra and others who differentiated the Prakritic languages from the Classical Sanskrit. These three languages are therefore overlapping each other. But as no living language in the world can remain without undergoing any modification, the Vedic Sanskrit which was a living language at one time, began to pass from its primitive stage to the derivative and corruptive stages; for in the Vedas themselves we see traces of mutations and corruptions. The Classical Sanskrit also exhibits a great deal of those modifications and corruptions which constitute the peculiar feature of the Prakritic languages. Take, for instance, the three allied forms *gṛbhṇāmi*, *gṛhṇāmi*, *ghiṇṇāmi*, the first of which is primitive; the second, derivative, because of the change of *bh* into *h*; and the third, Prakritic on account of the corruption of the word *gṛbhṇāmi* by the insertion of *i* for the vowel (properly a consonant) *ṛ*, the doubling of *n* and the amalgamation of the aspirate *h* with the initial *g*. The first two occur in the Vedas and the last in the Classical Sanskrit. The form *ōpiṣe* which is a Prakritic corruption of *āvapasē* (*ā* prefix, *vap*, 'to sow') occurs in the Rig Veda. The words *vauçaṭ* and *vaṣaṭ* (for *vahśat*), and *vaṭ*, a contraction of *vaṣat*, all meaning 'may he carry,' are Prakritic in their forms. A right understanding of these three stages is necessary for scientific investigations. But in the Dravidian languages which have been the spoken languages of Southern India for nearly twenty-four centuries, no such distinctions have come into existence.

With regard to the Dravidian languages, which are generally considered as belonging to the Turanian family, I would observe that I am not acquainted with any of the languages of the so-called family. The word Turanian is a negative term and means at most that the languages to which it is applied are not Aryan. In spite of the prevailing opinion of Dravidian scholars, I have brought the Dravidian languages within the pale of the Aryan family, and have succeeded, to a great extent, in connecting their vocables with those of the Aryan languages and their vernacular daughters, and in explaining their grammatical structure by reference to those of the latter languages, and hope that those scholars whose opinion differs from mine will begin to agree with me when they read my etymological dictionaries and comparative grammars. The Dravidian languages cannot, however, entirely be traced to the Classical Sanskrit to which they are related rather as younger sisters, but to the Vedic Sanskrit only; and in their philological importance they are greater than Latin, Persian and many other languages. As regards the religion, archæology, philosophy and history of Southern India, they are as important as Sanskrit itself and perhaps more. They are older than any classical language except Sanskrit, Latin, Greek and Hebrew, and to them we must look for a thorough knowledge of the intercourse which the Western nations had with the Hindus in Southern India and the mutual influence thus exerted. The subject is treated at full length in the Second Volume which is also in the Press.

In writing these volumes, the principal resources are derived from my own original investigations. I have published in the beginning of this volume a list of the names of authors to whom I am variously indebted for the valuable information received from their works. Foremost of them are Professors Bopp, MaxMüller and Whitney, the study of whose works suggested to me the method of my investigations and whom I regard as my teachers.

I have to thank Dr. Oppert, Professor of Sanskrit in the Presidency College and my collaborateur in the field of Philology, for his sympathy with, and his interest in, my linguistic researches.

In conclusion, I have to thank Dr. Duncan, the Principal of the Presidency College, for the special access he allowed me to the books of the College Library.

M. SESHAGIRI SASTRI.

MADRAS, *Sept. 1884.*

SCHEME OF TRANSLITERATION.

अ	*a*	ङ	*ṅ*	ब	*b*
आ	*ā*	च	*c*	भ	*bh*
इ	*i*	ౘ	*c̄*	म	*m*
ई	*ī*	छ	*ch*	य	*y*
उ	*u*	ज	*j*	र	*r*
ऊ	*ū*	ౙ	*j̄*	ल	*l*
ऋ	*ṛ*	झ	*jh*	व	*v*
ॠ	*ṝ*	ञ	*ñ*	श	*ś*
ऌ	*ḷ*	ट	*ṭ*	ष	*ṣ*
ॡ	*ḹ*	ठ	*ṭh*	स	*s*
ఎ എ	*e*	ड	*ḍ*	ह	*h*
ए	*ē*	ढ	*ḍh*	ळ	*ḷ*
ऐ	*ai*	ण	*ṇ*	ழ ഴ	*ḻ*
ఒ ഒ	*o*	त	*t*	ன	*ṉ*
ओ	*ō*	थ	*th*	ற റ	*ṟ*
औ	*au*	द	*d*	ః	*h*[1]
क	*k*	ध	*dh*	ఁ	*c*[2]
ख	*kh*	न	*n*	ం	*ṁ*
ग	*g*	प	*p*	ஃ	*h*[3]
घ	*gh*	फ	*ph*		

[1] *Visarga*. [2] *Ardhānusvāra*. [3] *Āydam* (Tamil).

LIST OF BOOKS
CONSULTED AND REFERRED TO IN THIS VOLUME.

1. Adams' Roman Antiquities.
2. Æschylus's Agamemnon.
3. Aufrecht's Uṇādisūtra with the Commentary of Ujjvaladatta.
4. Ākhyātacandrikā.
5. Āśvalāyanagṛhyasūtra and Gargyanārāyaṇa's Vṛtti.
6. Beames's Comparative Grammar of the Modern Aryan Languages of India.
7. Benfey's Sanskrit Grammar.
8. Bohtlingk and Roth's Sanskrit-English Dictionary.
9. Bopp's Comparative Grammar.
10. Bopp's Glossarium Sanskritum.
11. Bresslau's Hebrew-English Dictionary.
12. Burnell's Palæography.
13. Buttmann's Greek Grammar.
14. Catafago's Arabic-English Dictionary.
15. Cowell's Prākṛtaprakāśa.
16. Cox's Aryan Mythology.
17. Cox's Introduction to Mythology and Folklore.
18. Crusius's Homeric Lexicon.
19. Dvirūpakōśa.
20. Eadie's Biblical Cyclopædia.
21. Fallon's New Hindustani-English Dictionary.
22. Forbes's Bāgh-o-Bahar.
23. Forbes' Hindustani Grammar.
24. Forbes' Hindustani-English Dictionary.
25. Freund's Latin Dictionary.
26. Gesinius's Hebrew Lexicon.
27. Gladstone's Homeric Synchronism.
28. Gladstone's Homeric Primer.
29. Gladstone's Juventus Mundi.
30. Goldziher's Mythology among the Hebrews.
31. Græcæ Grammaticæ Rudimenta.

32. Haug's Essays on the Parsis.
33. Hesiod.
34. Hoernle's Grammar of the Gaudian Languages.
35. Homer's Iliad.
36. Homer's Odyssey.
37. Lee's Grammar of the Hebrew Language.
38. Liddell and Scott's Greek-English Lexicon.
39. L. N. R.'s "The Book and Its Story."
40. Matthiæ's Greek Grammar.
41. Max Müller's "Chips from a German Workshop."
42. Max Müller's Rig Veda Saṁhitā with Commentary.
43. Max Müller's Essays on the Science of Language.
44. Mēdinīkōśa.
45. Monier Williams's Sanskrit-English Dictionary.
46. Muir's Original Sanskrit Texts.
47. Oppert's "Ancient Commerce of India."
48. Oppert's Classification of Languages.
49. Oppert's Śukranītisāra.
50. Palmer's Persian-English Dictionary.
51. Ṛkprātiśākhya.
52. Roth's Yāska Nirukta.
53. Sayce's Principles of Comparative Philology.
54. Schleicher's Compendium of Comparative Grammar of Sanskrit, Greek and Latin.
55. Schmitz's Latin Grammar.
56. Smith's Dictionary of Greek and Roman Biography and Mythology.
57. Smith's Greek and Roman Antiquities.
58. Smith's Latin-English Dictionary.
59. Sophocle's Œdipus.
60. Taittirīyaprātiśākhya.
61. Whitney's Sanskrit Grammar.
62. Whitney's Study of Languages.
63. Zumpt's Latin Grammar.

And other works.

☞ A separate list of the books on Dravidian Languages consulted and referred to will be given in Volume II.

LIST OF ABBREVIATIONS.

Abl..........Ablative case.
Accus......Accusative case.
Ang.-Sax...Anglo-Saxon.
Arab.......Arabic.
Comp......Comparative degree.
Dan.........Danish.
Dat..........Dative case.
Egypt......Egyptian.
Eng..........English.
Fem.........Feminine gender.
Gaud........Gaudian languages.
Gen.........Genitive case.
Ger..........German.
Gr............Greek.
Heb.........Hebrew.
Hind.......Hindi and Hindustani.
Hom. Syn.Homeric Synchronism.
Icel.........Icelandic.
Inter........Interrogative.
Juv. Mund.Juventus Mundi.

Kan..........Kanarese.
Lat..........Latin.
Loc.........Locative case.
Mal..........Malayalam
Mas.........Masculine gender.
M. E........Middle English.
Neut........Neuter gender.
Nom.........Nominative case.
Pers.........Persian.
Plur.........Plural number.
Rel...........Relative.
Sans.........Sanskrit.
Sing.........Singular number.
Śukra.......Śukranītisāra.
Sup.........Superlative degree.
Tam.........Tamil.
Tait. Sam..Taittirīya Saṁhitā.
Tel..........Telugu.
Teut........Teutonic.
=............'equals,' or 'is equal to.'

COMPARATIVE TABLE

LANGUAGES.	VOW-						
	a	*ā*	*i*	*ī*	*u*	*ū*	*ṛ*
SANSKRIT ...	अ	आ	इ	ई	उ	ऊ	ऋ
GREEK ...	α	ᾱ ω	ι	η	υ	ῡ	—
TAMIL ...	அ	ஆ	இ	ஈ	உ	ஊ	[illegible]
TELUGU ...	అ	ఆ	ఇ	ఈ	ఉ	ఊ	ఋ
KANARESE ...	ಅ	ಆ	ಇ	ಈ	ಉ	ಊ	ಋ
MALAYALAM ...	അ	ആ	ഇ	ഈ	ഉ	ഊ	ഋ
HEBREW ...	אַ אֲ אֶ	אָ	י אִ	י אִי	ו אֻ	ו אוּ	—
ARABIC ...	ا	آ	يِ إِ	يِ إِي	و أُ	وُ أُو	—

OF ALPHABETS—I.

ELS.

ṝ	ḷ	ḹ	e	ē	ai	o	ō	au
ॠ	ऌ	ॡ	—	ए	ऐ	—	ओ	औ
—	—	—	ε	ει	αι ει &c.	ο	ω	αυ ου &c.
ஜூ	ள	ளூ	எ	ஏ	ஐ	ஒ	ஓ	ஔ
ౠ	ఌ	ౡ	ఎ	ఏ	ఐ	ఒ	ఓ	ఔ
ೠ	ಌ	ೡ	ಎ	ಏ	ಐ	ಒ	ಓ	ಔ
ൠ	ഌ	ൡ	എ	ഏ	ഐ	ഒ	ഓ	ഔ
—	—	—	אֶ אֱ אֵ	אֵ	אֵי	אֹ	אוֹ	אָו
—	—	—	ي اِ	ي اِ	ىَ اَ	و اُ	و اُ	وَ اَ

COMPARATIVE TABLE

LANGUAGES.	CONSO-				
	k	*kh*	*g*	*gh*	*ṅ*
SANSKRIT ...	क	ख	ग	घ	ङ
GREEK ...	κ	χ	γ	—	γ*
TAMIL ...	க	𑌖	𑌗	𑌘	ங
TELUGU ...	క	ఖ	గ	ఘ	ఙ
KANARESE ...	ಕ	ಖ	ಗ	ಘ	ಙ
MALAYALAM ...	ക	ഖ	ഗ	ഘ	ങ
HEBREW ...	ךּ כּ ק	כ ח	גּ	ג	נ ן
ARABIC & PERSIAN.	ک ق	کھ خ	گ	گھ	ن

* *g* is used before three other letters of the guttural group to represent *ṅ*.

OF ALPHABETS—II.

NANTS.

c	*c̄*	*ch*	*j*	*j̄* or *z*	*jh*	*ñ*
च	—	छ	ज	—	झ	ञ
—	—	—	—	—	—	—
ச	—	ഛ	ஜ	—	ഝ	ஞ
చ	చ఼ †	ఛ	జ	జ఼ †	ఝ	ఞ
ಚ	—	ಛ	ಜ	—	ಝ	ಞ
ച	—	ഛ	ജ	—	ഝ	ഞ
—	—	—	—	—	—	—
چ	—	چه	ج	—	جه	[illegible]

† A dental sound as *c* and *j* in Mahrathi.

COMPARATIVE TABLE

LANGUAGES.	CONSONANTS.				
	ṭ	*ṭh*	*ḍ*	*ḍh*	*ṇ*
SANSKRIT ...	ट	ठ	ड	ढ	ण
GREEK ...	—	—	—	—	—
TAMIL ...	ட	ഠ	ഡ	ഢ	ண
TELUGU ...	ట	ఠ	డ	ఢ	ణ
KANARESE ...	ಟ	ಠ	ಡ	ಢ	ಣ
MALAYALAM ...	ട	ഠ	ഡ	ഢ	ണ
HEBREW ...	—	—	—	—	—
ARABIC AND PERSIAN ...	ٹ	ٹھ	ڈ ڑ	ڈھ	ن

OF ALPHABETS—III.

--(*Continued.*)

	t	*th*	*d*	*dh*	*n*	*p*	*ph*	*b*	*bh*	*m*
	त	थ	द	ध	न	प	फ	ब	भ	म
	τ	Θ θ	Δ δ	—	N ν	Π π	Φ φ	B β	—	M μ
	த	𑌥	𑌦	𑌧	ந	ப	𑌫	𑌬	𑌭	ம
	త	థ	ద	ధ	న	ప	ఫ	బ	భ	మ
	ತ	ಥ	ದ	ಧ	ನ	ಪ	ಫ	ಬ	ಭ	ಮ
	ത	ഥ	ദ	ധ	ന	പ	ഫ	ബ	ഭ	മ
	ת ט	ת	ד	ד	נ ן	פּ	פ	בּ	ב*	מ
	ت ط	تھ	د	دھ	ن	پ	پھ	ب	بھ	م

* Sounded like *v*.

COMPARATIVE TABLE

LANGUAGES.	CONSONANTS.							
	y	*r*	*l*	*v*	*ś*	*ṣ*	*s*	*h*
SANSKRIT ...	य	र	ल	व	श	ष	स	ह
GREEK ...	ι	Ρ ρ	Λ λ	Υ υ	—	—	Σ σ ς	‘*
TAMIL ...	ய	ர	ல	வ	ஶ	ஷ	ஸ	ஹ ஃ
TELUGU ...	య	ర	ల	వ	శ	ష	స	హ
KANARESE ...	ಯ	ರ	ಲ	ವ	ಶ	ಷ	ಸ	ಹ
MALAYALAM ...	യ	ര	ല	വ	ശ	ഷ	സ	ഹ
HEBREW ...	י	ר	ל	ו	—	שׁ	ס שׂ	ה ח
ARABIC & PER.	ي	ر	ل	و	—	ش	ث س ص	ه ح

* An inverted comma, originally ϵ, is inserted over initial vowels and *r* to

OF ALPHABETS—IV.

—(*Concluded.*)

ḷ	*ḻ*	*ṟ*	*ṉ*	*z*	*ps*	*ks*	*ẓ*	*a·*	*gh*	*f*	*zh*
ळ	—	—	—	—	—	क्ष	—	—	—	—	—
—	—	—	—	Z ζ	Ψ ψ	Ξ ξ	—	—	—	—	—
ள	ழ	ற	ன	—	—	க்ஷ	—	—	—	—	—
ళ	—	ఱ	—	—	—	క్ష	—	—	—	—	—
ಳ	ೞ	ಱ	—	—	—	ಕ್ಷ	—	—	—	—	—
ള	ഴ	റ	—	—	—	ക്ഷ	—	—	—	—	—
—	—	—	—	ז	—	—	—	ע†	—	—	—
—	—	—	—	ز ذ ظ	—	—	ض‡	ع†	غ	ف	ژ

represent *h*. † The silent *a*. ‡ Sounded as *d* in Arabic and as *z* in Urdu.

SCHEME OF VEDIC ACCENTS.

Udātta, and *Pracaya*, i.e., *Anudātta* following *Svarita*.	...not marked.
Anudātta preceding the *Udātta* and *Svarita*.	...marked as —
Svarita	,, |

There are three *Svaras* or accents in the Vedas; the *Udātta*, 'acute,' the *Anudātta*, 'grave,' and the *Svarita*, 'toned.' When more than one *Anudātta* precede an *Udātta*, all but the last are often sounded lower. The *Anudāttas* following a *Svarita* are sounded like *Udātta* generally and also called *Pracayas*. If we compare the above accents with the seven tones of a musical gamut, we can know the exact sounds of those accents. Let the *Udātta* be represented by any key on the piano and be marked as *C*, and स *sa* according to the Hindu method; then the two sounds of the *Anudātta* will be marked as *B* and नि *ni*, and *G* and प *pa* respectively. The *Svarita* will be sounded as *C* sharp and रि *ri*.[1] The *Pracaya svara*, as it is pronounced by the Brahmins of the *Taittirīya śākhā* and also by the Rig Vedis, is identical with the *Udātta* and therefore is equal to *C* and स *sa*. A long *Svarita* in the Rig Veda is split into two long sounds, the first of which is *Udātta* and the second *Svarita*.

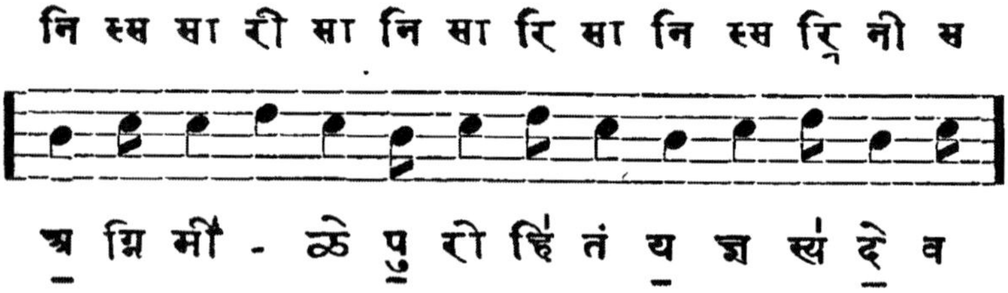

[1] It is called *śuddha ṛṣabha* by the Hindus.

नि स्स सा री सा सा री सा स न्नि सा रि सा

ऋ त्वि जं - हो तां - रं र त्न धा तं मं

Rig Veda, I. 1. 1.

दा प नि स्सा नी स सा री नी

चो द यि त्री सू नृ तां - नां

सा सा री सा स स नी सा

चे तं - ती सु म ती नाम्

Ibid, I. 3. 4.

CONTENTS.

[☞ Matters contained in the Foot-notes are inserted in brackets.]

INTRODUCTION.

A*

ANALYSIS OF THE ARYAN LANGUAGES.

SECTIONS. PAGES.

List I.—*Ātman Group.*

SECTIONS. PAGES.

SECTIONS. PAGES.

SECTIONS. PAGES.

SECTIONS. PAGES.

SECTIONS. PAGES.

INTRODUCTION.

I. Grammar and Etymology originated first among the Hindus and, having been incorporated with their sacred literature, were held in high esteem. Nearly four thousand years ago, when almost all the other nations of the earth were leading a savage life without any civilization, and without any learning, the Hindus had a sacred literature named Veda and some sciences which arose out of and for the study of the Veda, and among them were Grammar and Etymology. The Hindus learnt the Vedas by heart, closely attending to every word and every syllable, which they pronounced according to rules and with proper accents. They investigated the etymology of every word they found in the Vedas and enquired into its meanings. From such a study originated the Niruktas and the Prātiśākhyas in which are embodied the most complete classification of sounds according to the organs of pronunciation, the rules of the combination of vowels and consonants, and discussions on various parts of speech, and the like. Even in the Vedas themselves we can see the attempts of early etymologists to derive words; and their views and theories are, in some respects, better than those held by modern philologists. The Prātiśākhyas were followed by more systematic works on the subject called Vyākarana.

II. There are several works on the subject founded on different systems, of which the most important was that of Pāṇini which brought into desuetude all the other systems. It was written about twenty-six centuries ago and ever since has occupied the highest place in the grammatical literatures of the world. Making every allowance for its errors and imperfections and for the symbols and signs arbitrarily introduced on account of the system adopted, we can say that it is the most scientific grammar, analysing the grammatical forms on sound principles, and classifying the processes. These classifications and analyses are generally so correct that even modern philologists take them as fundamental principles in their scientific investigations. I may therefore rightly call Pāṇini the first philologist. But his system was not perfect and there were errors, and these could not be detected by persons who knew only Sanskrit and could not compare it with the kindred languages; for they felt the same contempt as the Greeks for the languages of other nations whom they called Mlēcchās (those that speak an unrefined tongue), as the Greeks called them *βαρβαροι*. These errors and defects have been discovered by the modern philologist in whose hands the science of grammar and etymology has assumed a new form and a new character. Instead of studying one language, deriving its words and grammatical forms independently and laying down arbitrary rules, he compares every word of a language with the corresponding ones in the other languages of the same family and discovers the general laws of letters and words, on which he founds his new science of language.

III. This young science is now rapidly growing and trying to attain to maturity and perfection. There are, however, persons who question the scientific character of philology and maintain that nothing is certain about it. They assert also that there are only a very few letters in each language, of which the vowels are nothing and that any consonant may become any other consonant. In fact, such is the taunt which the incipient science received at the hands of one of the greatest satirists of the world, Voltaire.[1] Satirical as it is, it is truth and nothing but truth, and in fact the crystallization of the whole truth of the science of philology. Charges of this kind may be brought against any science viewed in the light of an ignorant man for whom everything in the world is an independent element. If union is the principle of science, variety is the principle of ignorance.

Amidst the apparent confusion in the growth and development of a language there is a cosmos and harmony. The growth of a language takes place according to some order and this order is the foundation of the science of philology. There is a humorous anecdote of a Tamil man learning Telugu on the principle of analogy. He began his study with the Telugu word for a horse, viz. గుఱ్ఱము *gur̤r̤amu.* No sooner did he hear the word, than he was reminded of the Tamil word குதிரை *kudirai;* and he began to apply the analogy to every other word resembling குதிரை *kudirai;* and first of them was ஆனை *āṉai,* meaning 'elephant.' Like குதிரை *kudirai* the word ஆனை *āṉai* ends in the vowel *ai.* He began his conjecture thus. If the Telugu name for குதிரை *kudirai* (horse) be గుఱ్ఱము *gur̤r̤amu* (properly కుఱ్ఱము *kur̤r̤amu*), the name of ஆனை *āṉai* must be అఱ్ఱము *ar̤r̤amu.* Though this conclusion, based on the principle of analogy, is wrong in this particular case, yet it is the principle on which languages have been formed, and a person that is not capable of taking cognizance of this principle in the languages he studies, can never become a philologist. Let us see how this principle can be applied rightly. If the Tam. வரு *varu,* 'to come,' becomes వచ్చు *vaccu* in Telugu, Tam. தரு *taru,* 'to give,' must become తెచ్చు *teccu*[2] and பெறு *per̤u,* 'to

[1] Vide MaxMüller's '*Lectures on the Science of Language.*'

[2] By the same analogy போதரு *pōdaru* becomes పుత్తెచ్చు *puttеccu* and

get,' పుచ్చు *puccu*. If the Tam. கொனை *koṉai*, 'top,' assumes the form కొంగు *koṅgu* = కొనగు *konagu* = కొనై *kɔnai* + అగు *agu*, then வளை *vaḷai*, that is வணை *vaṇai*, must becc.ne వంగు *vaṅgu* = వణగు *vaṇagu* = వణై *vaṇai* + అగు *agv*. In Sanskrit the word वृष *vṛṣa* means 'a beast' and 'virtue.' If वृष *vṛṣa* meaning 'animal' is modified as ऋक्ष *ṛkṣa*, 'bear,' (properly, ऋष *ṛṣa*), by the elision of the initial व *v*, and then as *ursus* in Latin and *αρκτος* (properly *αρσος*) in Greek, and then this *ursus* is softened into अच्छ *accha*, 'bear,' in Sanskrit, is it not natural to expect that there should be the same or similar changes undergone by the word in the other meaning (viz. 'virtüe')? and our expectation is realized in the forms Sans. ऋत *ṛta*, 'right,' Gr. *αρτι*, 'just,' Lat. *ordo*, 'a straight row,' and Sans. अच्छ *accha*, 'good,' thus ऋक्ष *ṛkṣa* corresponding to ऋत *ṛta*, *αρκτος* and *ursus*, to *αρτι* and *ordo*, and अच्छ *accha*, to अच्छ *accha*. Vide *Vṛṣa* Group.

In Sanskrit, वृष *vṛṣa* means 'an animal,' 'bull,' 'r.t,' 'eminent,' and so on; of these meanings the most original is 'an animal'; and the word is modified as वृषभ *vṛṣabha* by taking the suffix व *va*, which is changed into भ *bha*. Now, वृषभ *vṛṣabha* is transformed into वर्षभ *varṣabha* by the guṇation of the vowel ऋ *ṛ*, गर्षभ *garṣabha* by the change of व *v* into ग *g* and गर्दभ *gardabha* by the change

---

ஏகுதரு *ēgutaru* ఏతెచ్చు *ētec̄cu*. But the words are modified as పుత్తెంచు *puttenc̄u* and ఏతెంచు *ētenc̄u* by the insertion of a nasal sound for the first *c*, and the Telugu Pandits derive them from పోవుతెంచు *pōvutenc̄u*, 'to cut off going,' ఏగుతెంచు *ēgutenc̄u*, as if the latter parts were తెంచు *te..c̄u*, 'to cut.'

of स *s* into द् *d*. Analogy leads us to expect a similar transformation of ऋषभ *ṛṣabha*. We see accordingly that ऋषभ *ṛṣabha* is, in its turn, metamorphosed into अर्सभ *arsabha* by the guṇation of the initial vowel ऋ *ṛ* and रास भ *rāsabha* by the transposition of the र् *r* to the beginning of the word.

Again take the form पृश् *pṛś*, which means 'back' or 'side,' and forms the radical part of पृष्ठ *pṛṣṭha*, 'back,' पार्श्व *pārśva*, 'side,' Lat. *prope*, 'near,' पर्शु *parśu*, 'rib,' पुच्छ *puccha*, 'tail,' मुष्टि *muṣṭi*, 'elbow,' पृत् *pṛt*, 'battle,' originally 'side,' पृतना *pṛtanā*, 'army,' originally 'side,' पर्द् *pard*, 'to fart,' Gr. *μετα*, Dor. *πεδα*, 'by side,' 'in the midst,' *παλιν*, 'back,' *πυγη*, 'tail,' *περδομαι*, *βδεω*, 'to fart,' Lat. *merda*, 'dung,' वर्चस् *varcas*, पुरिष *puriṣa* and पुरीष *purīṣa*, 'dung,' &c., is at last modified as विश् *viś*, Lat. *fæx*, 'grounds,' 'sediments,' and is further modified as विष्ठा *viṣṭhā* = विस् *vis* + आ *ā* = विस्सा *vissā* = विस्ता *vistā* = विष्ठा *viṣṭhā*. Compare Lat. *crista* = Gr. *κρας* + *a*, and the Gr. *ιστος*, Sans. इष्ठ *iṣṭa*, suffixes of the superlative degree of adjectives, = ईयस् *īyas* + अ *a*, ईयस् *īyas* being the suffix of the comparative degree (p. 111). In these words there is a series of meanings all originating from the radical one of 'side,' the transition being from 'side' to 'back,' to the fist (or elbow), to tail and at last to animal excrescence. If पृश् *pṛś* assumes the forms of पृष्ठ *pṛṣṭha*, &c., we may expect similar changes from the similar word वृष *vṛṣa*, meaning 'an animal.' The word accordingly has the following forms: बस्त *basta*, 'a goat,' बष्कयणी *baṣkayaṇī*, 'a cow that has yeaned long ago,' वशा *vaśa*, 'a cow,' पशु *paśu*, 'cattle,' मर्त्य *martya*, 'man,' वृष्णि *vṛṣṇi*, 'a goat,' गृष्टि *gṛṣṭi*, 'a cow that has yeaned once' for वृष्टि *vṛṣṭi*, मूष *mūṣa*, 'rat,' मार्जार *mārjāra*, 'cat,' पुरुष *puruṣa* and पूरुष *pūruṣa*, 'man,' वधू *vadhū*, 'woman,' विश् *viś*, 'man,' वेश *vēśa*, वेश्या *vēśyā*, 'whore,' विट *viṭa*, 'adulterer.' See the following table:—

Sans. पृश् *pṛś*	— Sans. वृष *vṛṣa*
,, पृष्ट *pṛṣṭa* ,, पर्शु *parśu* ,, पार्श्व *pārśva* Lat. *prope*	— ,, गृष्टि *gṛṣṭi* properly वृष्टि *vṛṣṭi*.
Sans. पर्द *parda* Gr. περδομαι, βδεω.	— ,, मर्त *marta*
Sans. पुच्छ *puccha* Gr. πυγη.	— ,, पुंस् *puṁs* developed into पुमांस् *pumāṁs*.
Sans. मध्य *madhya* Gr. πετα & μετα.	— ,, वधू *vadhū*
Sans. पार्ष्णि *pārṣṇi* Lat. *perna*, 'ham.'	— ,, वृष्णि *vṛṣṇi*
Sans. पाश *pāśa*	— ,, पशु *paśu* Lat. *pecus*, Sans. वशा *vaśā*
,, मुष्टि *muṣṭi*	— Sans. मूष *mūṣa* ,, मेष *mēṣa*
,, वर्चस् *varcas*	— ,, मार्जार *mārjāra*.

Sans. पक्ष *pakṣa*	—	Lat. *vacca* Sans. बस्त *basta* „ बष्कयणी *baṣkayaṇī*.
„ पुरीष *purīṣa*	—	„ पुरुष *puruṣa* „ पूरुष *pūruṣa*
„ विश् *viś* „ विष्ठा *viṣṭhā*	—	„ विश् *viś* „ वेश *vēśa* „ वेश्या *vēśyā* „ विट *viṭa*

Again the word आत्मन् *ātman* is modified in Sanskrit as अश्मंतम् *aśmantam* and in Persian آسمان *āsmān*, and this modification leads us to expect a similar one in the allied languages; and we accordingly find in Greek *ασαμινθος* applied to a tub used for a hot bath (p. 141). In Greek and Latin the same word आत्मन् *ātman* is metamorphosed into *κ' μινον* and *cuminum*, and though at first I did not know, yet by a continued search I succeeded in discovering the corresponding form in अजमोदा *ajamōdā* which is however not applied to cummin seeds but to bishop's weed (p. 142). If in Greek there exists a reduplicated form of *κανθος* as *ὑακινθος*, we hope to see a similar form in Sanskrit of the corresponding Sans. शोण *śōṇa;* and I have shown that the word कोकनद *kōkanada* is the required form, notwithstanding the apparent difference in the forms of these words (p. 150). In Kanarese the future participial adjective ends in *a* as well as the present and past participial adjectives; as, ಗೆಯ್ಯುವ *geyyuva*, 'who will do.' This form is the most original and is variously modified as in Tam. செய்யும் *śeyyum*. Analogy leads us to expect a form செய்யுவ *śeyyuva* which, however, does not exist. But the root கட *kaḍa*, 'to pass,' gives the required form as கடவ *kaḍava*, which answers to Kan. ಕಳಿವ *kaḷiva* which is a contraction of ಕಳಿಯುವ *kaḷiyuva*. The Tam. கடவ *kaḍava* must therefore be a contraction of கடக்குவ *kaḍakkuva*, originally கடயுவ *kaḍayuva* answering to Kan. ಕಳಿಯುವ *kaḷiyuva*. I can add a multitude of more instances, but what I have given is quite sufficient to prove the importance of the principle of analogy.

IV. The method of my study and observation is purely analytical and experimental, and though in possession of the rules and theories already given by ancient grammarians and lexicographers, I did not apply them in any case till I arrived at them by the very instances which I gathered during the course of my study. Care was taken to find corresponding words and grammatical forms in the allied languages and to institute close comparisons among them. I have thus been able to discover new laws of orthographical growth, decay and mutation, and by their means explain the etymologies of difficult words and the formations of complicated grammatical forms, of which some instances will be given lower down in this Introduction.

V. I have written a series of volumes under the designation of NOTES ON ARYAN AND DRAVIDIAN PHILOLOGY of which this is the first. It is entirely devoted to the description and illustration of the method of investigation which I have pursued. As the method consists in the analysis of the languages which are investigated, I have analysed the Sanskrit, Greek, and Latin languages into groups of allied words, and these groups are treated one after another. In conformity to the experimental and analytical character of my investigation, the above outline is filled up with grammatical and etymological matters which are introduced for the illustration of orthographical or other processes in an order quite different from that in which they will be arranged in a synthetic grammar. Thus, for instance, the Latin perfect and pluperfect forms are explained under the heading of the Sanskrit word '*svādu*' in the First Group, which is changed into '*suavis*' in Latin by the change of *d* into *v;* and for the illustration of this process the above perfect and pluperfect forms are introduced (p. 78). But they will occur in a synthetic grammar in the chapter on Verbs and under the heading of Tenses. Again, the Greek perfect forms ending in κα as πεφυκα are introduced under the Sanskrit termination '*vas*' which I suppose to have been changed in Greek into κοτ by the insertion of *k* for *v;* and this process is illustrated by the above perfect forms in which I discovered the same change and also the allied change of य *y* into *ka.*

VI. Words are of three kinds; first, those which are indivisible; second, those which are divisible and contain two parts, such as a root and a prefix, a suffix, or both; third, those that are composed of the above parts and contain in addition to them some orthographical outgrowths which are the excrescences in the natural development and growth of words. This classification is very important, inasmuch as we are dealing with a critical analysis of the words of kindred languages. The linguistic chemist, so to speak, must try to analyze a word completely and be able to account for the smallest residuum in the decomposition; and, in this analytical method, he must arrive ultimately at the most simple elements—elements which do not admit of a further analysis, nor contain common parts. In the synthetical method he must start from the simplest roots and derive words by the most natural processes.

This method has not been properly followed and is violated not only by the ancient but also by modern grammarians and philologists. To illustrate this linguistic aberration, I give here below a few instances.

VII. Pāṇini tells us that the augment आनुक् *ānuk* (आन् *ān*) is to be added to some masculine nouns such as इंद्र *Indra*, वरुण *Varuṇa*, &c., to get the feminine forms इंद्राणी *Indrāṇī*, वरुणानी *Varuṇānī*, &c. But how is this particle derived? Is it an arbitrary and extraneous addition or a natural growth? The question can be easily solved, if we know the changes which स *s* undergoes in Sanskrit and other languages. The letter स *s* is changed into न *n* as in Pāḷi नस् *nas*, Sans. सस् *sas*, 'he'; एन *ēna*, एष *ēṣa*, 'this'; ज्ञातम् *gñātam* (prop. ज्ञातन् *gñātan*), Gr. γνωτον, in which ον comes from the masculine ος; Sans. अहन् *ahan*, अहस् *ahas*, 'day;' and so on. From these examples we can clearly see that the स *s* of इंद्रस् *Indras* may be the source of the न *n* of इंद्राणी *Indrāṇī*. We may therefore derive the feminine form इंद्राणी *Indrāṇī* from the masc. इंद्रस् *Indras* by the addition of the fem. suffix ई *ī*; thus,— इंद्रस् *Indras* + ई *ī* = इंद्रन् *Indran* + ई *ī* by the change of स *s* into न *n* and इंद्रान् *Indrān* + ई *ī* by the lengthening of the अ *a* preceding न *n*, and at last, इंद्राणी *Indrāṇī*. Similarly we may explain the feminine form Διωνη from Διος. While we connect Δεσποτης with दिवस्पति *divaspati*, 'lord of Heaven,' the feminine form Δεσποινα may be derived from दिवस्पत्नी *divaspatnī* which is shortened into

Δεσποτυνη and then modified as Δεποινα by the elision of τ, which is represented by *i* as in ειμι for εσμι, and the change of the final η into *a*. Following the same theory we can derive पत्नी *patnī* from पतिस् *patis* + ई *ī* = पतिन् *patin* + ई *ī* = पत्न् *patn* + ई *ī* by the elision of the इ *i* preceding न *n*.

VIII. If all such forms may be explained by assuming the change of स *s* into न *n*, why should we bring in the unnecessary augment आन् *ān* (आनुक् *ānuk*)? Even supposing that there is such an augment, we do not get a physical explanation of this augment. Nor does it account for the form पत्नी *patnī* which is formed exactly like इन्द्राणी *Indrāṇī*, except as regards the process of the elision of the final इ *i* of पति *pāti*; nor for असिक्नी *asiknī*, 'a young female servant,' and पलिक्नी *paliknī*, 'an old woman,' of which असिक्नी *asiknī* = असितस् *āsitas* + ई *ī* = असित्न् *asi'n* + ई *ī* = असित्नी *asitnī* by the elision of अ *a* preceding न *n*, असिक्नी *asiknī* by the change of त *t* into क *k*, असितस् *asitas* meaning 'black,' (*sc.* in hair), therefore 'young' and not 'old.' Similarly can be derived पलिक्नी *paliknī* from पलितस् *palitas*, 'grey,' that is, 'having grey hairs.'

IX. Again, according to Pāṇini आन *āna* (शानच् *śānac*) is to be added to an Ātmanēpadi root to form the present participle, and when the root takes अ *a*, य *y*, and अय *aya* before the verbal suffix ते *tē*, then *m* is inserted before आन *āna* after those augments. But I have compared these suffixes मान *māna* and आन *āna* with the corresponding Gr. μενος and Lat. *bundus*, and *andus*, *endus* and *undus*, and ultimately traced them to the Sanskrit suffix मन् *man*. (Vide p. 112.)

X. In the Tamil grammars, the Tolkāppiyam, the Nannūl and the like, a list of சாரியைகள் *śāriyaigaḷ*, augments, is given, which, on a minute investigation, I have dissolved into simpler elements. Thus the augment அன் *an* in வந்தனன் *vandanan*, 'he came,' is traceable to the demonstrative adjective அனை *anai*; for வந்தனன் *vandanan* is composed of வந்த *vanda* and அனன் *anan*, வந்த *vanda*, the past participial adjective of வா *vā*, 'to come,' and அனன் *anan*, a contraction of அனையன் *anaiyan* = அனை *anai* + அன் *an*, meaning 'a man of that sort,' which, like the pronoun அவன் *avan*, is used merely as a personal suffix in the above verb வந்தனன் *vandanan*. The so-called குச்சாரியை *kuccāriyai*, the augment கு *ku*, in நடக்க *naḍakka*, 'to walk,' and உரைக்க *uraikka*, 'to say,' springs from the உடம்படுமெய் *uḍambaḍumey v* and *y*, as the words are modifications of the original forms, நடவ *naḍava* and உரைய *uraiya*, which are to be distributed respectively as நட *naḍa* + அ *a*, and உரை *urai* + அ *a*, and in which *v* and *y* are used to fill up the hiatus, and are changed into க *k*, which process prevails in the Aryan languages also, especially in Greek in which I have been able to explain some perfect forms by the analogy of the above Tamil forms. (pp. 116-118).

XI. In Telugu, we have such words as మ్రాఁకు *mrāṅku* 'tree,' వలఁకు *valaṅku*, 'beauty,' కొలఁకు *kolaṅku*, 'tank,' in which the particle కు *ku* is inorganically inserted in the singular optionally and in the plural necessarily. In the plural the part *ku* is an organic element and with the following part *ulu* is traceable to the Tamil plural termination *kaḷ* which is itself a corruption of the masculine plural pronoun அவர் *avar* shortened into வர் *var* and used as a personal suffix; and this connexion is clearly seen by comparing those forms with the corresponding Tamil ones, as మ్రాఁకులు *mrāckulu*, மரங்கள் *maraṅgaḷ*, వలఁకులు *valackulu*, பொலங்கள் *polaṅgaḷ*, కొలఁకులు *kolackulu*, குளங்கள் *kuḷaṅgaḷ*. The identity of the plural forms మ్రాఁకులు *mrāc-kulu* and மரங்கள் *maraṅgaḷ* can be easily seen. The Telugu language does not generally allow consonants at the end of words, but modifies them by the addition of the vowels అ *a*, ఉ *u* and ఇ *i*. Thus, the Tam. மரங்கள் *maraṅgaḷ* becomes மரங்களு *maraṅgaḷu*, and the part மரம் *maram* being contracted into ம்ராம் *mrām*, மரங்களு *maraṅgaḷu* assumes the form of ம்ராங்கலு *mrāṅkalu*. Compare Tam. கடைக்கண் *kaḍaikkaṇ*, Tel. క్రేఁగన్ను *krēcgannu*, 'a side-look;' Tam. கீழ்த்தொடை *kīḻttoḍai*, Tel. క్రీఁదొడ *krīcdoḍa*, 'the lower thigh'; Tam. பழங்கெம்பு *paḻaṅkembu*, Tel. ప్రాఁగెంపు *prācgempu*, 'old ruby'; Tam. புதுச்சீரை *puduccīrai* (properly குதுச்சீரை *kuduccīrai*[1]), Tel. క్రొంజీర *kromjīra*, 'new cloth;' in which Tam. கடை *kaḍai*, கீழ் *kīḻ*, பழம் *paḻam*, and புது *pudu* are shortened in Telugu into క్రే *krē* (క్ళే *kḷē*), క్రీ *krī* (క్ళీ *kḷī*); ప్రాఁ *prān* (ప్ళాఁ *pḷān*), and క్రొ *kro* (క్డొ *kdo*).

XII. Here I have to refer to another law of the Telugu language, viz., the law of the assimilation of vowels, according to which, contiguous vowels are assimilated as in అడిగి *aḍigi*, 'having asked' = అడుగు *aḍugu* + ఇ *i* = అడుగ్

---

[1] In the North Indian Vernaculars '*kōrā*' means 'new,' as in *kōrāpān*, 'newness,' and కోడి *kōḍi* is used by washermen in the sense of 'new cloth.' These are traceable to Tel. క్రొత్త *kotta*, and Tam. புத்த *putta*, 'new.'

aḍug + ఇ *i*, then అడిగి *aḍigi* by the change of the vowel ఉ *u* of డు *ḍu* into ఇ *i*. We have thus మ్రాంకల్ *mrāṅkalu* becoming మ్రాంకులు *mrāṅkulu*, which is modified as మ్రాఁకులు *mrāckulu* by inserting the ardhānusvāra ఁ instead of the pūrṇānusvāra ం. Similarly can be derived the forms వలఁకులు *valackulu* and కొలఁకులు *kolackulu*. [Vide Vol. II.]

But the Telugu grammarians analyzed them wrongly, distributing them as మ్రాఁకు *mrācku* + ఉలు *ulu*, వలఁకు *valacku* + ఉలు *ulu*, and కొలఁకు *kolacku* + ఉలు *ulu*, in which they thought *ulu* was the plural suffix and the remaining parts మ్రాఁకు *mrācku*, వలఁకు *valacku*, and కొలఁకు *kolacku* were stems in singular, and thus were compelled to add the particle *ku* to the singular forms of those words. But as there were already separate singular forms as మ్రాను *mrānu*, వలను *valanu*, and కొలను *kolanu* modified from the corresponding Tam. மரன் *maraṉ*,[1] பொலன் *polaṉ*, and குளன் *kuḷan*, the above inorganic addition of *ku* to the singular became optional.

XIII. Again the technical term ఔపవిభక్తిక *aupavibhaktika* is invented to be applied to a class of so-called augments such as *i*, *ti* and *ṭi*, of which the first I hold to be a genitive singular suffix and the next two are composed of *t* and *i* and *ṭ* and *i*. The initial consonants of the latter two augments are modifications of the final *y*, *d*, *n*, *l*, *r*, and *ṟ* of nouns, owing to the addition of the suffixes *i*, *in* and the like. They sometimes spring from the final *n* of the casal suffixes ఇన్ *in* and అన్ *an*, which are changed into *iṭ* or *inṭ* and *aṭ*.

---

[1] The Tam. ன *ṉ* is to be treated as ந *n* for all scientific purposes.

Thus, అలిచేతన్ *ālicētan*, 'by the wife,' corresponds to ஆள்கையால் *āḷkaiyāl*, 'by the hand of person.' The *i* in అలి *āḷi* is a genitive suffix and occurs in దానిచేతన్ *dānicētan* (Tam. அதன்கையால் *adankaiyāl*, Kan. ಅದರಕೈಯಿಂದ *adarakaiyinda*), and corresponds to the *a* of ಅದರ *adara*.

చేతన్ *cētan* = చేయి *cēyi* + అన్ *an* = చేయ్ *cēy* + అన్ *an* = చేత్ *cēt* + అన్ *an*, in which య *y* is changed into త *t* as it is changed into స *s* in చేసి *cēsi* = చేయు *cēyu* + ఇ *i*. Compare Sans. एधिषीष्ट *ēdhiṣīṣṭa* for एधियीस्त *ēdhiyīsta*, and Gr. Θετιδος for Θετιγος.

కంటన్ *kaṇṭan* = కన్ను *kannu* + అన్ *an* = కన్న్ *kann* + అన్ *an* = కణ్ట్ *kaṇṭ* + అన్ *an*, by the change of the second న *n* into ట *ṭ* and the consequent change of the previous న *n* into ణ *ṇ*. Compare Sans. स्वांतम् *svāntam*, 'heart' = स्वन् *svan* + अम् *am* = स्वन्नम् *svannam*; Lat. *mentes*, 'mind' = *men* + *es* = *mennes*; Tel. ఉండు *uṇḍu* = Tam. இர் *ir* + உ *u* = இன் *in* + உ *u* = உன் *un* + உ *u* = உன்ன் *unn* + உ *u*, = ఉన్ను *unnu*; Tel. పుండు *puṇḍu*, 'sore' = Tam. புண் *puṇ* + உ *u* = పుణ్ణు *puṇṇu* (Kan. ಹುಣ್ಣು *huṇṇu*).

Similarly comes *ṭ* in వింటన్ *viṇṭan* = Tam. வில்லால் *villāl*,[1] 'by bow'; పంటన్ *paṇṭan* = Tam. பல்லால் *pallāl*, 'by teeth'; నుదుటన్ *nuduṭan*, Tam. நுதலால் *nudalāl*, 'by the forehead,' (Sans. निटिल *niṭila*); వెంటన్ *veṇṭan*, వెన్నన్ *vennan*, Tam. வெரிநால் *verināl*, வெந்நால் *vennāl*, பின்னால் *pinnāl*, 'by back.'

గోటన్ *gōṭan* = గోరు *gōru* + అన్ *an* = గోట్ *gōṭ* + అన్ *an*, Tam. உகிரால் *ukirāl*, 'by the nail'; similarly నీటన్ *nīṭan*,

[1] The stem வில் *vil* becomes విన్ *vin* before అన్ *an*, so that విల్లన్ *villan* = విన్నన్ *vinnan* and then వింటన్ *viṇṭan*. Similarly పంటన్ *paṇṭan*.

Tam. நீரால் *nīrāl*, 'by water'; నెత్తుటన్ *nettuṭan*, Tam. உதிரத்தால் *udirattāl*, 'by blood,' (Sans. रुधिर *rudhira.*)

In the above examples the final *y*, *n*, *l*, and *r* of the Telugu nominal stems are changed into *t* and *ṭ*.

పేరిటన్ *pēriṭan* = పేరు *pēru* + ఇన్ *in* + అన్ *an* (Tam. பேரினால் *pērināl*) = పేరు *pēru* + ఇట్ *iṭ* + అన్ *an*, by the change of *n* into *ṭ*.

రెండింటన్ *reṇḍiṇṭan* = రెండు *reṇḍu* + ఇన్ *in* + అన్ *an* (Tam. இரண்டினால் *iraṇḍināl*) = రెండు *reṇḍu* + ఇన్న్ *inn* + అన్ *an*, by the doubling of *n* = రెండు *reṇḍu* + ఇంట్ *iṇṭ* + అన్ *an*, by the change of the second *n* into *ṭ* and the consequent change of the first న *n* into ణ *ṇ*; also రెండిటన్ *reṇḍiṭan* by the elision of ణ *ṇ*.

సరసంపుటలుక *sarasampuṭaluka* (Tam. ஸரஸத்தின் *sarasattin* + அழுங்கல் *aḻuṅgal*), 'amatory anger;' సరసంపుటలుక *sarasampuṭaluka* = సరసమ్ *sarasam* (Tam. ஸரஸம் *sarasam*) + ఇన్ *in* (Tam. இன் *in*) + అలుక *aluka* (Tam. அழுங்கல் *aḻuṅgal*), in which ఇన్ *in* is the genitive suffix. Here I have to observe that the final *am* of the Telugu and Tamil word *sarasam* is a neuter singular suffix corresponding to the *am* of Sans. दानम् *dānam* and *ον* of Gr. δωρον, and *at* of तत् *tat*, 'that;' and, of these Aryan neuter singular suffixes *am*, *ον* and *at*, the Gr. *ον* is original, being directly traceable to the masculine singular suffix '*os*.' When the genitive singular suffix *in* is added, the Tamil word changes its final *am* into *an*, corresponding to the Gr. *ον*; and hardens the *n* into *t*, as is seen in Sans. तत् *tat*, so that ஸரஸம் *sarasam* + இன் *in* + அழுங்கல் *aḻuṅgal* = ஸரஸந் *sarasan* + இந் *in* + அழுங்கல் *aḻuṅgal* = ஸரஸந்ந் *saraann* + இன் *in* + அழுங்கல் *aḻuṅgal* = ஸரஸத்த் *sarasatt* + இன் *in* + அழுங்கல் *aḻuṅgal*, by the hardening of *nn*. But the Tel. సరసము *sarasam* follows a different yet allied modification. Thus సరసము *sarasam* + ఇన్ *in* + అలుక *aluka* = సరసమ్ము *sarasamm* + ఇన్ *in* + అలుక *aluka* by the doubling of the final *m* of సరసము *sarasam;* then = సరసమ్పు *sarasamp* + ఇట్ *iṭ* + అలుక *aluka*, by the change of the second *m* into *p* and of the *n* of ఇన్ *in* into ట *ṭ* = సరసమ్పు *sarasamp* + ఉట్ *uṭ* + అలుక *aluka*, by the change of ఇ *i* into ఉ *u* as in గురువునకు *guruvunaku* = గురువినకు *guruvinaku* (Kan. ಗುರುವಿಂಗೆ *guruviṅge*, Tam. குருவிற்கு *guruviṟku*) = గురు *guru* + ఇన్ *in* + అ *a* + కు *ku*.

Tel. మిఱితన్ *miṟitan*, 'by elevation' = మిఱ్ఱు *miṟṟu* + ఇన్ *in* + అన్ *an*, in which మిఱ్ఱు *miṟṟu*, properly మిట్టు *miṭṭu*, is a corruption of Tam. மேடு *mēḍu* by the change of *ṭṭ* into *ṟṟ* as in కఱ్ఱ *kaṟṟa*, Tam. கட்டை *kaṭṭai*, 'stick.' మిఱ్ఱు *miṟṟu* + ఇన్ *in* + అన్ *an* corresponds to Tam. மேடு *mēḍu* + இன் *iṉ* + ஆல் *āl* and = మిఱ్ఱు *miṟṟu* + ఇత్ *it* + అన్ *an* by the change of the *n* of ఇన్ *in* into *t* = మిఱు *miṟu* + ఇత్ *it* + అన్ *an*, by the elision of one of the two *ṟ*'s.

XIV. In the Kanarese Grammar, Śabdamaṇidarpaṇa, in the chapter on Verbs, it is said that the particles ಅನೆಗಂ *anegam* and ಎನೆಗಂ *enegam* are to be added to the participial adjectives to indicate time, as ಬರುವನೆಗಂ *baruvanegam*, ಬರುವಿನೆಗಂ *baruvinegam*, 'at that and this time when he, &c., will come'; ಬಂದನೆಗಂ *bandanegam*, ಬಂದಿನೆಗಂ *bandinegam*, 'at that and this time when he, &c., came.' But ಅನೆಗಂ *anegam* and ಇನೆಗಂ *inegam* are not particles but are nouns in the dative case. ಅನೆ *ane* and ಇನೆ *ine* are demonstrative adjectives, meaning 'that' and 'this' respectively, and correspond to the Tam. அனை *anai* and இனை *inai* from which I have derived the demonstrative adjectives அன்ன *anna*, 'of that sort' and 'that,' and இன்ன *inna*, 'of this sort' and 'this,' and their modified forms அந்த *anda* and இந்த *inda* in Modern Tamil. By adding the dative suffixes Tam. கு *ku*, and Kan. ಗೆ *ge*, and the particles Tam. உம் *um*, and Kan. ಅಂ *am*, we get அனைக்கும் *anaikkum* and ಅನೆಗಂ *anegam*, radically meaning 'to that,' that is 'to that time,' and இனைக்கும் *inaikkum*, ಇನೆಗಂ *inegam*, 'to this,' that is, 'to this time,' which latter is modified into ఇన్కమ్ *inkam*, ఇన్కన్ *inkan* and at last ఇంకన్ *iṅkan* and ఇక్కన్ *ickan* and means 'now' and hence 'hereafter.' By adding '*anaikkum*,' and '*anegam*' to Tam. வருவ *varuva*, and Kan. ಬರುವ *baruva*, we get வருவனைக்கும் *varuvanaikkum* and ಬರುವನೆಗಂ *baruvanegam*, meaning 'to or at the time when he, &c., will come.' The *v* of the suffix *uva* being changed into *t* as in ಅವನು *avanu*, ఆతను *ātanu*, 'he,' வருவனைக்கும் *varuvanaikkum* becomes வருந்தனைக்கும் *varundanaikkum* and ಬರುವನೆಗಂ *baruvanegam* ಬರುವತನಕ *baruvatanaka*, and this yields the Tel. వచ్చుతనక *vaccutanaka*.[1]

XV. Again the particle ಅಳೊಡಂ *aloḍam* is to be added to any root to indicate the time of completing the action. Thus ಗೆಯ್ಯಳೊಡಂ *geyyaloḍam* means 'after doing' = Tam. செய்ய லுடன் *śeyyaluḍan*. Comparing these two expressions we can easily see that the Kan. ಅಳೊಡಂ *aloḍam* = Tam. அலுடன் *aluḍan* in which the first part அல் *al* belongs to the verbal noun செயல் *śeyal* (Kan. ಗೆಯ್ಯಲ್ *geyyal*), 'the act of doing,' and உடன் *uḍan* (Kan. ಒಡಂ *oḍam*) is the instrumental suffix

---

[1] The latter part of this expression, viz. తనక *tanaka*, is modified in Hindustani as تک *tak* by the elision of *n*, and تلک *talak* by the change of *n* into *l* and means 'till.'

meaning 'with' or 'immediately after.' What an unscientific analysis and distribution! In Tamil no one would commit such an error. The Kanarese Grammarian, however, did not know the analysis of the expression and distributed it wrongly.

XVI. Such were the errors and mistakes of the ancient grammarians and philologists, and they have been handed down to us without any correction whatever. The duty of the philologist is to enquire into the nature and composition of every grammatical form and the etymology of every derivative word. Following this principle, I have been able to discover the affinities of many words and grammatical forms in the Aryan and Dravidian languages and have thus thrown much light on subjects which have remained in deep obscurity, in spite of all the attempts of lexicographers, grammarians and philologists.

XVII. The subject of this volume, as already mentioned, is the method of linguistic investigation pursued by me; and with the description and explanation of this method the book begins. Then follow lists of groups of words which are introduced to illustrate the method. The first list contains five groups each of which includes the corresponding words of the allied languages of the Aryan family, which are similar in form, and convey the same or allied ideas. The second contains the corresponding words of allied languages which express the same ideas and are allied in form. In the third are given the allied grammatical forms of the kindred languages, and I have then discussed the peculiarities of conjugation and proposed a new classification of them instead of the old. The First, Fourth, Sixth and Tenth are brought under one class, and the Second includes the Third, Seventh and the Yanluganta or the frequentative without any augment. The Fifth is referred to a separate class with the augment *u*, and the *n* of the so-called augment नु *nu* (श्नु *śnu*) has been shown to spring from a radical nasal and is therefore organic. In this class is included the Eighth which inserts *u* before the personal suffixes. In the Ninth class, the root ज्ञा *jñā* is shown as belonging to the Second, as the part जाना *jānā* of जानाति *jānāti* is only an organic development of ज्ञा *jñā* by the insertion of आ *ā* between ज *j* and ञ *ñ* and the consequent change of ञ *ñ* into न *n*. Compare Gr. γνωθι and Sans. जानीहि *jānīhi*. In the remaining roots मंथ् *manth*, ग्रंथ् *granth*, &c., the radical nasal is transposed to the end, and when आ *ā* is added before the personal suffixes, such as ति *ti* and ते *te*, we get मथ्न् *mathn* + आ *ā* + ति *ti* = मथ्नाति *mathnāti* and ग्रथ्न् *grathn* + आ *ā* + ति *ti* = ग्रथ्नाति *grathnāti*. In the Seventh the vowel अ *a* is inserted between the last consonant of the root and a preceding nasal, so that we get *na* in the midst of the root, which is wrongly treated as an augment. But in the Ātmanēpadi roots no augment is inserted, so that we get such forms as रुंद्धे *runddhē* from रुंध् *rundh* + ते *tē*.

According to my system, therefore, there are five classes, the First, the अ *a* class; the Second, आ *ā* class including the original Ninth class (श्नाविकरण *'śnāvikaraṇa*) and the subjunctive forms as भवाति *bhavāti*; the Third, इ *i* class which inserts इ *i* before the augment ति *ti*, as श्वसिति *śvasiti*, अनिति *aniti* and the like; the Fourth class which inserts

ई ī as ब्रवीति *bravīti*, बोभवीति *bōbhavīti* and such forms as अब्रवीत् *abravīt* and अबोभवीत् *abōbhavīt*; the Fifth, उ *u* class in which उ *u* is added to the root, as कुरुते *kurutē*, तरुते *tarutē*, अश्नुते *aśnutē* and the like.

XVIII. The etymological importance of my researches is as great as the historical, ethnological, and mythological. Etymology is to Philology what Chemistry is to Physical Science. It is the essential part of a dictionary, and the science of grammar is based upon a right etymology. But lexicographers and grammarians did not follow a strictly scientific method in their investigations. They assigned wrong and fanciful derivations to words and analyzed the grammatical forms in a way quite contrary to the fundamental laws of philology; and, in consequence, many errors have crept into the works of most writers on languages and grammars and dictionaries. It is therefore the duty of every-philologist to follow a strict method of investigation, and establish a system of sound principles derived from carefully analyzed facts. The etymology so established should be introduced into grammars and dictionaries. I need not bring in here examples, as every page of my work contains some illustrations of what I say. Such a critical investigation furnishes us with a set of psychological and orthographical rules by which we can determine the root of many a doubtful word and explain the construction of many a difficult grammatical form. We have been lately favoured with an Etymological Dictionary of the English Language by Mr. Skeat, Professor of Anglo-Saxon in the University of Cambridge. It has been compiled with great learning, and the author has therein embodied the results of the researches of many etymological scholars, and, in that way, has done a good service to the language. But in many cases, however, he has not settled the etymologies of words; and the failure must be attributed to the want of some definite rules to guide. Such rules can be derived only by a scientific comparison of the words and grammatical forms of a language with one another and with the corresponding ones found in the other allied languages of the family, as has been attempted in this work.

XIX. For instance, in the Second Group, that is, the *Śiras Group*, we arrive at a conclusion that in the Aryan languages the words for 'head,' 'crown,' 'hair' and 'horn' are allied and spring from the Sanskrit root शिरस् *śiras* and Gr. *καρ*. If we refer to the Etymological Dictionary of Mr. Skeat for the etymology of the word '*crest*' we can see there many allied words given under it and, among others, Lat. '*crista*' with which it is ultimately connected by the author; but with regard to the derivation we learn nothing, for the author says that 'the root of the word is uncertain.' The fact above mentioned, however, settles the etymology, as the word '*crista*' is only '*cris*' in another form, and means '*hood*.' In form it is allied to Gr. *καρ, καρα, κορυς, κρασ, κρανον,* and *καιτη*; Sans. शिरस् *śiras*, शृंग *sṛṅga*, कच *kaca*, and केश *kēśa*; Lat. *caput, crinis, cæsaries,* and *cornu*; which words mean 'head,' 'hair,' 'horn,' or 'crest.' Now applying the analogy we can connect the Lat. *crista* with the corresponding Sanskrit and Greek words mentioned above and derive it by the addition of the suffix *a* to *κρας*. Thus *κρας* + *a* = *κρασσα* = *κρισσα* = *krista* = *crista*.

XX. Referring to the Dictionary for the derivation of the English word '*hair*,' we learn that the word is found in many other forms and that the author is not certain about its root. Now, applying the above rule, we can easily suppose that English, which is mainly an offshoot of Anglo-Saxon, one of the languages of the Aryan family, must contain the corresponding words used in the respective ideas, and a slight acquaintance with English will suggest to any person the most common words 'head,' 'horn,' and 'hood,' 'hair.' The first and second of these words are evidently connected with the Gr. *κεφαλη* and Lat. *caput*, and Gr. *κρανον* and Lat. *cornu* respectively. 'Hood' is allied to Sans. कोटि *kōṭi*, Gr. *κωδια*, 'top,' चूडा *cūḍā* and चूला *cūlā*, 'crest,' and has changed the initial क *k* of कोटि *kōṭi* into *h*, as the word 'head' itself has done with the *k* of *κεφαλη*. There can be no doubt that the English word *hair* and Anglo-Saxon '*hair*' and '*her*' are modifications of *καρα*.

Under the word '*hat*' he gives the allied words such as the Ang-Sax. '*hæt*,' Dan. '*hat*,' Icel. '*hattr*,' and observes that it is probably connected with Lat. *cassis*, 'helmet,' which he derives from *skad*, 'to cover,' and cautions the reader not to confound the word with *kut* which is cognate with Eng. '*hood*.' But by the rule above mentioned we can at once settle the derivations and connect *hat*, as well as Lat. *cassis*, with Sans. कोटि *kōṭi*, 'top.'

XXI. Under the word '*cap*' which agrees in meaning with '*hat*,' though apparently differing in form, the author mentions some allied words such as *cape*, *cope* and Lat. *coppa*; but as these are in form and meaning allied to Sans. शिफा *śiphā*, 'head,' and शफ *śapha*, 'hoof,' of which the Eng. 'hoof' is a modification, they may be easily traced to the latter.

XXII. In the First Group, I have derived from आत्मन् *ātman*, स्व *sva*, 'own,' 'possession,' स्वर् *svar*, 'heaven,' modified as सुवर् *suvar*, and सुमेरु *sumēru*, and contracted into मेरु *mēru*, त्मन् *tman*, &c., meaning 'self,' 'soul,' 'spirit,' 'smell,' 'wind,' 'region of wind,' 'sky,' 'clouds,' 'water,' &c., and I may lay down a general rule to the following effect, that words which are similar to the above words in form and convey the above and allied ideas are allied to each other and are ultimately traceable to आत्मन् *ātman*. Referring to the Dictionary of Mr. Skeat for the etymology of the word '*heaven*,' we learn that it has allied forms in M. E. *heuen*, Ang.-Sax. *heofon*, *hiofon*, *hefon*, O. Icel. *hifinn*, and is of unknown origin. But its connexion with Sans. स्वर् *svar*, सुवर् *suvar* and Gr. Ολυμπος is settled by the above rule. (Vide p. 20.)

XXIII. With reference to the origin of the word '*have*,' we are informed by the lexicographer that it is from the Teutonic base, '*hab*.' This root he connects with the Lat. *capere*, 'to seize,' 'to hold'; Gr. κωπη, a handle; and the original idea must accordingly be 'to take' or 'to hold.' But by the above rule I would connect the word with Sans. स्व *sva* (Gr. ιδιο) of which Lat. *haveo* is a developed form by the change of स *s* into *h* and the insertion of the vowel *a* between स *s* and व *v*. (p. 14).

XXIV. Under the words '*self*' and '*soul*' he gives many allied words of the kindred languages and traces them to their original Teutonic sources, *selba* and *saivala*, respectively, and observes however that their origins are unknown. We can, however, conclude, *primâ facie*, that the two words must be the different forms of the same word as they are identical in form, except that the final consonant of *saivala* is metathetically transposed to the middle of the word; and this *primâ facie* conclusion is thoroughly established by the above rule by which they can be both connected with आत्मन् *ātman*.

XXV. Mr. Skeat traces the word '*smell*' to its original form *smoran*, 'to suffocate,' which ends with *r* instead of *l*. From आत्मन् *ātman* we get Sans. बाष्प *bāṣpa* (originally आस्प *āspa*) and Lat. *vapor*, Gr. *ατμος* and *ατμις*, 'vapor,' and नभस् *nabhas* meaning 'clouds,' 'vapour,' &c.; and we can, according to the rule, connect '*smell*' with Lat. *sibilus*, Sans. श्वस् *śvas*, and त्मन् *tman* from which last is derived the verb ध्मा *dhmā*, 'to blow.'

We can thus see the great utility of the method of investigation pursued by me and of the fundamental general rules of philology which are derived from the classification and the analysis of allied words according to that method. By the application of the rules to the other languages of the Aryan family, we can settle the etymologies of the corresponding words of those languages.

XXVI. The application of the rule may not be confined to the Aryan languages. I suspect very strongly that there must be more connection between the Aryan and Semitic families than hitherto discovered, perhaps, sufficient to warrant a radical union between them in one family. The Semitic languages have not yet been subjected to a scientific analysis by philologists. The laws of constructing words and grammatical forms, which present a striking contrast to those prevailing in the Aryan languages, have not been properly accounted for. The way in which they are enunciated are most unscientific in appearance. Unless these laws are simplified and reduced to fundamental facts, they must remain in deep oblivion. Take, for instance, the laws of guṇa, vṛddhi single and double, reduplication of radical forms, the insertion of the augment *a* in past tenses at the beginning of roots and so on, which were so many arbitrary processes as they were treated in our Sanskrit and Greek grammars, and which, when they were analyzed and simplified, appealed to our reason.

We learn from the English grammars that the roots *rise*, *lie* and *sit* are changed into *raise*, *lay* and *seat* respectively in the causal; and the vowel changes which take place seem to be arbitrary. But when we refer them to the general laws of lengthening the vowel of the first syllable of a word, which are in Sanskrit called guṇa and vṛddhi, we understand them better. There are many similar grammatical and verbal peculiarities in the Aryan languages, and, unless they are reduced to most general laws and are thus explained, they must remain arbitrary and unreasonable.

The same must be the case with the Semitic languages. "In no language," says Dr. Bresslau, "are found words and roots with so various and not unfrequently with opposite significations as in the Hebrew, besides the peculiarities in that remarkable tongue arising from the various paradigms." What is the cause of this? Why should there be so many roots which are not found in the actual usage? The limited comparison which I have instituted between the Aryan and the corresponding Semitic words leads me to think that there must be an ultimate connection between the Aryan and the Semitic languages. When the nation speaking these languages separated, the nucleus common stock must have been replenished with new matters which grew naturally and were created arbitrarily. A portion of the difference can be explained by reference to the ignorance of the ancient grammarians and lexicographers who had a system of traditions and beliefs regarding the language, instead of a scientific grammar and etymology; roots were coined to assign some etymon to every word, and grammatical forms were wrongly analyzed and new forms, coined on wrong analogies. When these were incorporated with the language, there arose some inconsistencies and complicacies which have eluded the closest scrutiny of philologists. This is the case with the Aryan languages, and must be equally so with the Semitic languages also.

Let us see how far we can compare the Aryan and Semitic words. In the Aryan languages the word आत्मन् *ātman* originates words expressive of the following ideas :—'sky, light, sun, day, wind, breath, deity, time, happiness, peace, health, colours such as white, yellow, and the like, beautiful, shining, burning, strength, youth, &c.' The words so derived resemble, both in form and meaning, the corresponding Hebrew and Arabic words :

Heb.	*Ṣabath*, 'rest,'	Sans.	स्वस् *svas*, 'happiness.'
,,	*Ṣelam*, 'peace,'	,,	शर्मन् *śarman*, ,,
,,	*Gabar*, 'to be strong,'	,,	कुमार *kumāra*, 'young.'
		Gr.	οβριμος, 'strong.'
,,	*Balag*, 'to shine,'	Sans.	भ्राज् *bhrāj*.
,,	*Ṣamar*, 'to watch,'	,,	स्मील् *smīl*, 'to close the eye,' the idea of closing the eye arising from that of winking.
,,	*Ṣafar*, 'to shine,'	,,	ज्वल् *jval*, 'shine.'
,,	*Ṣemeṣ*, 'sun,'	,,	दिवस् *divas*, by the change of द् *d* into *ṣ* as in '*Ṣen*,' दंत *danta*, 'teeth.'
,,	*Ṣua*, 'to be rich,'	,,	स्व *sva*, 'possession.'
,,	*Nafaṣ*. 'to breathe,'	,,	नभस् *nabhas*, 'wind.'
,,	*Nefeṣ*, 'breath,'	,,	,, ,,

Heb. *Ṣahan*, 'to be hot,'	Sans. स्वर् *svar*, ज्वल् *jval*, 'to shine.'
,, *Ṣem*, 'Third son of Noah.'	,, देव *dēva*, 'a deity,' (compare *ṣen*, *ṣafar*, *ṣemeṣ*, above given).
,, *Laban*, 'white,'	,, श्वेत *śvēta*.'
,, *Ṣaban*, 'tender,'	,, कोमल *kōmala*, 'soft.'
	Gr. *ἁβρος*, 'delicate.'
,, *Ṣuṣ*, 'to be white,'	,, शुच् *śuc*, 'to be pure.'
	,, शुचि *śuci*, 'white.'
,, *Yōn*, 'wine,'	Gr. *οινος*, 'wine.'
,, *Zaphah*, 'to look out,'	Sans. स्पश् *spaś*, 'to see.'
,, *Ur*, 'light,'	,, उषा *uṣā*, 'dawn.'
,, *Saraf*, 'to burn,'	,, ज्वर् *jvar*, 'to be hot.'
,, *Ṣafir*, 'beautiful,'	,, ज्वल् *jval*, 'to shine.'
,, *Barak*, 'lightning,'	,, भ्राज् *bhrāj*, 'to shine.'
,, *Faz*, 'refined as gold,'	,, भास् *bhās*, ,,
Arab. *Lebbek*, 'God,'	,, दिवस् *divas*, द्यौस् *dyaus*, 'God of Heaven.'
Heb. *Baaz*, 'fleetness,'	Gr. *βιος*, 'strength.'
,, *Ṣabah*, 'to extol,'	Sans. सभाज् *sabhāj*, perhaps स्वस् *svas*, 'happiness,' the original idea being 'to please.'
,, *Yom*, 'day,'	,, व्योमन् *vyōman*, 'sky.'

XXVII. In its bearing on Comparative Mythology the system of linguistic analysis adopted by me is very important and, in my opinion, will be attended with good results.

The Science of Comparative Mythology was, as it were, created by Prof. Max Müller and Mr. Cox, whom we ought to call fathers of the science as far as England is concerned. By comparing the Vedic theogony with the Homeric and Hesiodic versions and also their modified forms among the Teutonic and other branches of the Aryan nations, they have found a close alliance not only in the various details of the stories told concerning the personages connected with the theogonies, but also in the names applied to some of them. We know how each myth and story of a nation has a corresponding one in those of the other kindred nations kept up intact in its full integrity, slightly modified, or entirely metamorphosed into new shapes, and how the same myth among the same nations assumes a variety of forms, in each of which the nucleus of the story is repeated. Thus, for instance, in the Hesiodic theogony the 'Earth' under the names of *Gaia, Terra, Rhea,* and *Hera* becomes the wife of *Chaos, Ouranos, Cronus* and *Jupiter,* respectively. But these alliances are psychological and ethnological; and there is yet a connexion which is wanting, and that is formal or philological. We do not know why *Zeus* and द्यौस् *Dyaus, Uranus* and वरुण *Varuṇa, Hera* and इरा *Irā, Olumpos* and स्वर् *Svar,* and other personages who figure in the Aryan theogonies are so called. Are such corresponding names significant or mere words coined to be applied to an individual deity? But a scientific investigation of languages will clearly show that the latter can never be the case. Language is the result of a physical development of sounds and not an arbitrary and conventional growth. Most of the proper names of languages must be common names expressive of some particular idea, and, in spite of the apparent difference in their forms, can be traced to a few roots. This is the conclusion arrived at by my analysis of Sanskrit, Greek and Latin. I have assigned proper etymologies to the names of many deities who figure in the Vedas of Sanskrit and in the poems of Homer, Hesiod and Virgil. Many of the names have been traced to the word आत्मन् *ātman* which represents the First Group ; some, to the word शिरस् *śiras* which represents the Second Group ; and some, to वृषन् *vṛṣan* from which originate all the words of the Third Group.[1] As a psychological

---

[1] I give here a list containing the most important of the proper names derived in the book :—

A
Achaian
Achilles
Aditi
Adruades
Æthra
Agastya
Agni
Ahalyā
Ahanā
Ahura
Ajax
Aithra
Angellos
Aṅgiras
Apollon
Apsaras
Arethusa
Argos
Ariadne
Arthur
Asana
Āsara
Asura
Athamas
Atnēnē
Atlas
Ātrēya
Atri
Atrides
Atrius

B
Bādarāyaṇa
Barbaros
Baseleus
Bālakhilya
Bāṣkala
Bhāradvāja
Boiōtos
Brahman
Breareōs
Bṛhaspati

C
Caia
Caius
Chaos
Cheiron
Coeus
Cohus
Cottos
Covella

D
Da
Daitya
Danae
Danaos
Dānava
Danu
Despoina
Despotes
Diana
Diipetes
Dikte
Diônê
Dis
Diti
Dionusos
Duṣyanta
Dyaus
Dyōtanā

E
Echidna
Eos
Epiros
Europa
Evadne

F
Faunus

G
Ga
Gaia
Gandharva
Gautama
Gmā
Gnā
Gua
Guges

H
Hamadruades
Hanvanu
Heaven
Hebe
Hector
Hekatos
Helios
Hellas
Hellen
Hera
Hercules
Hesperos
Hestia
Hippotes
Hippotades
Huakinthos
Humen
Huperion

I
Ialkos
Iapetos
Iason
Ida
Iduia
Ilia
Ilion
Ilos
Indirā
Indra
Ino
Iokaste
Ion
Isis
Italia
Italos

J
Jacob
Japheth
Javan
Jebus
Jehoshua
Jehova
Jehu

connection has already been proved to exist among these names, so I have argued a philological one among them and made their alliance complete. Making allowance for the affinities and kindredships founded on accidental coincidences and resemblances of forms, a great part of my etymology seems, in my humble opinion, to be correct. If so, a connecting link is established by which we can thoroughly unite the myths of all the Aryan nations who were originally living together and are now separated by thousands of miles.

Twenty years ago Professor Max Müller traced the various forms of द्यौस् *Dyaus* and *Zeus* in the Aryan languages.

Jehudu
Joseph
Judah

K

Kailāsa
Kaṇṭhīrava
Kaṇva
Kapila
Kāśyapa
Kavi
Kārtavīrya
Kentauros
Kerberos
Kinnara
Kirāta
Koios
Kōkanada
Kolossos
Kosmos
Kronos
Kumāra

L

Laitma
Latinus
Latium
Latmus
Latona
Lemures
Lykos
Lyktos

M

Maināka
Mēna
Mēru
Minos
Minotauros

N

Naiades
Namuci
Naraka
Narkissos
Nephele
Neptunus
Nereides
Nereus
Nessos
Niobe
Notos

O

Odusseus
Oidipous
Olumpos
Osiris
Ouranos

P

Pan
Parūśara
Pegasos
Pelagos
Pelasgos
Peleus
Penelope
Phaethon
Phrugia
Pieros
Psuchē

R

Rāma
Rambhā
Ṛbhukṣan
Remus
Rhea
Roma
Romulus
Romus

S

Sagara
Saindhava
Samīra
Saramā
Sarasvatī
Sarpedon
Saturos
Serapis
Sindhu
Śiva
Śivā
Sumēru
Sura
Sūra

T

Tanau
Tanūnapāt
Tethus
Thebai
Theos
Thesbes
Theseus
Thessalia
Thetis
Titan
Tithōnos
Tituos
Triton

U

Ulysses
Ulyxes
Uśanas

V

Vivasvan
Vīrabhadra

W

Woden
Wuotan

Y

Yakṣa
Yavana

Z

Zephuros

His method suggested to me the possibility of making more comprehensive groups of the same kind. Attempts were already made to discover the origin of the Mythological names of the Aryan languages. Several words are derived by Mr. Cox in his Aryan Mythology and his Introduction to Mythology and Folklore, and part of his etymology is very creditable to him. Mr. Gladstone, in his 'Juventus Mundi,' refers to a book published by M. Jacoliot, which he, however, considers as untrustworthy. "It would be," he says, "a matter of great interest to know how far, apart from any theory, the names of the Hellenic divinities are really derivable from the Sanskrit: and in the recent work of M. Jacoliot, 'La Bible dans l' Inde,' a list of many of them is given with Sanskrit roots, in many cases seemingly appropriate." Certainly it must be in Sanskrit alone which is the most ancient and most cultivated of the Aryan languages that the etymology must be sought, and the failures of scholars who have tried to seek in that language the etymons of the names of the Vedic and Hellenic characters must be attributed to the erroneous methods they pursued, and not to any other cause.

It is really astonishing to see that the roots from which the proper names have sprung are not many and are very limited in number. It is equally astonishing that the names applied to many of the Vedic and Hellenic deities have been evolved from the word आत्मन् *ātman*, 'sky,' the prevailing radical idea of those words being 'heavenly' or 'bright.' Most of the names of the water deities are metamorphoses of the word सलिल *salila*, Gr. ἅλς. We are not the less surprised when we see that the names of Ṛṣis, such as पराशर *Parāśara*, भारद्वाज *Bhāradvāja*, बाष्कल *Bāṣkala*, बालखिल्य *Bālakhilya*, पैल *Paila* and बादरायण *Bādarāyaṇa*, गिरिश *Giriśa*, the name of Śiva,

कैलास *Kailāsa,* the name of the mountain in which he dwells, are traceable to the word शिरस् *śiras* from which have been derived the words गंधर्व *Gandharva, Kentauros, Satyr, Chiron* and *Cronos.*

XXVIII. Finally, I shall mention some linguistic and psychological conclusions to which my investigations lead. There may be errors committed by me and they may require corrections from competent scholars. This circumstance, however, does not much affect the conclusions which I am going to mention. By the analysis adopted by me, it would appear that the Aryan languages can be reduced to a few groups of allied words, of which five have already appeared in this volume, and a few more groups will be introduced in the succeeding volumes. In the treatment of the subject my intention has been to simply point out the application of the method and give a few important instances. The analysis was applied to Sanskrit, Greek, Latin and Anglo-Saxon, and, among these too, importance was attached to Sanskrit as the oldest and nearest representative of the mother language of the Aryan family. In some places Greek and Latin words corresponding to the Sanskrit have not been given, and left to be learnt from the existing dictionaries; and they will all be included in my 'Comparative Lexicon' which is under preparation. It can be easily seen that each word of each of the other allied languages of this family must be included in the group, in which the corresponding words of Sanskrit, Greek and Latin have been included. Perhaps the few groups to which I have tried to reduce all the allied languages may be split into more groups by the separation of some words wrongly included in one group. But this does not materially affect the conclusions which I am going to mention. The whole vocabulary of the Aryan languages has been evolved from a small number of words. What that number is we cannot determine; nor is it necessary to do so. A more important and surprising conclusion is that not only the whole vocabulary of languages has sprung from a few words, but also the very grammatical elements are traceable to one word आत्मन् *ātman!* I have shown, for instance, that the nominative, accusative, and genitive suffixes are remnants of the pronouns स *sa*, 'he,' and स्व *sva*, 'own,' and these are ultimately traceable to आत्मन् *ātman*. The conjugational suffixes, most of the personal pronouns and the majority of suffixes added to nouns and verbs to form derivative words, have been traced to the same source. In short, the greater part of the grammatical machinery has been traced to the single word आत्मन् *ātman*.

XXIX. It has been shown also that most of the verbs have sprung from nouns. In the *Ātman* Group itself have been derived many important and primitive verbal roots, as शुभ् *śubh*, स्वप् *svap*, सुख् *sukh*, दीव् *dīv*, जीव् *jīv*, दीप् *dīp*, द्युत् *dyut*, ज्युत् *jyut*, त्विष् *tviṣ*, तृप् *tṛp*, दृप् *dṛp*, लस् *las*, लक्ष् *lakṣ*, लज्ज् *lajj*, हस् *has*, दृश् *dṛś*, रुच् *ruc*, लोक् *lōk*, लोच् *lōc*, स्पश् *spaś*, स्वद् *svad*, पच् *pac*, मृड् *mṛḍ*, भास् *bhās*, भी *bhī*, ज्वल् *jval*, तप् *tap*, and क्षिप् *kṣip*; in the *Salila* Group सिंच् *siñc*, उंद् *und*, &c.; and in the *Vṛṣa* Group मुंष् *muṁṣ*, &c. It has been supposed by many that verbs must have preceded nouns, and this theory has been the source of many etymological and grammatical blunders. It will, however, be overthrown by the above and other examples. The word *heaven*, for instance, was hitherto derived from *heave*, 'to lift,' but I have shown in the book clearly that the contrary is the fact and that *heave* is derived from *heaven*. The importance and utility of the discovery is seen to a greater extent in the last three verbs, उंद् *und*, सिंच् *siñc* and मुंष् *muṁṣ*. In the *Salila* Group उंद् *und* and सिंच् *siñc* have been derived from उदन् *udan*, 'water,' and शीकर *śīkara*, 'drop,' respectively. उदन् *udan* is connected with वरुण *Varuṇa*, Ουρανος, Οκεανος, इन्द्र *Indra* originally a water god, &c., and शीकर *śīkara*, with सागर *sāgara*, 'ocean,' लहरी *laharī*, 'wave,' लवण *lavaṇa*, 'salt,' सिकत *sikata*, 'sands,' जंबाल *jambāla*, 'mud,' λιμην, 'harbour,' रुमा *rumā*, 'salt ocean,' रुमन् *ruman*, 'salt.' In उंद् *und*, the final *n* of उदन् *udan* is transposed to the middle of the word, and in सिंच् *siñc* the final *r* of शीकर *śīkara* is similarly transposed and changed into *n*. We thus see that the nasal in उंद् *und* and सिंच् *siñc* are radical. The conjugational form उनत्ति *unatti*, third per. sing. indicative, must therefore be distributed as उन् *un* + अ *a* + द् *d* + ति *ti*, in which अ *a* is inserted between the nasal and the following द् *d*, and to the root thus modified the personal suffix ति *ti* is added. According to this analysis the form must belong to the second conjugation, लुग्विकरण *Lugvikaraṇa*, and is not a separate conjugation (vide p. xx, *supra*). With regard to the root सिंच् *siñc*, we must have it enunciated as सिंच् *siñc* and not as सिच् *sic* as has been done in the Dhātupāṭha. As for the root मुंष् *muṁṣ*, it is enunciated as मुष् *muṣ* and in the conjugational form

मुष्णाति *muṣṇāti*, we have to add according to Pāṇini श्ना *ā* (श्ना *śnā*) to the root and derive the form from मुष् *muṣ* + ना *nā* + ति *ti*. But according to my analysis the form मुष्णाति *muṣṇāti* is to be distributed as मुंष् *muṁṣ* + श्ना *ā* + ति *ti* by the transfer of the nasal to the end of the root in the form of *n*; for मुंष् *muṁṣ* is borrowed from मूष *mūṣa* (μυσ) 'rat,' because the idea of stealth was represented by the action of a rat which takes away food and edible substances without the knowledge of the household. मुंष् *muṁṣ* must be a nasalized form of मुष् *muṣ* as पुंस् *puṁs* is of वृष *vṛṣa*. (Vide the *Vṛṣa* Group, and p. xx, *supra*).

XXX. We thus see that the majority of verbs have been derived from nouns only. It may be objected that the Sanskrit Dhātupāṭha contains about 4,000 roots, and that they cannot at all be derived from nouns. The objection, however, may be removed by supposing that the Dhātupāṭha is a grand attempt to derive every Sanskrit word from a primitive root; and this fact will be clearly seen by any one who studies the Uṇādisūtra and the commentaries on the Nighaṇṭus (Lexicons). In this attempt hundreds of roots which had never existed in the language have been created arbitrarily; and this unnatural element was incorporated with the language, especially in its secondary stage (Classical Sanskrit). A critical analysis, therefore, of the language must exclude all the alien elements.

XXXI. With reference to the psychological or logical part of the results of my investigation, I have to remark that, assuming that thought and language progress side by side and depend upon each other, man in the primitive age must have had a limited knowledge and a limited language; and in this possession he occupied a condition of which childhood is the best representative; and as the twofold property was enriched, the difference became wider and wider till at last he attained to the present condition of being. For instance, he had the notion of an animal, and expressed it by the word वृष *vṛṣa* which was applied to a man and an ox; and this word assumed the following forms as he acquired the ideas of new animals; as वृक *vṛka*, 'wolf' and 'quadruped,' मृग *mṛga*, 'quadruped' and 'deer,' पशु *paśu*, 'cattle,' Lat. *vacca*, 'cow,' बस्त *basta*, 'sheep,' ऋश्य *ṛśya* and पृषत *pṛṣata*, 'deer,' ऋच *ṛkṣa*, 'bear,' उलूक *ulūka*, 'owl,' उलूपी *ulūpī*, 'an alligator,' Eng. '*wolf*,' Gr. *αλωπηξ*, and Lat. *vulpes*, 'fox,' फेरु *phēru* and फेरव *phērava*, 'jackal,' Lat. *lupus*, 'wolf,' *Roma*, 'the city of Rome,' Romulus and Remus, of which the latter is a modification of Romus, meaning radically 'wolf' (which meaning was the source of the myth of their having been suckled by a wolf) and corresponding to the Sans. राम *Rāma*, 'son of Daśaratha,' which word also must have originally signified a wolf and was applied to the prince, referring to his courage and strength; मार्जार *mārjāra*, 'cat,' Lat. *martes*, 'a marten,' मुसली *musalī* (Tam. முதலை *mudalai*), 'lizard,' Sans. गृष्टि *gṛṣṭi*, 'boar,' and 'a cow that has yeaned once,' मेष *mēṣa*, 'sheep,' महिष *mahiṣa*, 'buffalo,' (cf. महिला *mahilā*, 'woman'), ओतु *ōtu*, 'cat,' बिडार *biḍāra*, उद्र *udra*, *otter*, उंदरु *undaru*, 'mouse,' and so on; and in its application to man it is transformed into मनुष्य *manuṣya*, मानुष *mānuṣa*, मर्त्य *martya*, मानव *mānava*, पुंस् *puṁs* (modified as

पुमंस् *pumaṁs* by the insertion of *a* between the nasal *m* and *s* and the addition of a second nasal between *a* and *s*), पुरुष *puruṣa,* पूरुष *pūruṣa,* विश् *viś,* विट *viṭa,* वधू *vadhū,* 'woman,' वेश *vēśa,* and वेश्या *vēśyā,* 'whore.' I shall give another instance. The verbal roots Gr. *γραφω,* 'to write,' *γλυφω, γλαφω* and Lat. *sculpo,* 'to engrave,' are not original roots, but are borrowed from the name of stone, such as Sans. ग्रावन् *grāvan,* from which are to be derived Gr. *λαος, λευς* and Lat. *lapis,* in which the initial *g* is cut off. But in the Latin *scribo* the initial *g* is changed into *c,* and the letter *s,* added to the beginning of the word. The Sans. लिख *likha* may be traced to the Gr. *γραφω*; and the ख *kha* of लिख *likha* may be a modification of *φ*. ग्रावन् *grāvan* is shortened into ग्रा *grā* and then developed into two syllables as गिरा *girā* from which form may be derived गिरि *giri,* 'mountain,' and by the change of ग *ga* into श *śa* शिला *śilā,* 'stone,' and शैल *śaila,* 'mountain.' The Tam. வரி *vari,* Tel. వ్రాయు *vrāyu,* and Kan. ಬರೆ *bare,* 'to write,' are corruptions of ग्रा *grā.* Perhaps Sans. शिल्प *śilpa,* 'art,' particularly stone-masonry, may be referred to the Gr. *γλυφη,* 'engraving,' and लिपि *lipi* to *γραφη,* 'writing.' From this it is clear that the roots meaning 'writing,' 'engraving' were originally borrowed from the name of stone. This conclusion applies not only to the Aryan languages but also to the Semitic languages. The so-called trileteral root *ktb* from which are evolved various forms, such as *katb,* 'writing,' *kātib,* 'writer,' *maktūb,* 'written,' *taktīb,* 'causing to write,' *iktāb,* 'dictating,' *kitāb,* 'book,' and *kitābat,* 'inscriptions,' is nothing but a modification of the Gr. *γραφω.* In this way we can clearly see that as one word is developed into so many forms, and all these allied forms are traceable directly or indirectly to the original word, just in the same way the meaning of the original word is modified in various ways, and these modified and allied ideas can be connected directly or indirectly with the original idea. In some cases the original idea is so much modified that the alliance is not clear. The language or the creative genius of its speakers depends on the principle of analogy, and works out the existing resources in preference to arbitrary coining. The ancient Romans, for instance, who had never seen an elephant before, saw one for the first time in the army of Pyrrhus in Lucania, they called it *Luca bos*, meaning thereby 'Lucanian ox.' What a mistake that was! We that are very familiar with the elephant think that no one would commit such a mistake. But even in the difference between a cow and an elephant which is very striking, there is a similarity; viz., an elephant is a quadruped and has tusks which answer to the horns of an ox, and the genius of Romans like that of any other nation worked out the existing resources of the language instead of coining a new name for an elephant and used it till they got the right names of the animal, viz., *eliphas* and *eliphantus*, from Sans. ऐरावत *airāvata*, 'celestial elephant,' through Gr. *ελεφας*.

From these examples we clearly see that language was developed in proportion as ideas were. Words did not deal with things as they were, but only as they were conceived by men. Names were given to things with reference to qualities, actions, conditions and the like, and to the latter with reference to their associations. Sometimes the connection was real, and sometimes merely imaginary and arbitrary. In this book general laws relating to such applications have been enunciated according to contexts and illustrated by proper examples. The words expressing the ideas of shining and laughing, for instance, are connected in the Aryan languages, the former producing the latter, and this law is found even in the Hebrew language.[1] The same idea produces those of fear, hesitation and shame; for when a person shines, his brilliancy may cause fear in the minds of the spectators, or it may expose the person who shines and thus make him shy or ashamed. (Vide pp. 74-77). Many more laws have been given in the book; and I simply refer the readers to them as it is unnecessary to quote them here.

In conclusion, I have to remark that I adopted a certain method of investigation not hitherto adopted in the analysis of the Aryan languages and entirely followed the course which my investigation took of itself. New facts and laws were discovered in some particular cases and they were applied to other cases. Thus my method has been inductive and deductive. But there may be errors both in the inductions and deductions, owing to the erroneousness and incompleteness of the laws, and also owing to the mistakes committed in the application of those laws. I have, however, ventured to put forward the results of my researches before the people more as a student desirous of learning from them than as a scholar presuming to teach them. I am, therefore, prepared to receive most thankfully every correction and improvement in my work, and to withdraw any statement or give up any conviction, in my homage to TRUTH and in my adoration to HIM who is the abode of

TRUTH.

"Veritas a quocunque dicitur, a Deo est."

[1] Vide Goldziher's Hebrew Mythology, p. 93.

NOTES

ON

ARYAN AND DRAVIDIAN PHILOLOGY.

METHOD OF LINGUISTIC INVESTIGATION.

PHILOLOGY, A PHYSICAL AND A METAPHYSICAL SCIENCE.

PHILOLOGY is the science of language and is therefore a physical as well as a metaphysical science. A language is a monument of the nation speaking it. It is as such of a twofold aspect. As it is an embodiment of the national thought and intellect, it is a metaphysical monument of the nation. As a nation progresses from a primitive condition to a highly civilized one, the intellect of the nation also receives a proportionate culture, and their language keeps pace with their intellect. Though speech is not absolutely necessary for thinking, an advanced state of knowledge can never be reached without the means of language. If this be the case with a man individually, much more so will this be with a society. The sum of knowledge which we possess now is the aggregate of what our ancestors inherited from their forefathers and what each of them acquired by his own original researches and added to the then existing stock, and all this was handed down by oral precepts in ancient times and by means of writing in subsequent times. The immemorial intellectual heirloom of our ancestors and the addition which each of them made to the stock could not have reached us if there had been no language to communicate human ideas and thoughts with, and human knowledge could not have made so much progress. Language is therefore closely connected with human thought and intellect.

Next, a language is the means of the expression of thought for men, and, as such, reducible to a number of words, and then again to a number of sounds (letters). Letters are articulate sounds. Acoustics is the science of sounds in general. Whatever is heard or perceived by the organ of hearing is called a sound. A sound has other characters; it is pleasing or unpleasing. The pleasantness and unpleasantness of a sound arise respectively from the regularity and irregularity of vibrations of the body which produces the sound. Sounds which are pleasant are musical; and music is the science of pleasant sounds. But what is musical may not be articulate, and music has nothing to do with consonants. Sounds which are distinctly produced by human voice from the various organs of pronunciation are called articulate. But I should observe here that the above definition is somewhat arbitrary and that what is articulate in one language may not be considered so in another. Thus, the letter *f* which is an articulate sound in English, is not so in Sanskrit and the Dravidian languages. The Arabic غ *gh* is not found in any European or Indian languages. In Sanskrit the most unscientific vowels, ऋ *ṛ*, ॠ *ṝ* and ऌ *ḷ*, ॡ *ḹ*, were adopted as vowel sounds in a later stage of the language, and they are not found in any other languages of the world. In Sanskrit the letters ट *ṭ*, ठ *ṭh*, ड *ḍ*, ढ *ḍh*, ण *ṇ*, श *ś*, ष *ṣ*, क्ष *kṣ*, ळ *ḷ* and a few others did not exist in the primitive stage of the language, and the same is the case with ψ and ξ in Greek. The cerebral letters were entirely unknown to the Ancient Aryan languages, and came into existence in several languages of the family after the separation of the original Aryan nation. In the Dravidian languages the letters ழ ḻ and ள ḷ were derived both in form and sound from Sans. ळ *l*, and represent the latter, often standing for other letters, such as ष ṣ, ड ḍ, &c. In the same way, the Dravidian ற ṟ called in Telugu śakaṭarēpha and the ன ṉ of Tamil sprang from ட[1] *t* and ந *n* respectively. In Sanskrit the visarga and the Tamil aspirate written as ஃ and called *āydam* came into existence as modifications of the sound *h*. The Telugu ardhānusvāra is a modification of the anunāsika sound represented by ں in the Vedas and in the North Indian vernaculars, and is allied to the ں *nūn* of the Arabic alphabet and can be ultimately connected with Sans. न *n*. The dental *th, dh,* though found in Anglo-Saxon, were not adopted in English which is derived from that language. The digamma F which represented the letter '*f*' in the Ancient Greek language was discorded in the later stage. The Vedic ḷ (as the cerebral ḍ is pronounced in the Rig Veda when it comes between two vowels) is not found in Modern Sanskrit. Of the sounds which can be called articulate, each language has adopted some, leaving the rest as inarticulate.

---

[1] In many ancient Tamil Inscriptions which I have studied, and in the Table of Ancient Tamil Alphabet given by Dr. Burnell in Vol. I, Part VIII, *Indian Antiquary*, this letter appears in forms which are allied to those of *t* and ṭ; and after a careful examination I have come to the conclusion that this form is a modification of that of the dental *t* used in the inscriptions and of that representing the cerebral ṭ in common writing till the introduction of printing in Southern India. As the sound ṭ is only a modification of *t*, the form for ṭ was taken from that used for *t*. In many cases, the śakaṭarēpha is inserted arbitrarily for Sans. र *r*.

The science of language is consequently metaphysical on the one hand, and, on the other, physical.

2. As ideas or the things to which they belong are connected, the words which are applied to them are also connected in their orthographical forms. In the material world, we see at a cursory glance innumerable things entirely different from one another. But the scientific man will see that, different as they are, they can be classified into a small number of groups or categories as earth, water, fire, air and empty space. But the chemist makes a critical analysis of the material substance of every kind, and says that they can be reduced to about sixty-five elementary substances. The whole universe or cosmos is divided, first, into astral systems or starry clusters; secondly, into individual systems; thirdly, into individual components of these systems; fourthly, into substances; fifthly, into molecules; and sixthly and at last, into atoms. I quote the following passage from Mr. Atkinson's Natural Philosophy :—

"It has been ascertained that all the various forms of matter with which we are acquainted may be resolved into about sixty-five different kinds, which are called simple substances or elements, to express that each only contains one kind of matter. Many of these are very rare, and are found in very minute quantities; others are more widely diffused, and have important uses, but are not abundant; and the great mass of the universe is made up of about fourteen; the non-metallic or metalloids are oxygen, hydrogen, nitrogen, silicon, carbon, sulphur, phosphorus, and chlorine; and the metals, aluminum, potassium, sodium, calcium, magnesium, and iron. Very few of these elements occur in nature in the free state; by far the greater number of the substances we know are compound; that is, formed by the union of two, three or four of these elements. Thus, water consists of hydrogen and oxygen; marble, of carbon, oxygen and calcium; muscular tissue, of carbon, hydrogen, oxygen and nitrogen. The number of substances containing more than four elements is very small."

3. Similarly, the linguist should divide the whole language into words; and each word is to him what a substance is to the chemist. When analyzed into its components, each word will contain one or more elements and may be classified into three kinds:—first, words which contain a mere root without any other element as Eng. *I*; (Ang. Sax. *ich*). The words of this kind, though admitting of no verbal analysis, can be orthographically analyzed by a comparison of them with the allied words in the same language and the corresponding words of the other languages of the family; next, words which are composed of a root or a primitive word of the above description and a suffix or a prefix or both, as Sans. अस्मि *asmi*, 'I am,' संपत् *sampat*, 'fortune,' and आविरस्मि *āvirasmi*, 'I come out.' Thirdly, those that contain in addition to the root and a suffix, a prefix, or both, some nexus or connecting link as *y*, *v*, *w*, and other letters, and the outgrowth produced by the rules of combination of letters and the like prevailing in the language, as in स्वयंभुवा *svayambhuvā*, 'by Brahma,' in which *v* is inserted between स्वयंभू *svayambhū* and the instrumental suffix आ *ā*; दत्रिम *datrima*, 'which is given,' in which *r* is inserted to strengthen त *t* of the suffix तिम[1] *tima*, which corres-

[1] The same termination तिम *tima*, which is, as shown above, modified as त्रिम *trima* by the addition of र् *r* to त *t*, assumes

ponds to Gr. σιμος as in ἁλωσιμος, 'easy to take,' πτωσιμος, 'fallen, slain,' βασιμος, 'accessible,' Κρισιμος 'decisive or critical,' and to Lat. *tivus* as in *dativus, captivus*; हगंस *hagmsa*, which stands for हंस[1] *haṁsa*, 'a swan,'

---

the form of लिम *lima*, in पचेलिम *pacēlima*, 'which is to be cooked,' from पच् *pac*, 'to cook,' भिदेलिम *bhidēlima*, 'which is to be broken,' from भिद् *bhid*, 'to break.' Cf. श्रोत्रिय *śrōtriya* for श्रोतिय *śrōtiya*, 'a Vedic scholar' from श्रुति *śruti*, 'the Veda.'

[1] As '*yuvan*,' contracted into *youn* and with *n* strengthened by *g*, becomes *young* in English, so '*haṁ*' in हंस *haṁsa* becomes *hang*, and by metathesis becomes '*hagṁ*' the anusvāra preceding *g* coming after it. This pronunciation is not mentioned in the Prātiśākhya and is mentioned in the śikshās only. I. think therefore that this is a Dravidian pronunciation originating from a desire on the part of the reciter to strengthen the unsteady and weak anusvāra; and the pronunciation prevails in the Dravidian languages to a great extent; e. g., Tamil பசு *paśu*, 'yellow,' as seen in such compounds as பசும்பொன் *paśumpoṉ*, taking the following ம் *m*, becomes பசும் *paśum*, is modified as பைம் *paim* and then பயின் *payiṉ*. To this பயின் *payiṉ*, *d* is added to strengthen the final consonant and then the vowel இ *i* for the sake of pronunciation. Thus we get பயின்டி *payiṇḍi*, which is in Telugu modified as పసింది *pasindi*, and then పసిడి *pasiḍi*, meaning 'yellow.' Similarly we have మామిడిపండు *mūmiḍi-paṇḍu* = மாவின்பழம் *māviṉpaḷam*, Tamil மாவின் *māviṉ* = மா *mā*, 'mango tree' + இன் *iṉ*, gen. termination meaning 'of,' assuming the form of మామిడి *māmiḍi*, in the Telugu language. Similarly, also, பீர் *pīr* + காய் *kāy*, (பீர் *pīr*, a creeper, காய் *kāy*, its fruit), becomes பீரங்காய் *pīraṅkāy*, by the insertion of the augment அம் *am*. See Tolkāppiyam Puḷḷimayaṅgiyal, Sūtra 70.

"பீரெஙகிளவி யம்மொடு சிவணும்."

Pīreṉkiḷavi yammoḍu śivaṇum.

'The word பீர் *pīr* will take the augment அம் *am*.'

பீரங்காய் *pīraṅkāy* assumes the form பீரங்குகாய் *pīraṅqukāy* by strengthening ங் *ṅ* with கு *ku*, which corresponds to ग् *g* in Sans.

in the Yajur Veda and in which गं॒ *gṁ*, pronounced somewhat like *gim*, is used for the *anusvāra* sound: and so on.

Most of the conjugational and declensional forms are derivatives containing several parts.

4. By a careful comparison of the words of one language which are connected in forms and meanings, with the corresponding words of the other languages of the same family, we can trace them to their simplest sources and be in a position to explain the derivation of each of them. We can also become acquainted with the principles on which each grammatical form is constructed and get a clear insight into its component parts. This is the method in which the philologist must conduct his linguistic investigations and solve all questions connected with the derivations of the words of a language and the analysis of its grammatical forms. This is not a quite new scientific method and need not be specially noted here but for the very limited use made of it in linguistic researches; and, when we look into the results achieved by philology even in the most cultivated languages of the world, viz. Sanskrit and Greek, we shall see that, with some exceptions, the most learned and intelligent scholars have fallen back and have contented themselves with what could be gathered about the surface and have not dived below the depth already reached.

हगं॒स *hagṁsa*, then பீராகுங்காய் *pīrakuṅkāy*, by the transfer of ங் *ṅ* and கு *ku*, and at last shortened into பீர்க்குங்காய் *pīrkkuṅkāy*, by the elision of அ *a* of ர *r* and the euphonic doubling of க *k*. But in the Telugu బీరకాయ *bīrakāya*, corresponding to the Tam. பீர்க்குங்காய் *pīrkkuṅkāy*, no such orthographical outgrowth is seen. This is the best way, I think, to account for the peculiar pronunciation of the Yajur Vedi Brahmins.

5. Now I shall give a brief account of what has been done in the Aryan and Dravidian philology.[1] Taking the Comparative Grammar of Mr. Bopp, we can say that it is really a great work and, as the first of the kind, a most admirable one. It is the only systematic and complete work on the subject and has not yet been surpassed or rivalled. But it is not sufficient and does not solve all questions and difficulties; and in addition to this, I may say that there are errors which require corrections. After the gigantic progress which that great pioneer of linguistic science made, his followers did not go much beyond his limit. This is the case with the Comparative Grammar of the Aryan languages. As for comparative lexicons, we have Bopp's Comparative Lexicon, Benfey's Dictionary and Mon. Williams' Dictionary and the like in which attempts have been made to bring under each word the corresponding words of allied languages for comparison but without much success.[2] But if we refer to Latin and Greek dictionaries of which we may take Smith's and Liddell and Scott's Dictionaries as the best representatives we have, we must observe that the case is equally unsatisfactory. With great deference to their scholarship and their immensely useful works, I beg to observe that the authors have failed to discover the alliance of many words in the same language and have treated words which are allied in form and meaning as different primitive words, and that they have equally failed to avail them-

---

[1] I request that my readers will be good enough to understand that I make these remarks very generally and that they are to be taken with much limitation.

[2] It is to be regretted much that, even in the St. Petersburgh Sanskrit Dictionary, no attempt was made to find out the right etymology of words.

selves of the results achieved by the past and contemporary philologists. The same remarks may be applied to the various works on the grammars, we have, of the other classical languages of Europe individually.

Coming to the Indian Vernaculars, I have to observe that within the last twenty years two Comparative Grammars have been produced, one written by Mr. Beames styled "A Comparative Grammar of the Modern Aryan Languages of India," and the other, by Dr. Hoernle styled "Grammar of the Gaudian Languages," and to these we may add a small book produced by the former with the title of "An Outline of Indian Philology." As for the Dravidian Languages, the Comparative Grammar written by Dr. Caldwell which is the first work of the kind is to the Dravidian languages what Bopp's Comparative Grammar is to the Aryan languages. It is an elaborate and interesting work in which the learned author has shown his researches and scholarship to a great extent.

I may next mention Dr. Gundert's Malayalam Dictionary in which the author has attempted to introduce under each word the corresponding words of the other Dravidian languages with some success.[1] But speaking generally of the results produced by the above and other philologists, I have to observe that the success achieved by them is very limited and much remains to be done, and that this is partly owing to the imperfection of the knowledge which the linguists possessed of the languages which they have treated and partly to their failure to give a wide application to the method above described.

---

[1] I cannot omit mentioning here the 'Kanarese Dictionary on the Comparative Method' which was promised five years ago by the Rev. Mr. Kittel of Mercara, who is one of the best Kanarese scholars in this Presidency and has done much for Kanarese literature and from whom we may expect much.

6. Now, to return to the scientific method of the philologist. He should classify all the allied words of one language and the corresponding words of the other languages of the family into one group, and if he continues this method in the analysis of the kindred languages and forming groups of allied words, he will arrive ultimately at a number of groups. He will then be able to see that each individual word of each group bears some orthographical affinity to the rest of the group and that all words of the group are traceable to one primitive word from which the other words can be reconstructed by orthographical changes which take place according to certain phonetic laws and which are to the linguist what evolution is to the chemist, with this difference that the orthographical changes which produce so many words from a primitive one partly depend on the peculiar construction of the organs of speech of the nation who speak it and partly on the will of the speaker, and the thought he wants to express. The Ang.-Sax. *cunnan*, 'to know,' for instance, should give us the past tense form '*cuthe*' and not '*could*' with an *l* as we now spell it.

7. The above method of grouping is of two kinds, one being the grouping of all words bearing some analogy in their forms and some connection in their meanings and then tracing their forms and meanings to their proper sources in the group itself as in the first of the following lists. This belongs to a higher stage of philology, which is accessible only to advanced scholars. The other kind of grouping consists in classifying together the corresponding words of the allied languages of the same family, which express the same idea as in the second of the following lists; as, Sans. अहम् *aham*, Gr. εγω, Lat. *ego*, Ang.-Sax. *ich*, and so on. There are, however, exceptions; *e. g.*, Sans. द्युस् *dyus* and Gr. ολυμπος are con-

nected with स्वर् *svar*, as shown lower down, while Lat. *cœlum* and the older form of it, *coelus*, are traceable to a group of words which originally conveyed the idea of 'a hole,' such as Sans. सुषि *suṣi*, गुहा *guhā*, कुल *kula*, कुहर *kuhara*, कोटर *kōṭara*, Gr. κευθω and κευθμων. The novitiates must begin their study of philology and their researches first in this method, for the chances of errors are fewer and the conviction is more certain than is the case with the other method.

8. As for the grammatical forms and derivative words, the second kind of the groupings abovementioned is to be followed. The philologist should take a grammatical form or a derivative word of one language and compare it with what is corresponding in the kindred languages.[1] Whatever may be the changes and outgrowths concealing the real origin of many of the allied forms and words, there may be some or at least one in which we can see a clear trace of the component parts; and we can apply the analysis thus arrived at to the rest of the corresponding forms and words. If, however, there be a peculiar part or residuum in the composition of them, it can be accounted for by some orthographical laws already existing or to be discovered hereafter. But if, after a careful investigation, we are not able to explain away the residuum, we may then, very generally, infer that the grammatical form or word, which thus baffles a clear and complete analysis, must be an unconnected one.

To illustrate what I say I shall give the following four lists, of which the first will contain five groups of the corresponding words of the allied languages of one family

---

[1] Here too there are exceptions; e. g., Sans. द्वितीय *dvitīya* is formed from द्वि *dvi*, 'two,' and तीय *tīya*, a termination modified

expressing the same and allied ideas; the second, many groups, each of which contains the corresponding words of the allied languages expressive of the same idea; the third, the corresponding grammatical expressions; the fourth, derivative words.

List I.

First Group, which I call *Ātman Group* as it is represented by the word आत्मन् *ātman.*[1]

9. Take the Sanskrit word शुभ *śubha*, 'good,' शोभन *śobhana*, 'good,' and शुभ् *śubh*, 'to shine.' It is easy to connect them; for there is not much difference in their forms. But the verb शुभ् *śubh*, 'to shine,' seems to be a little far in meaning from शुभम् *śubham*, 'good;' but what is good is attractive or beautiful by association. The two ideas are therefore connected. In Sanskrit स्वम् *svam* [स्वर् *svar* and स्वस् *svas*, 'heaven and happiness']

---

from त्य *tya*, and is found in Gr. τριτος and τριταιος and Lat. *tertius;* but the corresponding Greek and Latin words are differently formed, e. g. Gr. δεοτερος (Sans. द्वितर *dvitara*) is composed of δεο, 'two,' and τερος, a termination of the comparative degree; and Lat. *secondus* comes from *sequor*, Sans. सच् *sac*, Gr. ἑπομαι, and is a present participial adjective form of the root meaning 'following.' Similarly, Tam. ஒன்று *onṟu* (radically ஒன்னு *onnu*), Kan. ಒಂದು *ondu*, and Tel. ఒకటి *okaṭi*, meaning 'one,' are differently formed; for the former two are radically the same forms, while the last, Tel. ఒకటి *okaṭi*, is a contraction of ఒరువది *oruvadi*, ఒరు *oru*, Tam. ஒன்று *onṟu*, అది *adi*, Tam. அது *adu*, 'that,' meaning radically 'that which is one.' The real Telugu word corresponding to Tam. ஒன்று *onṟu*, and Kan. ಒಂದು *ondu*, is ఒండు *oṇḍu*, which is replaced in the common language by ఒకటి *okaṭi*, and is confined to literary language only. (*Vide* Vol. II.)

[1] *Vide* Note 1, p. 14. *Vide* the Semetic Analogy at the end of the List.

means 'happiness,' and from this word I derive the above three words शुभम् *śubham*, शोभनम् *śobhanam* and शुभ् *śubh*. The words शिवम् *śivam*, 'good,' शिवस् *śivas*, 'God Śiva,' शिवा *Śivā*, 'his wife,' also, are modifications of the same root स्वम् *svam*. But स्वम् *svam* is only of one syllable, and the connection between it and शुभम् *śubham*, &c., and शिवम् *śivam*, &c., which contain two syllables, may appear improbable. We may, however, take such examples as स्वर् *svar*, सुवर् *suvar*, 'heaven,' and स्वर्ग *svarga*, सुवर्ग *suvarga*, 'heaven,' and see that the monosyllabic स्वम् *svam* is modified by the insertion of *u* and *i* into शुभम् *śubham* and शिवम् *śivam* respectively. शिव *śiva* is modified as शेव *śēva* and क्षेम *kṣēma*, 'happiness,' the former being used in the Vedas. स्वम् *svam* is contracted into शम् *śam*, 'happiness.' Gr. ἴδιος,[1] 'one's own,' Ang.-Sax.

---

[1] स्व *sva* is modified as δια by the change of स *s* into δ and व *v* into ια, (Sans. य *y*) and ι is prefixed simply for pronunciation as 'o' in ολυμπος (स्वस् *svas*,) which is explained lower down.

It is this word स्व *sva*, which is converted into स्य *sya*, and is used as a genitive suffix. As स्वम् *svam* becomes ἴδιον in Greek, it becomes உடை *uḍai* in Tamil by the insertion of *u* at the beginning, and means 'possession,' 'property.' உடைய *uḍaiya* is used in Modern Tamil as the genitive suffix and is derived from உடை *uḍai*, and answers to Sans. स्य *sya*, and to Gr. ου. Tam. உடைமை *uḍaimai*, 'possession,' is formed exactly as Sanskrit स्वत्वम् *svatvam* (old form स्वत्वन् *svatvan*) and Gr. ἰδιωμα(τ) and agrees with the latter words in meaning. Compare Gr. κτημα(τ) 'possession.' Tel. కలిమి *kalimi*, 'wealth.'

habban, 'to have,' and Lat. *habeo*, 'to have,' are derived from स्वम् *svam*, meaning 'possession or property' and connected with स्वर् *svar*, 'heaven.'[1] To this स्वर् *svar* meaning 'happiness,' are traceable the Gr. *ολβος*, 'happiness,' Lat. *salvus* 'well,' 'sound' and perhaps the Eng. *happiness, happy* and *hap* which are usually derived from Fr. *happer*, 'to snatch,' and also Lat. *aveo* and *haveo*, 'to be happy,' and Sans. सुख *sukha*,[2] Gr. *ὑγιεια*, 'health,' 'soundness of body,' *ὑγιης*, 'sound,' 'healthy,' &c., in which *v* of स्व *sva* is changed into *kh* and *g*. The same idea is expressed in Latin by the word *salvus* of which '*halvus*' is simply a modification. स्व *sva* is contracted into सु *su* and *ευ*, 'good.'

10. Gr. *ολβος* and Lat. *salvus* seem to be metathetical modifications of स्वर् *svar* and स्वस् *svas*, 'happiness,' the final *r* coming to the middle of the word and being changed

---

[1] I shall assume here that the most original idea of this group is found in आत्मन् *ātman*, which I have taken as the representative of this group and which I shall mention hereafter. आत्मन् *ātman* means 'self,' that is 'I' or 'Soul,' Wind or breath, and all the other meanings are traceable to those two. The change of meanings may be as follows: from wind, region of wind, that is sky, the firmament, heaven, the region of Gods which is supposed to be above the sky, earth, the sun, moon, other planets, clouds, rain, snow, water, vapour, smoke, &c., and from the idea of 'I' or 'Self,' own, possession, property, wealth, happiness and so on.

आत्मायत्नधृतिस्वांतस्वभावपरमात्मसु। जीवबुद्धिशरीरेषु॥
Ātmāyatna dhṛtisvānta svabhāva paramātmasu, jīvabuddhi śarīrēṣu.
Nānārtharatnamālā.

[2] सुख *sukha*, being wrongly analyzed into सु *su* + ख *kha*, produced the word दुःख *duhka*, 'sorrow,' दुस् *dus* + ख *kha*. From सुख *sukha* are derived Arab. شوق *shauq*, Pers. شوخ *shōkh*, 'playful,' Tel. సోకు *sōku*, 'a spirit,' 'to be entranced.' సొక్కు *sokku*, 'charm.'

into *l*. Sans. सर्व *sarva*, 'happy,' 'whole,' is also allied to it.[1] Connected with स्वस् *svas* are the Gr. σωζω, σαω, and σωω, 'to keep alive,' and Sans. श्वस् *śvas*, Gr. φυσαω and Lat. *sibilo*, 'to breathe' and also Sans. स्वस्ति *svasti*, and Gr. σωστεον, 'it is to be saved,' and Sans. शर्मन् *śarman*, 'happiness,' केवल *kēvala*, 'sole, entire,' क *k* being inserted for स *s* of स्वर् *svar*, Sans. कुशल *kuśala*, 'welfare,' Pers. خوشامد *hkuṣāmad*, 'flattery,' خوش *hkuṣ*, 'pleased,' خوشی *hkuṣī*, 'happiness.'

11. Here I would mention the Ang.-Sax. *heofon, heofen, hefon* and *heben* and the English derivative *heaven*. This group is usually derived from Ang.-Sax. *hefan*, 'to raise or lift,' in Bosworth's Anglo-Saxon Dictionary, Angus's English Grammar, and other works; and this is the view held universally about the origin of the word. The final syllable *en* would then be a corruption of *ed*, *n* standing for *d* as in 'shap*ed*,' 'shap*en*,' the past tense forms of the verb to 'shape' as in Sans. त्रात *trāta* and त्राण *trāṇa*, 'protected,' from त्रा *trā*, to 'protect,' त *t* and न *n* being past participial terminations.

---

[1] सर्वतातिम् *sarvtatim*, 'happiness,' सर्व *sarva*, 'happy.'

Rig Veda, X. 100, 1; 36, 14.

Similarly Sans. सकल *sakala*, 'all,' Gr. οχλος, 'a throng of people,' seem to be traceable to the same source and also Sans. समस्त *samasta*, Gr. πασ, Gen. παντος, shortened from οπας, a form directly derived from समस्त *samasta*.

[2] I would derive the Arab. سلامتي *salāmati*, 'safety,' from Sans. शर्मन् *śarman*, by the change of *r* into *l* and the insertion of the vowel *ā* between *l* and *m*.

But if we compare *heaven* with Sans. स्वर् *svar*, 'heaven,' सुमेरु *sumēru*, and मेरु *mēru*, which last two words will be mentioned hereafter, we can easily see that the word is not to be derived from *hefan*, 'to heave,' but is to be connected with Sans. स्वर् *svar*, consonant with consonant, as *h* with स *s*, *f* with व *v*, and *n* with र् *r*. Analogy is, moreover, in favour of my supposition, for the idea of 'up' is derived from that of the region of sky, wind or air, with which the idea of 'Heaven' is to be connected.

12. Compare the following list:—

SANSKRIT.	GREEK.	LATIN.	ANG.-SAX.	ENGLISH.
उपरि *upari*,	ὑπερ.	*super*.	*ofer*.	over
परि *pari*	περι, περ	*per*	*for*	for
उप *upa*,	ὑπο	*sub*	*upp*	up
अव *ava*, as in				
अधर, *adhara*,				
अधम *adhama*,				
अधस् *adhas*, and				
अवर *avara*, and				
अवम *avama*.				
——	——	——	*ufan*	above.
——	——	——	*ufa*	——
——	——	——	*ufon*	——
उपर *upara*[1]	ὑπεριων[2]	*superus*,	*ufera*	upper.
उपम *upama*[3]	ὑπατος,[4]	——	*ufema*	upmost.
——	——	——	*upha*	——

[1] 'Clouds,' 'near.' [2] 'Sun-god.' [3] 'Similar.' [4] 'Highest.'

SANSKRIT.	GREEK.	LATIN.	ANG.-SAX.	ENGLISH.
	οφρα, 'that or in order that.'			
	οψε, 'at length.'			
	οψια, 'the latter part (of the day).'			
	ὑψι, 'aloft.'			
ऊर्ध्व[1] *ūrdhva*,	*αιπυς* } *αιπος* }	——	——	——
——	*ἠλιβατος*	——	*lyft, luft*	'heaven or atmosphere.'
ऋष्व *ṛṣva*.	*ολυμπος*	——	——	——

The first words of the above list, उपरि *upari*, *ὑπερ*, &c., may be connected with Sans. स्वर् *svar*, the idea of 'sky' originating that of 'high.' In Sanskrit, उपरि *upari* is shortened into परि *pari*, by the elision of the first vowel, and into उप *upa*, by that of the final syllable रि *ri*. Similarly are formed from Gr. *ὑπερ*, Lat. *super*, Ang.-Sax. *ofer*, respectively, Gr. *περι*, *περ* and *ὑπο*, Lat. *per* and *sub*, and Ang.-Sax. *for* and *upp*, *ufon*, *ufa*, *upha*, *&c.* In Sanskrit, अव *ava* meaning 'down' must be a modification of उप *upa*, and, in अधर् *adhara*, अधम *adhama*, and अधस् *adhas*, is still more modified owing to the contact of त *t*. अधर् *adhara*,[2]

---

[1] Gr. *αρδην* or its full form *αερδην* and Latin *altus*, 'high,' Sans. अट्ट *aṭṭa*, 'lofty' and अट्टालक *aṭṭālaka*, 'an apartment on the roof of a house,' seem to be allied to it.

[2] In these words अव *ava* is changed into अह *aha* by the change of व *v* into ह *h*; and, when तर् *tara*, तम *tama* and तस् *tas* follow, ह *h* is united with त *t* and changes it into ध *dha*; as,

'low' or 'mean' = अव *ava* + तर् *tara*, in which अव *ava* means 'down' and तर् *tara* is a suffix of the comparative degree; and अधम *adhama*, 'meanest,' 'lowest' = अव *ava* + तम *tama*, in which तम *tama* is a suffix of the superlative degree; अधस् *adhas*, 'down or downwards' = अवतस् *avatas*, तस् *tas* being an adverbial suffix corresponding to the Gr. θεν.

सधस् *sadhas* = सह *saha* + तस् *tas* as in सधस्थस् *sadhasthas*, 'an attendant,' सध्र्यंच् *sadhryañc*, 'an attendant' = सधस् *sadhas* + अंच् *añc* = सधर् *sadhar* + अंच् *añc* by the change of स् *s* into र् *r* = सध्र् *sadhr* + अंच् *añc* by the elision of the penultimate अ *a* and then = सध्र् *sadhr* + य् *y* + अंच् *añc* by the insertion of an extraneous य *y* between ध्र् *dhr* and the vowel अ *a* (as in सम्यंच् *samyañc* = सम् *sam* + अंच् *añc* and तिर्यंच् *tiryañc* = तिर् *tir* + अंच् *añc*, तिर् *tir* being contracted from तिरस् *tiras*.) Similarly, in Tamil அது *adu*, 'that,' இது *idu*, 'this,' and உது *udu*, 'yonder,' are written as அஃது *ahdu*, இஃது *ihdu*, and உஃது *uhdu*, respectively, in the first of which the āyda letter 'ஃ' (Sans. ह *h*) is inserted as a modification of வ *v* of அவ் *av* (and ஒ *o*), which stands for Sans. सस् *sas*, Pali and Prākṛtic सो *sō*, and Greek ὁ, the aspirate sound of which is lost in Tamil. அ *a* is a modification of ஒ *o*, and is used generally, but the latter which is more original reappears before the termination து *tu*; thus அது *adu* becomes ஒது *odu*, then அவ்து *avdu*, அவ் *av* being put for ஒ *o*, then அஃது *ahdu*, வ *v* being changed into ஃ *h*. But this aspirate sound is universally seen in the Kanarese language in both of its dialects, in the demonstrative adverbs, as Kan. ಅಹಗೆ *ahage*, Tam. ஆங்கு *āngu*, 'so'; Kan. ಇಹಗೆ *ihage*, Tam. ஈங்கு *īngu*, 'thus;' Kan. ಎಹಗೆ *ehage*, Tam. ஏங்கு *ēngu* (obsolete) or யாங்கு *yāngu*, which is used in its place and means 'where;' and the modern forms ಹಾಗೆ *hāge*, ಹೀಗೆ *hīge*, and ಹೇಗೆ *hēge* corrupted into ಹ್ಯಾಗೆ *hyāge*.

But in अवर् *avara* and अवम *avama*, the root अव *ava* remains unchanged and the suffixes अर् *ara* and अम *ama* are modifications of तर् *tara* and तम *tama* by the elision of the initial *t*. Compare परम *parama*, Lat. *supremus*, Gr. ὑπατος. In Gr. οψε, οψια and ὑψι, the *r* of ὑπερ is changed into σ. Οφρα is a modification of ὑπερ like Ang.-Sax. *ofer*; Eng. *above* is derived from *ab* + *ufa*, 'high.'

Sans. ऊर्ध्व *ūrdhva* seems to be a modification of स्वर् *svar*, which, by the insertion of a euphonic ऊ *ū* at the beginning as in Gr. Ολυμπος, Sans. स्वर् *svar* and उलूखल *ulūkhala*, Gr. δοιδυξ [see § 13], and, by the transposition of *r*, becomes ऊर्स्व *ūrsva* and then ऊर्ध्व *ūrdhva* by the change of स *s* into ध *dh*, and is connected with ऋष्व *ṛṣva*. It is from this word ऊर्ध्व *ūrdhva*, I think, that the Greek words αιπυς, 'high,' 'steep,' and αιπος, 'high,' are to be derived by the elision of र् *r* and ध *dh* and the change of *υ* into *p*. Compare the following :—

SANSKRIT.	GREEK.
उद्वह् *udvah*, 'to marry.'	οπυιω, οπυω,
उद्वहस् *udvahas*, 'son,'	υιος,
अध्वन् *adhvan*,	{ οιμος / οιμη } a way or path, by the elision of ध *dh* and the change of *v* into *m*.
Sans. श्लेष्मन् *ślēṣman* / Gr. φλεγμα (τ)	Gr. λαπη by the elision of γ and the initial φ.
Lat. *sagnus* / Sans. असृक् *asṛk*	Gr. αἷμα by the elision of *g* and the change of *ν* into *m* and of the initial *s* into *h*.
Sans. चिह्नम् *cihnam* / Lat. *signum*	Gr. σημα, by the elision of *g* and the change of *n* into *m*.

Sans. रुग्ण *rugṇa*, 'sick,' Gr. λοιμος, 'plague,' by the elision of ग *g*, the change of ण *n* into म *m*, and र् *r* into λ.

Sans. ऋष्व *ṛṣva* means 'high,' 'lofty,' as in the following Vedic passage :—

अज्रा इंद्रस्य गिरयश्चिदृष्वाः Rig Veda. VI. 24. 8.

Ajrā indrasyagirayaścidṛṣvāh.

'Even lofty mountains are surmountable to Indra.'

Gr. Ολυμπος corresponds to Ang.-Sax. *lyft* or *luft*, 'heaven,' 'atmosphere,' with this difference: that the euphonic *o* found at the beginning of the Greek word is not found in the Anglo-Saxon and the *t* which is found at the end of *lyft* disappears in Ολυμπος. As for the other consonants there is a clear affinity letter to letter, as *l* to λ, *f* to μπ. From *lyft* are derived Eng. *loft*, 'height,' *lofty*, 'high,' *aloft*, 'high,' and *lift*, 'to raise.' But *lyft* bears a closer alliance to स्वर् *svar* than it does to Ολύμπος, and can be connected with *heafon*, *heofen*, *hefon* and *heben*, the स *s* of the Sans. स्वर् *svar* being changed into *h* in *heafon*, &c., as it is changed into *l* in *lyft*. I would therefore trace Sans. उपरि *upari*, Lat. *super* and all the allied words and derivatives in the above list, the Eng. *heaven* and the Ang.-Sax. *heofon*, &c., *lyft* and *luft* to स्वर् *svar*. As in Sanskrit and Greek we have क्षिप् *kṣip*, σκηπτω, σκιμπτω, σκιπτω and also σκιπω, 'to throw,' and ηλιβατος, 'steep,' 'high' from स्वर् *svar*, so have we Ang.-Sax. *liften*, Icel. *lypta*, 'to lift,' Eng. *lift*, *sift*, Ang.-Sax. *hefan*, 'to lift,' Eng. *heave*, and Lat. *levo*, all traceable to the same root स्वर् *svar*.

13. From स्वस् *svas* and स्वर् *svar*, 'heaven,' 'happiness,' which gave us स्वम् *svam*, 'happiness,' and सुवर् *suvar*, 'heaven,' I derive सुमेरु *sumēru* and मेरु *mēru*[1] by the change of *v* into *m*, the idea of sky or heaven giving the idea of 'high.' Lat. *superus* 'above,' Gr. Ὑπεριων, Sans. सुपर्वन् *suparvan*, 'a deity,' पर्वत *parvata*,[2] 'clouds' and Gr. Ολυμπος, a high wall on the Macedonian frontier of Thessaly which was believed to be the abode of the gods, and the way to which was guarded by thick clouds, are allied to Sans. स्व *sva* (and स्वर् *svar*) which is changed into सुव *suva*,[3] as already shown in शुभ *śubha*, and then becomes लुप *lupa*, by the change of *s* into *l*[4] and *v* into *p*. Compare Lat. *liber*, Sans. स्वैर *svaira*, 'free.' लुप *lupa* is modified into लुंप *lumpa* by the insertion of *m* before *p*. The vowel *o* may have been inserted before the word for the sake of pronunciation; and the addition of a vowel to the beginning of a word often occurs in Sanskrit and Greek; as,

---

[1] Gr. Ἠπιρος, a large country in the north-west of Greece, which is elevated, Πιερια, a district in Macedonia, and Πιερος, a king of Emathia; Tam. மேடு *mēḍu*, Tel. మిట్ట *miṭṭa*, 'elevation,' Kan. ಮೇಲ್ *mēl*, Tam. மேல் *mēl*, Tel. మీదు *mīdu*, which are modifications of Sans. परि *pari*, Gr. περι, and are traced to the syllable वर् *var* of स्वर् *svar*.

[2] पर्वत *parvata* comes from पर्वन् *parvan* (πειρατ), 'end' = परिमन् *pariman* = उपरिमन् *upariman*, Gr. Ὑπεριων.

[3] From सुव *suva* we get सुम *suma*, which is changed into क्षुम *kṣuma* and then क्षौम *kṣauma*, 'an airy room on the top of a house.' Similarly can be derived from सुवर् *suvar*, Vedic सुमत् *sumat*, क्षुमत् *kṣumat*, 'happy,' and सुवितम् *suvitam*, 'happiness.'

[4] Vide § 31.

SANSKRIT.	GREEK.
अद्भुतम् *adbhutam,*	*θαυμα* (*τ*), 'wonder.'
भ्रू *bhrū,*	*οφρυς,* 'eyebrow.'
चल *cala,*	*οκελλω,* 'to move.'
एडूक *ēdūka,*	*τειχος,* 'a wall.'
अनीक *anīka,*	*νεικος,* 'battle.'
मिह् *mih,*	*ομιχω,* 'to make water.'
नख *nakha,*	*ονυξ,* 'nail.'
दन्त *danta,*	*οδους,* 'teeth,' *οδαξ,* 'with teeth.'
दभ्र *dabhra,*	*ελαφρος,* 'small,' 'light.'
लज्ज् *lajj,* 'to be ashamed,'	*ελεγχω,* 'to put to shame.'
ग्लै *glai,*	*οκλαζω,* 'to sink down.'
लेश *lēśa,*	*ολιγος,* 'few,' 'small.'
दु *du,*	*οδυσσομαί,* 'to be grieved.'
अश्रु *aśru,* 'tear,'	*ολοφυρομαί,* 'to shed tears,' in which the radical part is *λαφυρά* which contracted into *λαφρα* answers to *δακρυ,* *φ* standing for *κ* of *δακρυ,* Latin *lacrima* and *dacrima.*
मृज् *mṛj,*	*ομοργνυμι,* 'to wipe out.'
निंदा *nindā,*	*ονειδος,* 'reproach.'
उलूखल *ulūkhala,*	*δοιδυξ,* 'a pestle,' which by metă-thesis becomes *δοικαδα* and then *δυχαδα* and, by the change of *δ* into ल *l,* and the euphonic insertion of उ *u* before the word, is transformed into उलूखल *ulū-khala.*

SANSKRIT.	GREEK.
नर *nara*,	*ανηρ*, 'a man.' Sans. अंडीर *aṇḍīra*,[1] 'a man.'
नामन् *nāman*,	*ονομα* (τ), 'a name.'
सभाज् *sabhāj*,	*ασπαζομαι*, 'to embrace.'

Sans. सभाज् *sabhāj* being modified from स्वज् *svaj*, 'to embrace' which latter in Tamil becomes தழுவு *taḷuvu*, Kan. ತಬ್ಬು *tabbu*, 'to embrace,' Tel. డొబ్బు *dobbu*, 'to cohabit with a woman,' Hindi شاباش *ṣābāṣ*, 'bravo,' has received an additional *a* at the beginning in the Gr. *ασπαζομαι*.

In the above examples a vowel is inserted at the beginning of a word for the purpose of euphony. But Gr. Ολυμπος may be derived from स्वर् *svar*, by metathesis as Lat. *salvus* and Gr. *ολβος*, 'happiness,' were derived; and in that case the initial *o* must be aspirated as a modification of स *s* and, as the *o* however is not aspirated, we may also suppose that the aspirate sound was lost.

14. Next comes the word सस् *sas*, 'to sleep,' which is a contraction of स्वस् *svas*, 'happiness.' Similary, I derive from स्व *sva* and सुख *sukha*, स्वप् *svap*, 'to sleep,' Lat. *sopio*, 'to put to sleep,' Gr. *ὑπνος*, 'sleep,' Sans. स्वप्न *svapna*, and the corresponding words of other languages and their derivatives. स्वाहा *svāhā*,[2] a word applied to the Gods, and

---

[1] In the sūtra कांडांडादीरन्नीरचौ *kāṇḍāṇḍādīrannīracau* (V. 2, 111), Pāṇini derives अंडीर *aṇḍīra* from अंड *aṇḍa*, 'testicle' and ईर *īra*, a suffix indicating possession.

[2] Yaska mentions स्वाहा *svāhā* among the synonyms of वाक्

स्वधा[1] *svadhā*, applied to the Manes, both meaning 'happiness,' correspond to the word स्वस्ति *svasti*, applied to men, as स्वस्त्यस्तुते *svastyastutē*, 'may there be happiness to you.' स्वाहा *svāhā* seems to be a modified form of स्वस् *svas*, by inserting *h* for the final *s* and adding *ā* to the end and lengthening the preceding vowel *a*. But in स्वधा *svadhā*, *ā* is added to स्वस् *svas*, and *h* is changed into *dh*.

15. Next, from स्वस् *svas* we proceed to दिवस् *divas*, Gr. Ζευς, Δις, Διος (Sans. दिव्य *divya*), Θεος, Διωνη, Lat. *Deus*, and *Jovis*, *Juno*, *Janus* and *Diana*. दिवस् *divas* originally meant 'Heaven,' as in दिवस्पति *divaspati*,[2] द्यौस्पितर् *dyauspitar*, Gr. Ζευσπατηρ and Lat. *Jupiter*, and, when contracted, becomes द्युस् *dyus*, and द्यौस् *dyaus*, 'Heaven,' द्युस् *dyus*, द्यस् *dyas*, and तिथि *tithi*, 'a day.' दिवस *divasa*, which comes directly from दिवस् *divas*, also, means 'a

---

vāk, 'speech,' and derives it in the following way:—

स्वाहेत्येतत्सु आहेतिवा स्वावा गाहेतिवा स्वंप्राहेतिवा स्वा
Svāhētyētatsu āhētivā svāvā gāhētivā svamprāhētivā svā
हुतं हविर्जुहोतीतिवा ॥ (Nirukta, 8-20.)
hutam havirjuhōtītivā.

[1] स्वधा *svadhā* is mentioned by him among the synonyms of water' and 'food.' From this may be derived सुधा *sudhā*, 'nectar.'

[2] In the word दिवस्पितृ *divaspitṛ*, Gr. Ζευσπατηρ, the word पितृ *pitṛ*, πατηρ, is added to दिवस् *divas*, Ζευς, as μητηρ to Γη in Γημητηρ which is found in an older form as Δημητηρ, Demiter or Ceres, the goddess of agriculture and rural life and mother of Persephone.—Max Müller's '*Science of Language*,' Lecture X.

day.' दिन *dina*, 'a day,' is a modification of द्युस् *dyus* by the change of *s* into *n*.

In the Latin word *Jupiter* the द्य *dya* of द्यौस् *dyaus* is changed into *j*, as also in *Jovis*, *Jupiter*, 'God,' *Juno* the wife of Jupiter, and *Janus*, 'the sun-god.' As ज्या *jyā* is the wife of द्यौस् *dyaus*, Δη of Ζευς, so is *Juno*, the wife of Jupiter. Compare *Caius* or *Gaius* and *Caia*, which will be mentioned lower down. The change of the *s* of द्यौस् *dyaus* into *n* in *Juno* and *Janus*, is like that taking place in Sans. क्षोणी *kṣōṇī*, 'earth', Gr. Διωνη, the mother of Venus, दिन *dina*, 'a day,' Eng. *dawn* and Lat. *Diana*, the daughter of Jupiter and Latona, sister of Apollo, (Latona answering to Sans. द्योतना *dyōtanā*, 'the goddess of dawn') and Gr. Ζαν, Doric form for Ζην, 'Ζευς.'

16. To this word द्यस् *dyas*[1] or दिवस् *divas* may be traced the Ang.-Sax. *daeg*, *daga*, *dah*, Eng. *day* and *dawn* (Ang.-Sax. *dagian*); Sans. सद्यस् *sadyas*, 'now,' अद्य *adya*, 'to-day,' द्यवि *dyavi*, 'in the day,' तदा *tadā*, 'then,' a contraction of तदम् *tadam*, तदानीम् *tadānīm*, which is a modification of तदम् *tadam* + इत् *it*, तदम् *tadam*, Lat. *tandem*, meaning 'then' and इत् *it*, 'also or even,' Vedic सदमित् *sadamit*,[2] which is composed of सदम् *sadam*,

---

[1] I derive प्रादुस् *prādus*, 'brightness,' 'openness,' from प्र *pra*, 'much,' and द्युस् *dyus*, 'day,' 'brightness.'

[2] पाहिसदमिद्विशायुः.—Rig Veda, I. 27, 2.
Pāhisadamidviśāyuh.
'Protect (me) always everlasting.'

'always,' and इत् *it*, 'even,' इदा *idā* and इदानीम् *idānīm*, now;' perhaps Lat. *donicum* and *donec*, 'as long as' or 'while,' *denique* and *demum*, 'at last,' 'at length,' *tamdiu*, 'so long,' *quondam*, which is a modification of *quumdam*, 'at a certain time,' 'at one time,' *diu*, 'by day,' and *dum*, 'while;' Gr. τηνικα, τηνικαδε, 'at this or that part of the day,' τηνικαυτα, 'at this particular part of the day,' δην, Dor. δαν, 'for a long while,' δη and ηδη, 'now,' 'already,' δαι, 'then,' as in 'τι δαι,' 'what then,' ἡμερον, σημερον, Doric σαμερον and Attic τημερον, 'to-day,' of which the Doric σαμερον may be metathetically modified as μασερον and, by the change of *m* into *v*, may give us the Sans. वासर *vāsara*,[1] 'a day.' I hold ἡμαρ to be a corruption of दिवस् *divas* or स्वस् *svas*, as well as the Lat. *tempus* (-*oris*), 'time,' by a natural change. Though Lat. *tempus* is usually derived from *temno*, 'to cut,' I would trace it to दिवस् *divas*.

17. Next come the Sans. ह्यस् *hyas*, 'yesterday,' श्वस् *śvas*, 'to-morrow,' which may very easily be connected with Sans. द्यस् *dyas*, 'day,' by the change of *d* into *h* and *ś*. The Gr. χθες is a modification of ह्यस् *hyas*, and has ह् *h* strengthened into χ and य *y* changed into *s* and then hardened into θ. Lat. *here* and *heri* are modifications of the same root ह्यस् *hyas*. Compare Sans. गद् *gad*, कथ् *kath*, 'to say,' चक्ष् *cakṣ*, 'to say,' शंस् *śaṁs*, 'to say or praise,' which are all allied forms and are contracted into ख्या *khyā*, 'to say or proclaim,' and क्श्या *kśā*, a modification of the same.

---

[1] Or, it may better be derived from अतस *atasa*, 'brightness,' by the addition of *v* to the beginning of the word. (Vide अतस *atasa*.)

If $\chi\theta\epsilon\varsigma$ and *here* or *heri* are derived from ह्यस् *hyas*, I do not see any reason why द्यस् *dyas*, which gives श्वस् *śvas*, may not be modified as *cras* in Latin, the processes of change being somewhat like those in $\chi\theta\epsilon\varsigma$, द्यस् *dyas* becoming *gyas*, *gsas*, *ksas* and at last *kras*, that is, *cras*.[1] The Sanskrit words सम *sama*, 'a year' and समय *samaya*, 'time,' seem to be traceable to दिवस् *divas*.

---

[1] Compare the following:

शेयते *śēyatē*, 'they sleep,' becoming शेरते *śēratē*, शी *śī*, 'to sleep;' एधेयन् *ēdhēyan*, 'they may grow,' एधेरन् *ēdhēran*; in which two instances य *y* is changed into र् *r*.

एधियीस्त *ēdhiyīsta*, 'may he grow,' एधिषीष्ट *ēdhiṣīṣṭa* in which य *y* is changed into स *s*. (Vide List III, Conjugation.)

एधियीसन् *ēdhiyīsan*, 'may they grow,' एधिषीरन् *ēdhiṣīran*, in which स *s* is changed into र् *r* and य *y* into स *s*.

This law prevails to a great extent, also, in the Dravidian languages; *e.g.*

Sans. कैकेयी *kaikēyī*, Tam. கைகேசி *kaikēśi*, 'a wife of Daśaratha, father of Rama.'

Sans. क्रिया *kriyā*, Tam. கிரிசை *kiriśai*, Kan. ಕೆಲಸ *kelasa*, 'work,' Sans. कृ *kṛ*, 'to do.'

Tel. చేసి *cēsi*, 'having done,' చేయు *cēyu*, 'to do' + ఇ *i*, past participial termination.

In these instances *s* is used for *y*.

Tam. வாயி *vāyi*, Tel. వాయించు *vāyiñcu*,(Sans. वाद् *vād*, 'to play on a musical instrument'), Kan. ಬಾರಿಸು *bārisu*.

Tam. பாய் *pāy*, 'to flow,' Kan. ಹಾರು *hāru*.

In these instances *r* is inserted for *y*.

It would appear from the examples that Lat. *kras* may directly come from *hyas*, or from Gr. $\kappa\theta\epsilon\varsigma$ ($\kappa\sigma\epsilon\varsigma$) by the change of σ into *r*.

18. द्योस् *dyōs* is further modified as दोस् *dōs,* and, by the addition of *ā* at the end, becomes दोषा *dōṣā,* meaning 'night.'[1] From द्युस् *dyus,* we get द्युष्टम् *dyuṣṭam* or द्युष्टि *dyuṣṭi,* and, by the change of *d* into *v,* व्युष्टम् *vyuṣṭam* or व्युष्टि *vyuṣṭi,* व्युष्टम् *vyuṣṭam* meaning 'dawn or daybreak' and व्युष्टि *vyuṣṭi,* 'dawn,' 'felicity' or 'happiness,' and also दिष्टम् *diṣṭam,* 'fortune,' the decree of deity, in which last three स्त *st* is inserted for स *s* as in स्वस्ति *svasti* = स्वस् *svas* + इ *i,* स्वस् *svas,* 'happiness,' विष्टप *viṣṭapa,*[2] properly विस्तप *vistapa,* from विश्व *viśva,*[3] 'all' and विषु *viṣu,* 'everywhere.' दिवम् *divam,* दिवा *divā,* 'day,'

---

[1] The Sanskrit word दोस् *dōs* and its modification दोषा *dōṣā,* meaning 'arms,' though identical in form with that which means 'night,' have no radical connection with it. I connect them with Sans. उरस् *uras,* 'breast,' Lat. *thorax,* Gr. θωραξ, Ang.-Sax. *throte, throtu* and Eng. *throat,* Tam. தோள் *tōl,* 'arms,' and தொண்டை *toṇḍai,* 'throat' and also Sans. क्रोड *krōḍa,* 'the space between the shoulders,' in which last the θ of the Gr. θωραξ is represented by *k.*

[2] विष्टप *viṣṭapa* is simplified as विटप *viṭapa* by the elision of the ष *ṣ* and means 'extension as of a tree.' Also विष्टप् *viṣṭap* in the Veda.

[3] Compare also the following:

वृष *vṛṣ,* 'a bull,' गृष्टि *gṛṣṭi,* 'a cow that has yeaned once.' Vide the *Vṛṣan Group.*

ग्मस् *gmas,* गभस्ति *gabhasti* (q. v.)

पृश् *pṛś,* 'back' (as in पार्श्व *pārśva,* 'back'), पृष्ठ *pṛṣṭha,* 'back,' मुष्टि *muṣṭi,* 'elbow,' Gr. πυγη, Sans. पुच्छ *puccha,* 'tail.'

are contractions of दिवस् *divas*. दिवस् *divas* gives also the words दिव् *div*, 'to shine,' 'to rejoice,' देव *dēva*, 'a god,' and देवता *dēvatā*, 'deity,' जीव् *jīv*, 'to live,' दीप् *dīp*, 'to shine,' ज्वल् *jval*, 'to shine,' and ज्वर् *jvar*, 'to be hot,' and the kindred words in other languages. दिव् *div*, taking the suffix मन् *man* (Gr. *μεν*, 'men,' Lat. *men*), becomes दिव्मन *divman*, then द्युमन् *dyuman* and द्योमन् *dyōman*, (the *u* of द्यु *dyu* taking its guṇa form ओ *ō*) and at last व्योमन् *vyōman*, by the change of *d* into *v*, as in व्युष्ट *vyuṣṭa* and व्युष्टि *vyuṣṭi*. This word, by the way, is shortened into व्युम् *vyum*, and is changed into वियुम् *viyum*, by the insertion of *i* between *v* and *y*, and, by the addition of *u* at the end, வியுமு *viyumu*, and then வியும்பு *viyumbu*, by the use of *b* to strengthen *m*, and at last விசும்பு *viśumbu*, by the change of *y* into *ś*; விசும்பு *viśumbu* in Tamil means 'sky.' In Sanskrit व्योकार *vyōkāra* means 'a polisher of metals' or 'an iron-smith.' I see in this the word द्यौ *dyau* which, being modified as द्यो *dyō*, becomes व्यो *vyō*, by the change of *d* into *v* as in द्योमन् *dyōman*, व्योमन् *vyōman*.

कासर *kāsara*, 'buffalo,' कस्तूरी *kastūrī*, 'bos grunniens,' Gr. *καστωρ*, 'the beaver.' Vide *Vṛṣan Group*.

स्वस् *svas*, 'happiness,' समस्त *samasta*, 'whole' (*q. v.*)

कुसुम *kusuma*, 'flower,' कौस्तुभ *kaustubha*, 'a precious stone worn by Viṣṇu,' कुस्तुंबुरु *kustumburu*, 'coriander.' I think the latter two words are derived from कुसुम *kusuma*, the original idea of which is 'hollow', 'round.'

व्यो *vyō* means 'brightness' and व्योकार *vyōkāra,* 'one who makes brightness.' This word व्योकार *vyōkāra* is, therefore, rightly applied to a polisher of metals, and then comes to mean, also, an 'iron-smith.' The word व्योषम् *vyōṣam,* also, meaning the three medicinal plants, 'black pepper, long pepper and dry ginger,' which are believed to possess good medicinal virtues and therefore to remove sickness and give *brightness* to the countenance, comes from द्यौस् *dyaus.*

19. Now to make the reader understand the change of *d* into *v,* I shall introduce other examples which are, also, derived from the same root and in which the same change has taken place. From दिवस् *divas,* 'heaven,' we have दिवस्वान् *divasvān,* which, by the change of *d* into *v,* becomes विवस्वान् *vivasvān,* meaning 'sun.' As दिवस् *divas* is changed into विवस् *vivas* in विवस्वान् *vivasvān,* so the latter विवस् *vivas* is further changed into वियत् *viyat,* by the insertion of *y* for *v,* and *t* for *s,* and means 'heaven.' From वियत् *viyat,* we get वयस् *vayas,* 'a bird,' contracted into विस् *vis,* 'a bird,' विह *viha,* 'sky,' in which *h* stands for *y,* and *t* is cut off, and which occurs in विहग *vihaga,* विहंगम *vihaṅgama,* 'a bird,' विहायस् *vihāyas,* and विहा *vihā,* 'heaven.' वीक *vīka,* 'heaven or wind,' is another form of विहा *vihā,* and is found in विकिर *vikira* modified as विष्किर *viṣkira,* 'a bird,' in which latter *s* is used as in बष्कयणी *baṣkayaṇī,* Lat. *vacca,* 'cow,' to strengthen *k.* विहा *vihā* and वीक *vīka* are given in the Uṇadisūtra.

20. It is surprising to see that, while Jupiter is known by allied words in the other kindred languages, as Ζευς, Ζευσπατηρ, *Jovis, Tiu, Woden* and so on, in Sanskrit he is to be called गुरु *Guru*, गीष्पति *Gīṣpati*, धिषणा *Dhiṣaṇa*, इज्य *Ijya*, जीव *Jīva*, आङ्गिरस *Āṅgirasa*, वाचस्पति *Vācaspati*, none of which is connected with the above words. But I suspect that, in the word बृहस्पति *Bṛhaspati*, which has assumed a strange form by the addition of the vowel ऋ *ṛ* instead of इ *i* to ब *b* to strengthen it, the real alliance is concealed. (Vide दृश् *dṛś* and the rule under it.) If so, the word बृहस्पति *Bṛhaspati* should be बिहस्पति *Bihaspati*, and a corruption of दिवस्पति *Divaspati*, and is to be applied to Indra as the now lord of विहस् *vihas*, 'heaven,' a word already derived from दिवस् *divas*. When the word was thus differentiated in form a separate origin was assigned to it, as consisting of बृहत् *bṛhat*, 'great,' 'speech,' and पति *pati*, 'lord.' बृहस्पति *Bṛhaspati* is called वाचस्पति *Vācaspati* in the Yajur Veda.

बृहस्पतये वाचस्पतये नैवारंचरुम्. I. 8, 10.

Bṛhaspatayē vācaspateyē naivōramcarum.

'The nivāra cake should be offered to Brahaspati, lord of speech.'

वाग्घिबृहतीतस्याएषपतिः Chāndogya, I. 2, 11.

Vāgghibṛhatī tasyā ēṣapatiḥ.

'Speech is bṛhati ; this (Aṅgiras), its master.'

This derivation is not, however, given in the Nirukta where the word is distributed as बृहत् *bṛhat* + पति *pati*, बृहत् *bṛhat* being mentioned among the synonymes of महत् *mahat*, 'great,' and the same origin is given in the Vārtika on the sūtra (VI. 1,157) of Pāṇini's Aṣṭādhyāyī :—

तद्बृहतोः करपत्योः *Tadbṛhatōh karapatyōh.*

When the words कर *kara* and पति *pati* are combined with तद् *tad* and बृहत् *bṛhat* respectively, the final consonants of the latter two words are changed into स *s*, as तस्कर *taskara* and बृहस्पति *Bṛhaspati*. तस्कर *taskara* will however be connected with Lat. *dexterous* and shown to be the comparative degree of दक्ष *dakṣa*. Vide the last Group.

These mistaken derivations of the word बृहस्पति *Bṛhaspati* brought into existence such names as बृहतांपति *Bṛhatāmpati*, वाक्पति *Vākpati*, गीष्पति *Gīṣpati*, &c., and changed the position of Jupiter from that of the sovereignty of Heaven to that of the mastership of speech and the priesthood of the gods.

In the Vedic theogony Jupiter lost the sovereignty of Heaven which he enjoyed in the Hesiodic—a position universally assigned to him in the Aryan mythology. When the Aryans separated, this position was usurped by Indra whom the Hindus called दिवस्पति *Divaspati*.

बृहत् *bṛhat*[1] being contracted into बृह् *bṛh* and taking the suffix मन् *man*, becomes ब्रह्मन् *Brahman* and is applied to what is great, knowledge, hence to the Vedas, the Brahman, the creator, and a Brahmin. As वाक् *vāk*, 'speech,' is associated with Bṛhaspati, so सरस्वती *Sarasvatī*,[2] the goddess of speech, originally a river goddess, is associated

[1] The Tamil word வியன் 'big,' 'large,' 'great,' which is probably derived from बृहत् *bṛhat*, 'great,' has softened the vowel ऋ *ṛ* into इ *i* and, when it means 'sky,' must be connected with Sans. वियत् *viyat*. Tam. வியாழன் *Viyāḻan* is, also, traceable to वियत् *viyat*.

[2] सरस् *saras*, 'water' and the suffix वत् *vat*, 'having.'

with Brahman. In the sense of greatness and vastness the word ब्रह्मन् *Brahman* has yielded in Greek *μορμω* which has, however, degenerated in meaning and is applied to anything hideous, or a bugbear.

We thus see that the transformation, which the word विहस्पति *Vihaspati* underwent, has called into existence two Vedic characters बृहस्पति *Bṛhaspati* and इन्द्र *Indra* who cannot be compared to any in the mythology of other Aryan nations.

The modification of the word विहस् *vihas* into बृहस् *bṛhas* has also taken place in बृहत् *bṛhat*, 'large,' a word which I derive from विहस् *vihas*, 'heaven,' the idea of heaven giving that of vastness or extensiveness as seen also in विश्व *viśva*, 'all,' विषु *viṣu*, 'everywhere.' From विहस् *vihas* we get वहस् *vahas* and then बहल *bahala*, बहुल *bahula* by the change of the final स *s* into ल *l* as in Gr. *μεγαλ*, Sans. महस् *mahas* (vide p. 42). बहल *bahala* is shortened into बहु *bahu*, Gr. *παχυς* and *πολυς*, Sans. भूरि *bhūri*, पुरु *puru* and Lat. *multus*.

21. द्योमन् *dyōman* is shortened into द्युमन् *dyuman*, and by the addition of अम् *am* at the end and the elision of the अ *a* of म *ma*, becomes द्युम्नम् *dyumnam*, 'wealth,' a source of happiness. द्युम्नम् *dyumnam* is modified as स्युम्नम् *syumnam*, 'happiness,' and सुम्नम् *sumnam* (Gr. *ὑμνος*), 'happiness,' thence, 'a hymn.'

22. From द्यौस् *dyaus* we get द्योस *dyōsa* by the addition of the vowel *a*, द्योन *dyōna* by the change of *s* into *n* as in द्युस् *dyus*. दिन *dina*, and स्योन *syōna* by the change of *d* into *s*. स्योन *syōna* and its modification स्यून *syūna* are words used in the Vedas, स्योन *syōna* meaning 'happiness,' 'beautiful,' 'light,' 'sun,' and स्यून *syūna*, 'light,' 'sun,' &c and allied to सून *sūnu*, Eng. *sun*, Ang.-Sax. *son*, Lat. *sol*, Sans. सूर *sūra* and सूर्य *sūrya*. स्यून *syūna* gives us स्यूम *syūma* by the change of न *n* into म *m*. It is a Vedic word meaning 'light,' 'happiness,' and is modified as सोम *sōma*, 'moon.'

23. द्यौस् *dyaus* is shortened into द्या *dyā*, and becomes ज्या *jyā*, by the change of *d* into *j* (as in *Jupiter*, दिवस्पति *divaspati*) ; ज्या *jyā* means 'earth,' 'mother,' 'bow-string.' Compare Gr. $\gamma\eta$ and $\gamma\epsilon\alpha$, $\gamma\hat{a}$, Doric and Aeolic for $\gamma\eta$, and $\delta\hat{a}$, Doric. ज्या *jyā* means first 'earth,'[1] and corresponds to $\gamma\upsilon\alpha$, $\gamma\eta$, $\gamma\epsilon\alpha$, &c., and had an original form as द्या *dyā*, 'sky,' allied to the Doric form $\delta\hat{a}$ of $\gamma\eta$. The next meaning is 'a bow-string' which seems to be a secondary one; for the primary one is, no doubt, 'a curve or arch' which is preserved in the corresponding Greek word $\beta\iota o\varsigma$, 'a bow.' The word ज्या *jyā* is found also in its original form द्या *dyā*, when it means a 'bow-string.' I therefore conclude that the name of sky, द्या *dyā*, was applied to a bow, which resembles the sky on account of its curved appearance; but in Sanskrit, the word which was so applied to the bow originally, was subsequently transferred to the bow-string. ज्या *jyā* also means 'strength, power, or excessive force,' an idea derived from the sky or bow, and answers to Gr. $\beta\iota\alpha$, 'bodily strength.'

24. As Sans. द्या *dyā* is modified as ज्या *jyā* (Gr. $\gamma\upsilon\alpha$), so we have another modification of each of the above two words. By the elision of य *y* we get दा *dā* and गा *gā*

---

[1] ज्यामौर्वी मातृभूमिषु *jyāmaurvī mātṛbhūmiṣu*.—*Nānārtha Ratnamālā*. The word came to mean also 'mother' as the earth was considered mother and द्यौस् *dyaus*, 'heaven,' father.

which answer respectively to Gr. δα, and γῆ (γα). Δα is changed into δη as in Δημητηρ, an old form for Γημητηρ. Lat. *Ceres*. But the form दा *dā* does not exist in Sanskrit but is modified as इडा *iḍā* (इदा *idā*) which is pronounced in the Rig Veda as इळा *iḷā*, and इरा *irā*. इडा *Iḍā* is a Vedic Goddess or the earth, the wife of Dyaus; and this Idā may be identical with Iδα who nourished Ζευς whom his mother Ῥεα placed in her care to protect him from Κρονος, her husband, who was devouring all her children. Gr. Ῥεα and ερα are modified forms of Sans. इडा *Iḍā*.

25. But ज्या *jyā* undergoes a further transformation by the change of *y* into *v*, and then into *m*, and becomes ज्मा *jmā*, meaning 'earth.' But this ज्मा *jmā* is again changed into ग्मा *gmā* by the change of ज *j* into ग *g*; or we may derive ग्मा *gmā* directly from द्या *dyā* by the change of द *d* into ग *g* and य *y* into म *m*. It is also metamorphosed into क्ष्मा *kṣmā*, by the change of ग *g* into क्ष *kṣ* and, by the insertion of अ *a* between क्ष *kṣ* and म *m*, is at last developed into two syllables as क्षमा *kṣamā*, 'earth,' and Gr. χαμαι,[1] क्षमायां *kṣamāyām*, 'on the earth.' क्षमा *kṣamā* is found in the Veda in the form of क्षम् *kṣam*[2] as in,—

यथांचिद्वृद्धमतस मग्नेसंजूर्वसिक्षमिं. Rig Veda, VIII. 60-7.

Yathācidvṛddhamatasa magnēsaṁjūrvasikṣami.

'O God of fire, just as you burn dry sticks[3] on earth.'

---

[1] The word χαμαι is in the locative case and does not occur in other cases.

[2] Also as क्षामा *kṣāmā* as in द्यावाक्षामा *dyāvākṣāmā*, 'Heaven and Earth.'

[3] I take अतस *atasa* as meaning a tree. Vide the word further on.

It is from the word ग्मा *gmā*, I think, that the Vedic ग्ना *gnā*, which is interpreted variously in the Nighaṇṭu and Sayanā's Commentary and in the St. Petersburg Dictionary, is derived.

26. ग्ना *gnā* passes from the meaning of 'the earth' to that of 'a woman' and is modified as अंगना *aṅganā*. From ग्ना *gnā* are to be derived Sans. जानि *jāni*, 'wife,' जनी *janī*, 'daughter-in-law,' जनि *jani*, 'a woman,' Gr. ρυνη, Pers. زن *zan*, Tam. நங்கை *naṅgai* and மங்கை *maṅgai*, 'a woman.' As ग्ना *gnā* comes from द्या *dyā*, so the form ग्नुस् *gnus* comes from द्युस् *dyus* and, by the change of ग *g* into स *s*, assumes the form of स्नुस् *snus* from which we may derive स्नुषा *snuṣā*, Gr. νυος, Lat. *nurus*, 'a daughter-in-law.' ग्नुस् *gnus* is also modified as गोसिन् *gōsin* by metathesis, and जोषित् *jōṣit* by the change of ग *g* into ज *j* and the hardening of न *n* into त *t*. जोषित् *jōṣit* means 'a woman' and is modified as जोषा *jōṣā*, योषित् *yōṣit* and योषा *yōṣā*. The form ग्नुस् *gnus* is changed into गुनक् *gunak* by inserting क *k* for स *s*, and then गणिका *gaṇikā*, 'a whore,' to which I trace the oblique cases of γυνη, Gen. γυναικος, Accus. γυναικα, Pl. γυναικες and γυναικων in all of which κ appears at the end.

Sans. योषित् *yōṣit* is modified as *uxor* in Latin by the insertion of *x* for *s*; and this modification occurs very frequently in Sanskrit, Greek and Latin and has concealed the close alliance of many a word in these languages. I therefore give a few examples.

Sans. लस् *las*, 'to shine,' लक्ष् *lakṣ*, 'to see.'

Sans.	पाश *pāśa*,	पक्ष *pakṣa*, 'side.'
,,	काश *kāśa*,	कक्ष *kakṣa*, 'a kind of grass.'
,,	लेश *lēśa*, 'small' (Gr. ολιγος)	लिक्षा *likṣā*, 'louse.'
,,	शेव *śēva*,	क्षेम *kṣēma*, 'happiness.' (p. 13)
,,	सुवर् *suvar*,	क्षौम *kṣauma*, 'a lofty apartment in a house.' (p. 21)
,,	,, ,,	क्षिप *kṣipa*, 'to throw.' (p. 20) (Gr. σκηπτω.)
,,	मशक *maśaka*,	मक्षिका *makṣikā*, 'a fly.'
,,	सुषि *suṣi*, 'hole'	कुक्षि *kukṣi*, 'belly,' the original idea of कुक्षि *kukṣi* being 'hollow.'
,,	सम् *sam*,	Gr. ξυν, 'with.' ,, συν
,,	ईषिका *īṣikā*, 'grass'	इक्षु *ikṣu*, 'sugarcane.'
,,	इषीका *iṣīkā*	
,,	वृषन् *vṛṣan*,	उक्षन् *ukṣan*, 'ox.'
,,	वृष् *vṛṣ*,	उक्ष् *ukṣ*, 'to pour.'
,,	निश् *niś*	Gr. *νυχ, νυκτος*, Lat. *nox, noktis* 'night,' wherein *ks* is put for श *ś*, (that is, स *s*), and then is hardened into *kt*.

For the guidance of the reader, I would here mention that wherever the letter श *ś* occurs in Sanskrit it may be treated as स *s* for all scientific purposes, and that the modern Aryan vernaculars often restore the original sound as Sans. क्रोश *krōśa*, कोस् *kōs*, 'a short distance'; पाश *pāśa*, पास् *pās*, 'side.'

27. द्यौस् *dyaus* is also modified as already shown into द्यस् *dyas* and द्युस् *dyus*, meaning 'a day.' From द्यस् *dyas* we get ज्मस् *jmas*, as we get ज्मा *jmā* from द्या *dyā*, and, by the change of *s* into *n*, ज्मस् *jmas* is modified into ज्मन् *jman*, meaning 'sky' or 'earth'. I derive from ज्मस् *jmas*, ग्मस् *gmas*, which and the two former also are Vedic words meaning 'earth,'[1] गमस् *gamas*, by the insertion of *a* between *g* and *m*, and then गभस् *gabhas*, by the change of म *m* into भ *bh*; and this गभस् *gabhas* gives us गभस्ति *gabhasti*,[2] as स्वस् *svas*, स्वस्ति *svasti*: गभस्ति *gabhasti* means 'light.' Again द्यौस् *dyaus* becomes द्योस् *dyōs*, ज्योस् *jyōs*, ग्योस् *gyōs*, and ग्मोस् *gmōs*, the processes of changing द्योस् *dyōs* into ग्मोस् *gmōs* being similar to those taking place in changing द्या *dyā* into ग्मा *gmā*. But ग्मोस् *gmōs* may be altered into ग्नोस् *gnōs* by the change of *m* into *n*, and when

---

[1] त्वंविश्वस्यमेधिरदिवश्चग्मश्चराजसि

Tvam viśvasyamēdhira divaścagmaśca rājasi. I. 25, 20.

"O wise Varuṇa! thou shinest on all the earth and heaven."

अबोध्यग्निर्ज्मः *Abōdhyagnirjmah.*

"The God of fire was awakened on earth." Rig Veda I. 157, 1.

अभिक्रत्वेंद्र भूरधज्मन् *Abhikratvēndrabhūradhajman.*

Rig Veda VII. 21-6.

"O Indra, thou hast by thy deeds excelled on earth."

[2] Or, it may be derived directly from दिवस् *divas*, and be a connecting link between दिवस् *divas* and युवस् *yuvas*, which latter will be mentioned further on.

n is hardened into *t*, we have ग्तोस् *gtōs*; and by changing *g* into *k* and aspirating *t* and *k*, we have ख्थोस् *khthōs*. This last form ख्थोस् *khthōs* may become χθων in Greek by the change of *s* into *n*, as in द्युस् *dyus*, दिनम् *dinam*, 'day,' and द्यौस् *dyaus*, स्योन *syōna*. In Greek, χθων means 'earth,' and Sans. क्षोणी *kṣōṇī* can be easily derived from it by the addition of the feminine suffix *ī*, and inserting क्ष *kṣ* (क *k* + ष *ṣ*) for χθ as we do ξ for κς in Greek.

28. द्युस् *dyus* becomes द्युत् *dyut* by the change of स *s* into त *t* and means 'to shine'; and द्युत् *dyut* is also modified as ज्युत् *jyut* by inserting ज *j* for द् *d* as in ज्या *jyā*, द्या *dyā*. द्युस् *dyus* may also assume the form of त्विष् *tviṣ*, 'to shine,' by hardening the initial द् *d* into त *t*, cerebralizing the final स *s* into ष *ṣ* owing to the contact of the preceding *i* and changing *y* into *v* and the vowel उ *u* into इ *i*. The word त्विष् *tviṣ* seems to be allied to श्वित् *śvit*, the root of श्वेत *śvēta*, 'white,' and the idea of white may be derived from that of shining. श्वेत *śvēta* is modified as श्येत *śyēta* which also assumes the form of श्येन[1] *śyēna* by the change of त *t* into न *n*. श्येत *śyēta* is contracted into शिति *śiti* and सित *sita*, which words mean 'white' and 'black,' respectively.[2] I think that the idea of black is not radical and

---

[1] वर्णादनुदात्तात्तोपधात्तो नः—IV. i. 39. Pāṇini.
Varṇādanudāttāttōpadhāttōnaḥ.

[2] शितीधवलमेचकौ.—*Amara*, Canto III.
Śitīdhavalamēcakau. शिति *śiti* means 'white' and 'black.'

is attached to the word only by mistake or by a remote connection. श्वेत *svēta* may become विशद *viśada* by metathesis and by the change of त *t* into द *d*.

29. From श्वेत *svēta* we may get पीत *pīta*, 'yellow,' by the elision of the initial consonant, and from पीत *pīta*, पीतन *pītana* and पिंजर *piñjara*, 'yellow orpiment' and मंजिष्ठा *mañjiṣṭhā*, 'a kind of yellow wood,' of which the first part मंज *mañja* seems to be a modification of पीत *pīta* by the change of प *p* into म *m*. The Tamil word பசு *paśu* and மஞ்சள் *mañjaḷ*, 'yellow,' have modified पीत *pīta* similarly. I feel no doubt that the meaning and form of the Vedic मंश्चतु *maṁścatū*,[1] 'yellow,' point to the same origin.

The word occurs in the Rig Veda in the passage (VII. 44-3.)

दधिक्रावाणं बुबुधानो अग्निमुपब्रुव उषसंसूर्यंगाम् ।

Dadhikrāvāṇambubudhānōagnimupabruva uṣasaṁsūryaṅgām,

ब्रध्नंमंश्चतोर्वरुणस्य बभ्रुंतेविश्वास्मद्दुरितायावयंतु ।

Bradhnanimaṁścatōrvaruṇasyababhruṁtēviśvāsmadduritāyāvayantu.

'Knowing the horse called Dadhikrāvan, I praise Agni, Ushas, Sun, the cow and the great dun-colored (horse) of yellow Varuna.' Let them remove our sins.

30. As द्यौस् *dyaus* is modified as द्या *dyā* and becomes ग्या *gyā* and then ग्मा *gmā* as already noticed, it may

---

[1] The word is derived by Sāyana as,—

मन्यमानान्स्तुवतोजनान्चेतयतेजानातीति; यद्वाभिमन्यमानांश्चातयतेनाशयतीतिमंश्चतुः

Manyamānānstuvatōjanān cētayatējānātīti ; yadvābhimanyamānāṁścātayatēnāśayatītimaṁścatuḥ.

also be modified as ग्यौस् *gyaus* and then ग्मौस् *gmaus* and at last ग्नौस् *gnaus* by the change of *m* into *n* as in ग्मा *gmā*, ग्ना *gnā*. This form ग्नौस् *gnaus* is again modified as ग्लौस् *glaus* by the change of न *n* into ल *l*. ग्लौस् *glaus* means 'moon,' and with its form changed into गोल *gōla* is applied to what is spherical. From गोल *gōla* we get Gr. *βωλος*, by the change of *γ* into *β*, as in *βους*, Sans. गौस् *gaus* (q. v.). ग्लौस् *glaus* is changed into ग्लप्स *glapsa*,[1] 'a bunch as of fruits,' Lat. *globus*, *glomus*, 'a sphere,' *gleba*, 'a lump of earth.' गुल *gula* and गुड *guḍa*, 'a lump of sugar,' have shortened the *o* of गोल *gōla* into उ *u*, and produced the verbal roots गुड् *guḍ*, 'to cover,' घुट् *ghuṭ*, घुण् *ghuṇ*, घूर्ण् *ghūrṇ*, 'to turn,' 'to roll,' and the nouns गुलिका *gulikā*, 'a pill,' and घुटिका *ghuṭikā*, 'ankle,' so called on account of the round knotty bone projecting in that part of human body. गुण *guṇa* is a modification of

---

[1] अथास्यैयुग्मेनशलाटुग्लप्सेनत्र्येण्याच शलल्यात्रिभिश्चकुश
Athūsyaiyugmēna śalāṭuglapsēna trēṇyācu śalalyātribhiścakuśa
पिञ्जूलैरूर्ध्वंसीमन्तंव्यूहति ॥ *Āśvalāyana Gṛhyasūtrā.*
piñjūlairūrdhvam sīmantam vyūhati.

शलाटुग्लप्सेनतरुणफलसंघातेन । शलाटुरितिअपक्वानां
Śalāṭuglapsēnataruṇaphalasaṅghātēna, śalāṭuriti apakvānām
फलानांसमाख्या । ग्लप्सइतिस्तबकउच्यते । औडुंबरस्तबकेन
phalānām samākhyā, glapsa itistabaka ucyatē, auḍumbarastabakēna
शास्त्रांतरेदृष्टत्वात् ॥ *Gārgyanārāyaṇavṛtti.*
śāstrāntarē dṛṣṭatvāt.

गुल *gula* or गुड *guḍa* by the change of the second consonant into ण *ṇ*. Though the word गुण *guṇa* has several meanings, it is not one word. In its form we see two different words derived from two different sources. As meaning 'a rope,' 'bowstring,' 'repetition' (as in गुण् *guṇ*, 'multiply,' 'to repeat,' गुणनम् *guṇanam*, 'multiplication,' गुणनिका *guṇanikā*, 'repetition'), गुण *guṇa*[1] is to be derived from ग्लौ *glau* as shown above. But when it means, 'quality,' 'nature,' 'property of material substances,' 'unimportant,' &c., it is to be traced to जन् *jan*, 'to be born'; for quality, nature, &c., are born in the thing in which they are found.

31. As दिवस् *divas* assumes the form of वियस् *viyas*, and then विह्स् *vihas* as already shown, it assumes further changes. विह्स् *vihas* is modified as मह्स् *mahas*, 'light' and महत् *mahat*, 'great.' (Compare बृहत् *bṛhat*, 'great').

मह्स् *mahas* means the fourth of the seven worlds which are above earth in the sky one above another, and in this meaning the word is modified as मह्र् *mahar* by the change of स *s* into र् *r*. As the modified form of अतस *atasa*, 'air,' viz., अतल *atala* called into existence a new nether world and the corresponding Gr. Ατλας, just so did the above modified form of विह्स् *vihas*, 'sky,' call into

---

[1] गुणोमौर्व्यामप्रधानेरूपादौसूददन्द्रिये ।
Guṇōmaurvyāmapradhānē rūpādausūdaindriyē,
त्यागेशौर्यादिसत्वादिसंध्याद्यावृत्तिरज्जुषु ।
Tyāgēśauryādisatvādi sandhyādyāvṛttirajjuṣu,
शुक्लादावपिवत्याञ्च ॥ *Mēdini.*
Śuklādāvapivatyāñca.

existence a new world above the sky. Compare भूर् *bhūr*, 'earth,' भुवर् *bhuvar*, 'the world above the earth,' the latter of which is merely a modification of the former and also सुवर् *suvar* from स्वर् *svar*, 'heaven.'

By the change of the final स *s* into ल *l*, महस् *mahas* becomes μεγαλ in Greek and, by the addition of the termination ος, μεγαλος. But in the corresponding Lat. *major*, the middle syllable हीय *hīya* of महीयस् *mahīyas* (Gr. μειζων) is shortened into ह्य *hya* and then changed into *j* as द्य *dya* into *j* in *Janus*, and in *magum* महस् *mahas* has undergone a contraction by the elision of the penultimate vowel अ *a* and the change of the final स् *s* into न *n* as in अहस् *ahas*, 'day,' अहनि *ahani*, loc. case, अह्ना *ahnā*, instr. case; ऊधस् *ūdhas*, Gr. ουθαρ, 'udder,' ऊधनि *ūdhani*, loc. case in the Vedas, ऊध्न *ūdhna* at the end of compound words.

The change of स *s* into ल *l* often takes place in the Aryan languages whether in the beginning or the end of a word; e.g.

Sans. सून *sūna*, 'sun' or 'a luminous body in heaven,'	Lat. *luna*, 'moon.'
,, सीमन् *siman*,	,, *limes* (*itis*), 'limit.'
,, स्वर् *svar*,	Gr. Ολυμπος, 'Heaven.'
,, सरट *saraṭa*,	,, λακερτα, 'a lizard.'
,, स्वैर *svaira*,	Lat. *liber*, 'free.'
,, सैंधव *saindhava*, 'belonging to the sea.'	Gr. λαιτμα, 'the deep sea.'
,, सस्यम् *sasyam*,	,, ληιον, 'a crop' or 'crop of corn.'

Sans. शण *saṇa*, — Gr. λινον, 'flax.'

" सव्य *savya*, — " λαιος, " σκαιος, Lat. *laevus*, " *scaevus* } 'left.'

" सिंह *siṁha*, — Gr. λεων, " λυγξ, Lat. *leo* (*n*), } 'a lion.'

" शंबूक *śambūka* allied to कंबू *kambū*, शंख *saṅkha*, Gr. κογχη, Lat. *concha*, Sans. काकणी *kākaṇī*, Gr. κοχλος, καλχη, χαλκη. } Lat. *limax* (*cis*).

As from दिव *diva* we get विय *viya* and विहा *vihā*, 'sky,' as shown already, so from this we get महा *mahā* which is modified, also, as मही *mahī*. Both the words महा *mahā* and मही *mahī* are used in the senses of 'a cow' and 'earth.' महा *mahā* is modified as माहा *māhā* and माहेयी *mahēyī* (Vide गौस् *gaus*). वियस् *viyas* is modified as वयस् *vayas* as I have already shown, and then मयस् *mayas*, a word used in the Vedas in the senses of 'pleasure,' 'happiness,' 'food,' &c. From मयस्[1] *mayas* I derive a form मयूस् *mayūs* by changing the अ *a* of य *y* into ऊ *ū* and from this form, the word मयूख *mayūkha* by the change of स् *s* into ख *kh*. A similar process has taken place in the Gr. βοιωτια, a word derived from βοιωτος, the son of Ιτονος who was the son of Deucalion and a king of Thessaly and the inventor

---

[1] मयस् *mayas* is alied to Gr. βιος, 'course of life,' 'lifetime.'

of the art of polishing metals. βοιωτια is the name of a country of Greece, the mountains of which, especially Helicon, was frequented by the Muses. Some connect the word with βους, 'an ox,' and think that the name radically signified the land of pasture for cows. I would however trace it to मयस् *mayas* (Gr. βιος, 'lifetime') and ultimately to द्यौस् *dyaus*.

32. The words दिति *diti* and अदिति *aditi* are correlative terms evolved out of द्युस् *dyus*, like तिथि *tithi*. अदिति *aditi* is applied to the earth, cow, the mother of the Gods, and speech, and दिति *diti* is coined as an antithesis to अदिति *aditi*. The initial अ *a* of अदिति *aditi* is euphonic as in इडा *iḍā*. To this class belongs the Gr. τιτυος.

कोनोमह्याअदितयेपुनर्दात्पितरंचदृशेयंमातरंच॥

Kōnōnahyāaditayēpunardātpitarañcadṛśēyammātarañca.

'Who will give me back to the great earth, that I may see my father and mother?'—Rig Veda, I. 24, 1.

अदितिर्द्यौरदितिरन्तरिक्षमदितिर्मातासपितासपुत्रः

Aditirdyauraditirantarikṣamaditirmātāsapitāsaputrah.

विश्वेदेवाअदितिः पंचजनाअदितिर्जातमदितिर्जनित्वम्॥

Viśvēdēvāaditih pañcajanā aditirjātamaditirjanitvam.

Rig Veda, I. 89, 10.

'Aditi is Heaven; Aditi, sky; Aditi, mother. He is father and son; he is all the gods, five peoples. He is birth, and the source of birth.'

In this passage Aditi refers to all-pervading power—a conception realized only in Ζευς by the Greeks and the use of the masculine demonstrative pronoun leads us to think that Aditi is here applied to the highest god.

As the word अदिति *aditi* is a mere modification of द्युस् *dyus*, the initial अ *a* is an extraneous addition. The radical part दिति *diti* seems to have been modified as क्षिति *kṣiti*, 'earth.' अदिति *aditi*, like मही *mahī* and पृथिवी *pṛthivī*, is frequently associated with द्यौस् *dyaus*, 'heaven,' in the Vedas. दिति *diti*, her counterpart, was originally a deity invoked with other deities. But she became the mother of Giants (दैत्य *daitya*) subsequently. The Gr. Τιτυος was the son of Gaia or of Jupiter by Elara. He was of a gigantic size and his mother died in travail. He offered violence to Latona and, as a punishment for this, he was placed in Hell where his liver was continually devoured by a serpent.

The word अदिति *aditi* leads us to the Greek Οδυσσευς which is formed from द्यौस् *dyaus* or द्युस् *dyus* exactly like the former, both of them containing the euphonic addition of a vowel. In the corresponding Latin *Ulysses*, the δ of the Greek word is changed into *l*, a change for which many instances have been given in this List; as, *Laios*, *Latona*, Ιλιον, Ιλυς, &c. Οδυσσευς was king of Ithaca whose return from Troy to Ithaca forms the subject of a poem of Homer, called Odyssey.

33. Here I would mention another word formed from द्युस् *dyus* like तिथि *tithi* but different from the latter in having a nasal न *n* to represent the स *s* of द्युस् *dyus*. द्युस् *dyus* produces दनु *danu* as it does दिन *dina*, and दनु is modified as दानु *dānu*. These words originally mean 'a Heavenly being,' 'bright,' 'powerful,' and so on, and as such are applied to Indra, Maruts and other gods.

हतवृत्रंसुदानवइन्द्रेणसहसायुजा । मानोदुश्शंसईशत ॥

Hatavṛtraṁsudānavaindrēṇasahasāyujā | Mānōduśśaṁsaīśata.

Rig Veda, I. 23, 9.

'O, Maruts, accompanied by many Danus; kill Vṛtra with the aid of the powerful auxiliary Indra. May our enemies not flourish.'

But Sāyana takes दानु *dānu* to mean 'gift.' I should however think that the word is connected with द्यौस् *dyaus* and means 'bright,' 'powerful,' or 'strong,' and is here applied to a 'Heavenly being in general' or perhaps the adjective सु *su* specifies the meaning and makes the word mean only 'good spirits' (*sc.* Maruts.)

In the following passage it is applied to Indra :—

दानुरस्माउपरान्पिन्वतेदिवः Rig Veda, I. 54, 7.

Dānurasmāuparānpinvatēdivaḥ.

'Dānus (that is Indra) pours clouds to this sacrificer from heaven.'

But it is applied to Vṛtra in the following :—

धिष्वाशवःशूरयेनवृत्रमवाभिनद्दानुमौर्णवाभं ॥

Dhiṣvāśavaśśūrayēnavṛtramavābhinaddānumaurṇavābham.

'O, valiant Indra! hold that power by which you have killed the giant Vṛtra like a spider.'—Rig Veda, II. 11, 18.

In modern Sanskrit literature, the word दानव *dānava* always means the sons of दनु *danu*, who are evil spirits, or Rāksasas and are opposed to the gods.

The corresponding Greek word Δαναος did not share the same fate as its Sanskrit counterpart. Δαναος is the name of a son of Belus and Anchinœ, who was reigning in Egypt with his brother. Owing to the enmity which arose between the brothers, Danaus emigrated to Argos with his fifty daughters and, in course of time, became king of the place. His brother followed him subsequently and brought with him his fifty sons who had been promised to the daughters of Danaus. But the king did not like the match and caused all the bridegrooms to be put to death by his daughters; and all the sons-in-law were murdered except one who married Hypermnestra, one of the daughters. The sisters were purified of the murder by the order of Jupiter, but according to some account they were punished in Hell.

I may perhaps connect with Sans. दनु *danu*, the Gr. Δαναη, daughter of Acrisius, king of Argos, of whom Jupiter was enamoured, and who bore to him a son named Perseus.

Gr. Δαναοι, originally meaning 'subjects of Δαναος,' was subsequently applied to all the Greeks (as in Homer) and offers a very interesting contrast to the Sans. दानव *Dānava* which has degenerated in its meaning and is now applied only to Rākṣasas, or Giants. Compare the word असुर *Asura* which was dealt with similarly in Sanskrit literature and which will be mentioned hereafter.

34. Here I would mention two Greek words which are formed from द्युस् *dyus* as Sans. तिथि *tithi*, 'day,' (Vide § 15)—Θιασος, a company or procession of persons dancing and singing in honor of a god as of Bacchus, and Θησευς, the most famous Athenian hero and son of Ægeus (अहस् *ahas*, 'day') and Æthra (अतस *atasa*, 'sky.')

35. From द्यौस् *dyaus* we may derive Gr. Λαος, by the change of द *d* into λ as in λιθος, दृषद् *dṛṣad*, 'stone,' λαμπω, दीप् *dīp*, 'to shine,' लोच् *lōc*, लोक् *lōk*, 'to see,'

द्युस् *dyus*, 'day,' 'light,' and Latona द्योतना *Dyōtanā*. This derivation affords us a clue to explain the story of Laios and Jocasta (Ιοκαστη). Œdipus was the son of Laios. As the father had heard an oracle at Delphi that he would be killed by his own son, he exposed the child near the hill Kithairon. But the child was rescued and attained his age, and, while journeying to Thebes, he met his old father Laios and, in a duel which took place accidentally, he killed the latter. He continued his journey and met a monster called Sphinx who was laying waste the whole country with sickness and drought. He could not be defeated by any one except those who solved his riddles. When Œdipus approached the monster, the latter propounded his riddle as usual; and, when it was solved, he threw himself down from the summit of the mountain on which he had taken his seat; and the drought terminated with heavy showers of rain. The inhabitants of Thebes who had proclaimed that he who would deliver the country from the drought and sickness, should rule over the country and espouse the hands of Jocasta, the widow of the late king, offered to Œdipus the sovereignty of the country; and he thus became the king of the country and the husband of his own mother. But he was not allowed to rule long in peace and happiness. The sin of parricide was to be punished, and the Gods inflicted a plague on the city. When the people consulted the Delphian oracle, they were told that the plague was the result of the murder of Laios, and the murderer should be punished. In the long run, it became known that Œdipus was the murderer. In compunction for the sin committed Œdipus tore out his eyes and Jocasta committed suicide. Œdipus too died soon under the signal of Heaven. This story must simply refer to the heavenly phenomena which are of daily occurrence, viz., the brightness of the starry Heaven being absorbed in the rays of the sun when the latter makes his appearance in the east, which may be referred to in the sun's taking Ιοκαστη (गभस्ति *Gabhasti*), the wife of द्यौस् *Dyaus*, his father; the gradual dimness of the sun in the evening, which corresponds to the unhappy reign of Œdipus after he was installed on the throne of his father and married his own mother; his loss of brilliancy, which corresponds to the death of Ιοκαστη; and, at last, his setting in the west, which corresponds to Œdipus' going to Heaven.

The reason of my connecting the sun with Œdipus is the fact that he is described as the second husband of his mother.

मातुर्दिधिषुमब्रवंस्वसुर्जारः शृणोतुनः ।

Māturdidhiṣumabravaṁ svasurjārah śruṇōtunah,

भ्रातेंद्रस्यसखाममं ॥ VI. 55, 5.

Bhrātēndrasyasakhāmama.

'I spoke of the second husband of his mother. Let the lover of his sister, brother of Indra and friend of mine, hear us.'

दूरेदृशेदेवजातायकेतवे दिवस्पुत्रायसूर्यायशंसत ॥ X. 37, 1.

Dūredṛśēdēvajātāyakētavē divasputrāya sūryāyaśaṁsata||

'Praise Sūrya, farseeing, born of deity, knowing, and son of Divas (Heaven).'

The country which was governed by *Laios* was Θηβαι, Thebes, a name given to several cities of which the most important were the Egyptian and Bœotian; the symbolical meaning of which story is that Heaven personified is the ruler of Heaven, the place where he is to rule; for while Λαιος is द्यौस् *dyaus*, Θηβη, the singular form of Θηβαι, is only दिवा *divā*, or द्यावा *dyāvā*, 'Heaven.'

The word Jocasta may be shown to be a modification of Sans. गभस्ति *gabhasti*,[1] which I have already derived from स्वस् *svas* (through the forms द्यस् *dyas*, ग्यस् *gyas*, ग्मस् *gmas* and गमस् *gamas*), with which the Sans. युवन् *yuvan*, 'a youth,' युवति *yuvati*, 'a youthful girl,' Lat. *juvenis*, 'young,' and the corresponding Gr. ἥβος, 'youthful,' ἥβη, 'youth,' will be connected hereafter. गभस्ति *gabhasti* may be changed into गवस्ति *gavasti* by the change of भ *bh* into व *v*, into यवस्ति *yavasti* by the change of ग *g* into य *y*, and then Ιοκαστη by the change of व *v* into ग *g* and then into क *k* and of य *y* into ιο as in Ἰω (*v*), यवन *yavana*, (q.v.)

The last word that requires explanation is Οιδιπους which, as it is spelt, seems to be composed of two words, the latter being πους, Sans. पाद् *pād*, 'leg.' The name of the sun which most closely resembles Οεδιπους is अर्यमन् *aryaman* in which the first part अर्य *arya* being modified as अद्य *adya* by the change of र *r* into δ, may be changed into Οιδι by the elision of य *y* and the lengthening of the previous vowel अ *a* into οι.[2]

On the change of *r* into *ḍ*, compare :—

Sans. वीर *vīra*, 'strong,' Gr. βριαω, 'to be strong,'	Ved. वीडु *vīḍu*, 'strength.'
Gr. γυρος, 'round,'	Sans. गुड *guḍa*, 'lump as of sugar.'
Sans. शिखर *śikhara*, 'crest,' 'top,'	„ शिखण्ड *śikhaṇḍa*, 'the crest.'
„ रैवत् *raivat*, 'rich,'	Lat. *dives*, and *dis*.

[1] Or it may be derived from युवस् *yuvas*, 'bright,' 'young.'

[2] Vide αυτος.

Sans. द्वार् *dvār*, 'gate,' Gr. *θυρα*, धूर् *dhūr*, 'front,' which are modified as तुर् *tur* and *θυρ* in तोरण *tōraṇa*, 'festoon,' Gr. *θυρων* (*ωνος*), 'the doorway,' and तोलि *tōli*, as in प्रतोलि *pratōli*, 'high road.'	Sans. तुण्ड *tuṇḍa*, 'face.'

I would here observe that the letter ड *ḍ* was originally द् *d*; and I may lay down for the guidance of the readers that wherever a cerebral letter occurs in Sanskrit it must be traced universally to a corresponding dental letter, and that, for all scientific purposes, the cerebrals in Sanskrit must be treated as dentals.

The latter part of अर्यमन् *aryaman* cannot be supposed to have been changed into *πους*, unless we assume that the ancient Greeks assigned a wrong etymology to the word and so assimilated the latter part to the word *πους*, meaning 'leg.'[1] I may suggest instead of the above word द्युपद् *dyupad* radically 'going in द्यु *dyu*, heaven,' or द्युमत् *dyumat*, 'shining,' 'having light,' corrupted into द्युपद् *dyupad*; or still better स्वपद् *svapad*, 'going in Heaven' modified as श्वापद् *śvāpad* which in Sanskrit is applied to a 'wild beast,' 'beast of prey.' In this meaning it answers

[1] Compare Gr. Ατλας (αντος) which I have connected lower down with अतल *atala* and ultimately अतस *atasa*, 'sky.'

to the Gr. Οιδιπους, referring to the prowling of wild beasts. If the word श्वापद् *śvāpad*[1] be a corruption of स्वपद् *svapad* as conjectured, it will be the origin of the Gr. Οιδιπους. It may, as it is, be distributed as श्व *śva* + पद् *pad*, श्व *śva* meaning 'swelling,' from श्वि *śvi*, 'to swell,' पद् *pad*, 'foot,' meaning therefore radically 'swollen-footed.'

The story of Œdipus, however, has greater points of resemblance to the description of Agni and the anecdotes occurring in the Rig Veda regarding him. In many places Agni is called son of Heaven and Earth. In the night the sky becomes dark and the earth receives the light of fire and this daily scene may have been symbolized in the story of Œdipus. In the following passage Agni is said to fight with his father.

अवस्पृधिपितरंयोधिविद्वान्पुत्रोयस्तेसहसस्सूनऊहे ॥ V. 3, 9.

Avasprahipitaramyōdhividvān putrōyastē sahasassūna ūhē ||

'O, god of fire, learned son and son of strength, thou putst down in battle thy father who has borne thee.'

In the passages of the Rig Veda, V. 2, 1 and the following five, Agni is said to have been kept in secret custody by the youthful mother (युवतिर्माता *yuvatirmātā*) and the people to have askod his mother to deliver him up to the father and to have complained "that they were deprived of their cattle, and their leader had to fight with his enemies. There was drought in the country, and, in consequence, no sacrifice was performed. The enemies have seized the king and the houses of the inhabitants, and the hymns of Atri should recover them."

I quote the passage here below and translate it:

---

[1] It is usually derived from श्वन् *śvan*. 'dog.' पद् *pad*. 'to go.'

कुमारंमातायुवतिस्समुब्धंगुहाबिभर्तिनददातिपित्रे ।

Kumārammātāyuvatissamubdham guhābibhartinadadātipitrē

अनीकमस्यनमिनज्जनासः पुरः पश्यंतिनिहितमरतौ ॥ १ ॥

Anīkamasyanaminajjanāsah puraḥpaśyantinihitamaratau

कमेतंत्वंयुवतेकुमारंपेषीबिभर्षिमहिषीजजान ।

Kamētantvaṁyuvatēkumāram pēṣībibharṣimahiṣījajāna

पूर्वीर्हिगर्भःशरदोववर्धापश्यंजातंयदसूतमाता ॥ २ ॥

Pūrvīrhigarbhaśśaradōvavardhā paśyañjātaṁyadasūtamātā

हिरण्यदन्तंशुचिवर्णमारात्क्षेत्रादपश्यमायुधामिमानम् ।

Hiraṇyadantaṁśucivarṇamārāt kṣētrādapaśyamāyudhāmimānam

ददानोअस्माअमृतंविपृक्वत्किंमामनिन्द्राःकृण्वन्ननुक्थाः ॥ ३

Dadānōasmāamṛtaṁvipṛkvat kimmāmanindrāhkṛṇavannanukthāh

क्षेत्रादपश्यंसनुतश्चरंतंसुमद्यूथंनपुरुशोभमानम् ।

Kṣētrādapaśyaṁsanutaścarantam sumadyūthaṁnapuruśōbhamānam

नताअगृभ्रन्नजनिष्टहिषः पलिक्नीरिद्युवतयोभवन्ति ॥ ४ ॥

Natāagṛbhrannajaniṣṭahiṣaḥ paliknīrídyuvatayōbhavanti

केमेमर्यकंवियवन्तगोभिर्नयेषांगोपाअरणश्चिदास ।

Kēmēmaryakaṁviyavantagōbhir nayēshaṅgōpāaraṇaścidāsa

यईंजगृभुरवतेसृजंत्वाजातिपश्वउपनश्चिकित्वान् ॥ ५ ॥

Yaīñjagṛbhuravatēsṛjantvā jātipaśvaupanaścikitvān

वसांराजानंवसतिंजनानामरातयोनिदधुर्मर्त्येषु ।

Vasāṁrājānaṁvasatiñjanānām arātayōnidadhurmartyēṣu

ब्रह्माण्यत्रेरवतंसृजंतुनिंदितारोनिंद्यासोभवंतु ॥ ६ ॥

Brahmāṇyatrēravataṁsṛjantuninditārōnindyāsōbhavantu.

'The youthful mother keeps her son secretly confined and does not give him up to the father. The people do not see before them his (the son's) injured form placed in an unpleasant (place).'

'O, youth! what youth do thou keep as a devil (पेषी *pēṣī*) whom you brought forth as a matron (महिषी *mahiṣī*)? The child grew for the last (many) years and as the mother brought him forth, I saw him born.'

'I saw the child of golden teeth, of pure color and bearing weapons, from the neighbouring field. I am giving him nectar extensively; what can the people deprived of rain and sacrifice do me?'

'From the field I saw him wandering on his knee (सनुतः *sanutah*) happily and shining greatly like a herd (of cows). They did not (should not?) take, for he was born. Even old women become youthful.' (Regarding सनुतः *sanutah*, vide जानु *jānu*.)

'Who are those that took away the cattle from the men whose leader was not without battle? Let those who seized him give him up. Let the wise lead our cattle.'

'Enemies have seized the houses of the inhabitants and imprisoned their kings. Let the hymns of Atri restore him to the people and the calumniators be calumniated.'

The following passage occurs in the beginning of the commentary of Sāyana on the above passages and contains a tradition given in the Brāhmaṇa of Śāṭyāyana and another version of it given in the Taṇḍaka Brāhmaṇa. The tradition is quoted there for the explanation of the meaning of the passages.

शाट्यायनब्राह्मणोक्त इतिहास इहोच्यते ।

Śāṭyāyanabrāhmaṇōkta itihāsa ihōcyatē

राजा त्रैवृष्ण ऐक्ष्वाकु स्त्र्यरुणोऽभवदस्य च ॥ १ ॥

Rājātraivṛṣṇaikṣvāku stryaruṇōzbhavadasyaca

पुरोहितोवृशोजार ऋषिरासीत्तदाखलु ।

Purōhitōvṛśōjāra ṛṣirāsīttadākhalu

संगृह्णंतिरथान्राज्ञां रक्षणायपुरोहिताः ॥ २ ॥

Saṅgṛhṇantirathānrājñāṁ rakṣaṇāyapurōhitāḥ

त्र्यरुणस्यवृशोरश्मिं संजग्राहपुरोहितः ।

Tryaruṇasyavṛśōraśmiṁ sañjagrāhapurōhitaḥ

कुमारोवर्त्मनिक्रीडन रथचक्रेणघातितः ॥ ३ ॥

Kumārōvartmanikrīḍan rathacakrēṇaghātitaḥ

छिन्नःकुमारश्चक्रेण ममाराथपुरोहितः ।

Chinnaḥkumāraścakrēṇa mamārāthapurōhitaḥ

त्वंहंतास्येतिराजानं राजाचापिपुरोहितम् ॥ ४ ॥

Tvaṁhantāsyētirājānaṁ rājācāpipurōhitam

त्वंहंतास्यकुमारस्य नाहमित्यब्रवीत्तदा ।

Tvaṁhantāsyakumārasya nāhamityabravīttadā

यतस्त्वंरथवेगस्य नियंतातस्त्वयाहतः ॥ ५ ॥

Yatastvaṁrathavēgasya niyantātastvayāhataḥ

रथस्वामीयतोराजन् तस्मात्त्वंतस्यघातकः ।

Rathasvāmīyatōrājan tasmāttvantasyaghātakaḥ

एवंविवदमानौतौ इक्ष्वाकून्प्रष्टुमागतौ ॥ ६ ॥

Evaṁvivadamānautau ikṣvākūnpraṣṭumāgatau

तौपप्रच्छतुरिक्ष्वाकून् केनासौनिहतोद्विजाः ।

Taupapracchaturikṣvākūn kēnāsaunihatōdvijāḥ

तेऽब्रुवन्रथयंतारं हंतारंवृशसंज्ञकम् ॥ ७ ॥

Tēɀbruvanrathayantāraṁ hantāraṁvṛśasaṁjñakam

सवृशोवार्शनाम्नातङ्कुमारमुदजीवयत् ।

Savṛśōvārśanāmnātaṅ kumāramudajīvayat

एवमाख्यायतत्रैव पुनरन्यदुदीरितम् ॥ ८ ॥

Evamākhyāyatatraiva punaranyadudīritam.

यतइक्ष्वाकवोरागाद्धंतारंऋषिमब्रुवन् ।

Yataikṣvākavōrāgāddhantāramṛṣimabruvan

तस्मात्तेषांगृहेष्वग्नेस्तेजोनिर्गतमेषुच ॥ ९ ॥

Tasmāttēṣāṁgṛhēṣvagnēstējōnirgatamēṣuca

गृहेपाकादयोनासन्तत्कारणमचिन्तयन् ।

Gṛhēpākādayōnāsantatkāraṇamacintayan

वृशंकुमारहन्तारंयदवोचामतेननः ॥ १० ॥

Vṛśaṁkumārahantāraṁyadavōcāmatēnanaḥ

अपाक्रमद्धरोवह्नेराह्वयामवृशंवयम् ।

Apākramaddharōvahnērāhvayāmavṛśaṁvayam

इतिसंचिंत्यतमृषिमाह्वयामासुरादरात् ॥ ११ ॥

Itisañcintyatamṛṣimāhvayāmāsurādarāt

समागत्यततश्शीघ्रंतेषामग्नेर्हरोभवेत् ।

Samāgatyatataśśīghrantēṣāmagnērharōbhavēt

इतिवार्षेनसाम्नासौअकामयतपूर्ववत् ॥ १२ ॥

Itivārsēnasāmnāsauakāmayatapūrvavat

एवंगायन्सऋषिर्ब्रह्महत्यां

Evaṁgāyansarṣirbrahmahatyām

भार्याआतांत्रसदस्योर्नृपस्य

Bhāryajātantrasadasyōrnṛpasya

पिशाचवेषांहरआदायचाग्नेः

Piśācavēṣāṁharaādāyacāgnēḥ

गृहान्नीत्वाकशिपौस्थापयंतीम् ॥ १३ ॥

Gṛhānnītvākaśipausthāpayantīm

दृष्ट्वासम्यकतद्धरस्तोषयित्वा

Dṛṣṭvāsamyaktaddharastōṣayitvā

साम्नापश्चाद्योजयामासचाग्निम् ।

Sāmnāpaścādyōjayāmāsacāgnim

ततस्त्वतेजास्संजातोऽभवत्पाकादिपूर्ववत् ॥ १४ ॥

Tatassatējāssañjātōऽbhavatpākādipūrvavat

एवंशाट्यायनेनोक्तंताण्डकोक्तमथोच्यते ।

Evaṁśāṭyāyanēnōktantāṇḍakōktamathōcyatē

वृशः पुरोधाश्चभवत्त्रसदस्योर्महीपतेः ॥ १५ ॥

Vr̥śaḥpurōdhāabhavattrasadasyōrmahīpatēḥ

सरथंधावयन्राजाब्राह्मणस्यकुमारकं ।

Sarathaṁdhāvayanrājābrāhmaṇasyakumārakaṁ

चिच्छेदरथचक्रेणप्रमादात्सोब्रवीद्वृशं ॥ १६ ॥

Cicchēdarathacakrēṇapramādātsōbravīdvr̥śaṁ

पुरोहितेवर्तमानेत्वयिमांहंतिरागता ।

Purōhitēvartamānētvayimāṁhantirāgatā

एषात्वयापनेतव्याचर्षिमित्यब्रवीन्नृपः ॥ १७ ॥

Eṣātvayāpanētavyārṣimityabravīnnr̥paḥ

सच्चर्षिर्वार्शसाम्नातंकुमारमुदजीवयत् ॥

Sarṣirvārśasāmnātaṁkumāramudajīvayat.

'I shall here narrate the tradition mentioned in the Brāhmaṇa of Śāṭyāyana. There was a king named Tryaruṇa in the dynasty of Ikṣvāku, son of Trivr̥ṣṇa, and his priest, the sage Vr̥śa, son of Jara. The priests took possession of all the chariots for keeping them safe. The priest Vr̥śa took the reigns of the chariot of Tryaruṇa. A boy who was playing on the road was run over by the wheel of the chariot. Trampled under the wheel the boy died. The priest then said to the king, "Thou art the murderer of the boy." The king replied, "Thou art the murderer and not I. As thou art the regulator of the speed of the chariot, the child was killed by thee." The priest then rejoined, 'as thou art the owner of the chariot, thou art the murderer.' Thus disputing they came to ask the Ikṣvākus.

They asked the Iksvākus, "By whom was the boy killed"? They said that the charioteer whose name was Vṛśa was the murderer. Vṛśa revived the boy with a hymn called Vārśa. Having narrated thus, the author relates also something else in the same place. As the Ikṣvākus pronounced the Ṛsi to be the murderer, the brilliancy of the fire in their houses was lost, and cooking and other works were no longer performed; and they thought of the cause of that: "As we pronounced Vṛśa to be the murderer of the boy, our fire lost its brilliancy, therefore let us call him." Having thought thus they called the Ṛsi respectfully. Then the Ṛsi came and prayed as before that there be brilliancy in fire. Thus singing, he saw in the form of a demon the brāhman-murder arising from the wife of the king Trasadasyu, who, having taken away the brilliancy of fire to its house, was concealing it in her food, and, having propitiated the demon with his hymn, he restored the brilliancy to the fire. Then the god of fire became bright, and works such as cooking began as before.

'Thus was said by Śāṭyāyana; and I shall now say what has been said by Tāṇḍaka. Vṛśa was the priest of the king Trasadasyu. The king driving his car killed accidentally the son of a Brahmin by the wheel of his car. He said to Vṛśa, "While thou my priest art, murder camo to me; it must be removed by thee." Then the Ṛsi revived the boy by the hymn called Vārśa.'

Now comparing the story of Laius with that of Agni given in the commentary of Sāyana and that portion of it which is referred to in the Vedic passages quoted above, we get the following parallel conceptions: (1) The driving of a king in a car with his charioteer: (2) The death of a person. In the story of Laius, it is the king that dies and this event is caused by a duel arising accidentally between the king and Œdipus, but in the two versions of the story given by Sāyana a Brahmin boy is killed by being run over by the wheel of the car of a king. But I should observe here that there is no reference to that accident in the Vedic version of the story. Nor do we learn from it anything as to who the boy was, whether he was the son of the king or the son of a Brahmin. (3) In the story of Laius, the whole country suffers from anarchy, drought and famine and the same appears in the Vedic story; but there is no reference to those events in the story given by Sāyana which, however, alludes to the extinction of sacrificial fire and the ceasing of cooking and other works in houses. (4) In the Greek story the mother marries the son and in the Vedic the youthful mother is said to have kept her son, but in the story of Sāyana there is no allusion to neither of those events.

From these points of similarity, it appears highly probable that the story was purely Indian and migrated to Greece like many other stories with various additions and subtractions.

In the Indian Mythology, besides the two given in the above, there are many others which are like the story of Laius, in all of which the common feature is the intercourse like that between Œdipus and Jocasta; such as the stories of Indra falling in love with Ahalya, the wife Gautama, and of Moon being fascinated by Tārā, the wife of Jupiter.

36. As द्यौस् *dyaus* is modified as द्या *dyā*, दा *dā* and at last इडा[1] *iḍā* and इळा *iḷā*, so have we Ιλιος, the land of Ιλιον, Ιλιος or Ιλιον, the city of Ilus, the last two words exactly answering to Sans. दिवस् *divas* and दिवम् *divam* without the euphonic initial *i*. The war, therefore, which took place between the Greeks and the Trojans in the

[1] Vide p. 35, and the Semitic Analogy at the end of the List.

land of Ιλιον, was a war in Heaven in which the victory was gained by Hercules (अहस्कर *Ahaskara*) and Achilles (अहस् *Ahas*), which two will be mentioned hereafter.

In comparison with the words इळा *iḷā* and इडा *iḍā* and Ιλιος and Ιλιον, I may mention Lat. *Ilia* or *Rhea* and Gr. Ιδυια. Ilia was the daughter of Numitor, king of Alba, consecrated by her uncle Amulius to the service of Vesta. Idya (Ιδυια) was one of the Oceanides who married Æetes, king of Colchis, and by him became the mother of Medea.

In the Gr. Λαος there is no euphonic addition in the beginning of the word of such letters as η, ι, ει, ο, as in ηλιβατος (स्वस् *svas*); इळा *iḷā*, इडा *iḍā*, इरा *irā*, Ιλιος, Ιλιον, Ιδυια and *Ilia*, (Sans. द्या *dyā*, Gr. Δα); ειλαπαvη, 'banquet,' (Sans. तेमन *tēmana*, Gr. δειπνον, 'meal time'); and Ολυμπος (स्वर् *var*), and Οδυσσευς (द्युस् *dyus*). Vide the above words.

37. From द्यो *dyō*, we can derive द्योतन *Dyōtana* by the addition of the suffix तन *tana*, which intensifies the meaning. According to the Nirukta (I. 8.), द्योतना *Dyōtanā* is a name applied to the Goddess उषा *Uṣā*, and in the following passage it comes with अहना *Ahanā*.

गृहंगृहमहनायात्यच्छादिवेदिवेअधिनामादधाना

Gṛhangṛhamahanāyātyacchādivēdivēadhināmādadhānā.

सिषासंतीद्योतनाशश्वदागादग्रमग्रमिद्भजतेवसूनाम्॥

Siṣāsantīdyōtanāśaśvadāgādagramagramidbhajatēvasūnām.

I. 123-4.

'The God Ahanā every day goes to every house directly with much modesty; and Dyōtanā desirous of distributing comes frequently and receives what is best of wealth.'

द्योतना *dyōtanā* may be taken as a verbal noun of agency

from द्युत् *dyut*, 'to shine,' by the addition of the termination अन *ana*, द्युत् *dyut* + अन *ana* becoming द्योतन *Dyōtana*, by the gunation of the *u* of द्युत् *dyut*. But to this I prefer the former origin. We have many instances in which तन *tana* and तम *tama* are added to nouns as well as to adjectives in the Vedas. Thus is formed गौतम *Gautama*, 'the name of a sage whose wife was अहल्या *Ahalyā*.' गौतम *Gautama* is held to be a patronymic of गोतम *Gōtama*, which is only a modification of द्योतम *Dyōtama* = द्यो *dyō* + तम *tama*, द्यो *dyō* meaning 'light' or 'heaven,' and तम *tama*, the intensive suffix. Similarly are formed वृषन्तम *vṛṣantama*, 'brave' = वृषन् *vṛṣan* + तम *tama*, वृषन् *vṛṣan*, 'a bull' or 'chief;' अङ्गिरस्तम *Aṅgirastama*, 'the greatest Aṅgiras,' अङ्गिरस् *Aṅgiras* (Gr. αγγελλος), 'a sage,' and 'a bright planet in heaven,' &c.

Agni is called Aṅgiras in Rig Veda, I. 31, 1:

त्वमंग्नेप्रथमोअंगिराः *Tvamagnēprathamōaṅgirāh.*

'O! God of fire, you are the first Aṅgiras (bright.)'

In the following stanza he is called Aṅgirastama:—

त्वमंग्नेप्रथमोअंगिरस्तमः *Tvamagnēprathamōaṅgirastamah.*

Rig Veda, I. 31, 2.

'O! God of fire, you are the greatest Aṅgiras (bright.)'

Vide the word अंगिरस् *Aṅgiras* mentioned further on.

Similarly we have काण्वतम *Kaṇvatama* from काण्व *kaṇva* which radically means 'bright,' as अंगिरस् *Aṅgiras*, and is connected with कन् *kan*, Gr. γαναω, 'to shine.' Vide काण्व *Kaṇva*, which word will be explained lower down.

The words *Latinus* and *Latmus* and *Latona* are to be analyzed in the same way. As Latona consists of Sans. द्यौस् *dyaus* and तन *tana*, the termination *tona* correspon-ding to तन *tana*, so Latinus and Latmus must be distributed as *Laus* + *tinus* and *Laus* + *timus*, the latter parts *tinus* and *timus* answering to Sans. तन *tana* and तम *tama*. Compare Lat. *intimus, optimus, ultimus*, and Gr. ιφθιμος = ιφιος + τιμος, Sans. इभ्य *ibhya* + तमस् *tamas*.[1] Latinus was a son of Faunus and Marica and was the king of the aborigines in Italy, who were named Latini and the country Latium (Italy) from him. Latmus is a mountain of Caria near Miletus, and was famous for the residence of Endymion who was visited by Diana every night. For *Latona*, see p. 25.

To the same word द्योतना *Dyōtanā* may be traced the Teut. *Wodin*, appearing also in another form as *Wuotan*[2] and shortened in the English word *Wednesday*, Ang.-Sax. *Woden-es daeg* (Sans. द्योतनस्यदिवस *Dyōtanasyadivasa*), *es* being equal to Sans. स्य *sya*, genitive singular suffix.

In the Teutonic word *Wuotan*, the initial द् *d* of द्योतन *Dyōtana* is changed into ब *b* first and then व *v*. Compare विहस् *vihas*, Gr. βιος from Sans. दिवस् *divas*, 'sky.'

38. द्या *dyā* is modified as स्या *syā* and then as काया

---

[1] The words ιφθιμος and Sans. इभ्यतमस् *ibhyatamas* mean 'mighty' and 'wealthy' respectively and must be connected, though they are usually derived from different sources, e. g., ιφθιμος from ιφι, the dative plural of ις, 'strength,' and इभ्यतमस् *ibhyatamas* from इभ *ibha*, 'an elephant,' because the possession of elephants indicates wealth.

[2] Cox's Mythology of the Aryan Nations, Vol. I, p. 368. *et seq.*

chāya, Gr. σκια, 'light.' छाया *chāya*[1] is further modified as छवि *chavi* by the change of the final आ *ā* into इ *i* and of य *y* into व *v*. छवि *chavi* means 'light.' By a similar process we get from द्या *dyā*, Gr. Κοιος and Sans. कवि *Kavi* or काव्य *Kāvya* meaning Śukra, that is, the planet Venus. The original meaning of the word कवि *kavi* is 'bright' or the planet Venus, then 'bright with knowledge,' 'a sage,' 'a weaver,' 'a poet.' From कवि *kavi* are derived Gr. ὕφαινω, 'to weave,' 'to make a composition,' कुविंद *kuvinda* (ὑφαντης), 'a weaver,' in which the radical part कुव् *kuv* is nearer to the Greek root than to the Sanskrit. With कवि *Kavi* may be compared Gr. Κοιος, who was a son of Heaven and Earth, as mentioned in the following passage :—

. . . . . . *αὐτὰρ ἔπειτα*
Οὐρανῷ εὐνηθεῖσα τέκ' 'Ωκεανὸν βαθυδίνην,
Κοῖόν τε Κρεῖόν θ', Ὑπερίονά τ' Ἰαπετόν τε,

133-134, Hesiod's Theogony.

'Moreover, she having been brought to the bed of Heaven gave birth to Cœus, Crius, Hyperion and Iapetus.'

In his notes on the above passage Mr. Paley, a commentator, says: 'Κοῖος may mean intelligent from Κοεῖν, or perhaps 'sky.' (Compare *Cohus*, i. e., *coelum* quoted by Festus, and Juno Covella).'

I thoroughly agree with the commentators in thinking that the word *Cohus* is connected with *coelum* as it is allied to a class of words to which I have already referred when speaking of *coelum* (p. 11). It will be very interesting

[1] छाया *chāyā* means also the wife of the Sun, reflection, and shade.

for the readers to know that in Sanskrit, too, the sky is called गहनम् *gahanam* (गाथ *gātha*, '*βαθυς*,' depth, गाह् *gāh*, 'to dive'), महाबिलम् *mahābilam*, 'great pit,' and सुषिरम् *suṣiram*, 'pit,' the last word being mentioned in the Uṇādi Sūtra (I. 52) and taken by the commentator in the senses of 'a hole' and 'sky.'[1] But from what I have said we can easily see that Mr. Paley was wrong in connecting *Cohus* with Κοιος.

As for the other word *Covella*, however, I think with him that it is connected with Κοιος. *Covella* must be a feminine diminutive form of such a word as *Covus* which is identical with Κοιος, and is obsolete in Latin.

The above comparison of the word Κοιος with Sans. कवि *kavi*, settles its ultimate origin from स्वर् *svar*, 'heaven.'

Cœus was father of Latona (द्योतना *Dyōtanā*, q. v.), Asteria, &c., by Phœbe, and son of Uranus and Terra.

I would connect with कवि *kavi*, Gr. *σοφος*, 'learned,' 'wise,' *σοφια*, 'learning,' Lat. *sapio*, 'to be wise,' and *sapient*, 'learned,' and *caveo*, 'to be cautious.'

As we have in Greek Κοιος corresponding to कवि *kavi*, so have we in Sanskrit सूर *sūra* corresponding to सूरि *sūri*, both the words meaning 'a sage.' As Κοιος originally meant 'bright,' and, having been modified as कवि *kavi*, was applied to the planet Venus, then a sage, so did the word सूर *sūra* originally meaning 'bright,' 'the sun,' come to mean also 'a sage.' This word has already been connected with स्वर् *svar*, 'heaven.' (Vide p. 34.)

---

[1] सुषिरंछिद्रमाकाशश्च *Suṣiraṁchidramākāśaśca*. I. 52.
Ujjvaladatta's Commentary on Uṇādi Sūtra.

I have thus been led by my investigations to anticipate such a word as कव *kava* in Sanskrit, which is found only in the modified form of कवि *kavi*, and I have at last discovered the existence of the word in the former part of the compounds कवारि *kavāri*, कवसख *kavasakha*. They occur in the following passages :

दैवीपूर्तिर्दक्षिणादेवयज्यानकवारिभ्योनहितेपृणन्ति

Daivīpūrtirdakṣiṇādevayajyānakavāribhyōnahitepṛṇanti.

अथानरःप्रयतदक्षिणासोवद्यभियाबहवःपृणन्ति ॥

Athānaraḥprayatadakṣiṇāsōvadyabhiyābahavaḥpṛṇanti.

'The sufficient divine fee of the divine sacrifice is not refused (not given) by the enemies of the Kavas (*sc.* Aryans). If they please (the Gods), many men do so, having given the fee by fear of sin.'—Rig Veda, X. 107, 3.

I have differed from Sāyana for whose interpretation I refer the reader to the commentary of that scholar, and construed the passage in the following way :—

दैवीपूर्तिर्देवयज्यादक्षिणाकवारिभ्योनहीतिन; अथतेपृणन्ति,

Daivīpūrtirdēvayajyādakṣiṇākavāribhyōnahītina ; athatēpṛṇanti,

अवद्यभियाप्रयतदक्षिणासोबहवोनरःपृणन्ति॥

avadyabhiyāprayatadakṣiṇāsōbahavōnaraḥpṛṇanti.

कवारिभ्यः *kavāribhyaḥ* in the above passage would naturally refer to the enemies of the कव *Kava*, that is, I think, non-Aryans. This meaning is supported by the use of the word in the following passage :—

अपापशक्रस्ततनुष्टिमूहतितनूशुभ्रंमघवायःकवासखः।

Anāpaśakrastatanuṣṭimūhatitanūśubhrammaghavāyaḥkavāsakhaḥ.

Rig Veda, V. 34, 3.

'Indra who is powerful and the friend of the Kavas, destroys the bright-bodied enemies of ceremonies.'

But in the above passages Sāyana understands by the word कव *kava*, 'little,' 'despicable,' as in the word कवोष्ण *kavōṣṇa*, 'little warm,' in which कव[1] *kava* means 'little,' and in that meaning the word may be simply a development of the syllable को *kō* of कोष्ण *kōṣṇa*. But according to Dr. Haug, the author of the 'Essays on the Parsis,' there is a word of the same form as कवि *kavi* in the Zend which was applied to a priest of the Deva religion as opposed to the Ahura Mazda religion in contempt. But he says that it looks very strange that the same word कवि *kavi* should be applied to "the highly celebrated personages of Iranian Antiquity, such as Kavi Husrava (Kaî Khusro), Kavi Kavâta (Kaî Kabâd), Kavi Vîshtâspa (Kaî Gushtâsp), and has become, in its derived adjectival form "Kayanian," the designation of a whole dynasty of the ancient Bactrian rulers.' He then mentions such an expression as Kavâ Vishtâspa used instead of Kavi Vishtâspa and thinks that *Kavi* was modified as *Kava* to avoid the bad idea implied by the word. But I differ from him and think that *Kava* was the original form, and कवि *kavi*, a modified one, as सूर *sūra* and सूरि *sūri*, which I have derived from the same root स्वर् *svar*, from which were derived कव *kava* and कवि *kavi*. Answering to Lat. *Caius* and *Caia* which are used as titles to proper names, Gr. Κοιος, a son of Ουρονος and Γεα and Gr. σοφος, 'wise,' we should have कव *kava* for the oirginal form and not कवि *kavi*.

---

[1] Cf. कवतिर्यङ् *kavatiryaṅ*, 'a little harizontal.' *Tait. Sam. and Āpast. Śr. Sūtra.* Here कव *kava* points to the original क्व *kva*, 'which.'

Many other Sanskrit words which originally ended in अ *a*, have changed the final अ *a* into इ *i* and the original ending reappears when they come as the latter parts of compound words; e. g.,

अंगुलि *aṅguli*, 'finger,' from अग्र *agra*, 'top,' (*q.v.*); अंगुल *aṅgula* as in त्र्यंगुल *tryaṅgula*, 'having three inches.'

रात्रि *rātri*, 'night,' from लस्त्र *lastra*, 'brightness' (*q.v.*); रात्र *rātra* as in द्विरात्र *dvirātra*, 'two nights.'

सखि *sakhi*, 'friend,' from सह *saha*, 'with' (*q.v.*); सख *sakha* as in विष्णुसख *Viṣṇusakha*, 'friend of Viṣṇu.'

अक्षि *akṣi*, 'eye,' from अग्र *agra*, 'top,' or लक्ष् *lakṣ*, 'to see,' by the elision of the initial ल *l*; अक्ष *akṣa* as in पद्माक्ष *padmākṣa*, 'having lotus-like eye.'

सक्थि *sakthi*, 'thigh,' from जघन *jaghana*, 'abdomen;' सक्थ *saktha* as in दीर्घसक्थ *dīrghasaktha*, 'long-thighed.'

नाभि *nābhi*, 'navel,' from नभस् *nabhas* (Gr. ομφαλος), 'sky' (*q.v.*); नाभ *nābha* as in पद्मनाभ *padmanābha*, 'having lotus-like navel.'

For the convenience of the readers, I extract here the following passage from Dr. Haug's Essays on the Parsis, pp. 290-91.

"These two names, *kavi* and *karapan*, designate in the fullest sense all the spiritual guides of the professors of the Deva religion, who tried to put down the adherents of the Ahura Mazda religion, and we necessarily find, therefore, a bad meaning attached to them in the Gâthas. This appears the more strange, as the word *kavi* itself forms part of the names of highly celebrated personages of Iranian Antiquity, such as Kavi Husrava (Kaî Khusro), Kavi Kavâta (Kaî Kabâd), Kavi Vîshtâspa (Kaî Gushtâsp), &c., and has become, in its derived adjectival form "Kayanian," the designation of a whole dynasty of the ancient Bactrian rulers.

"Here the question naturally arises, how could a designation, which distinguished the bitterest enemies of the Zoroastrian religion, be applied to kings who were, like Kavi Vîshtâspa, believed to be its staunchest friends and protectors? The only reasonable answer is, that, before the outbreak of the schism, when the Iranians and Brahmans lived peacefully together, the Kavis were at the head of both communities; and that, on account of their violent opposition to the religious and social reforms which were adopted by some of the Aryan tribes, such as the Iranians, their very name was branded, and became a word of abomination with the Zoroastrians. But the designation having been already closely connected with their ancient history, and having become the constant epithet of some of their greatest heroes and kings, it was difficult, nay, impossible, to expunge it entirely in its good and high sense from the language. The adversaries of the Kavis, therefore, had to rest satisfied with a slight change of the hateful word when they wished to use it with a good meaning. Thus we actually find this word in the old texts, when forming part of the names of the great Iranian heroes and kings, changed from its only true and original form *Kavi* into *Kavâ*, as for instance, *Kavâ Vîshtâspa*, instead of *Kavi Vîshtâspa*."

I should, however, as already stated, think that the Zend word was *Kava* in its original form and subsequently modified as *Kavi*. As applied to proper names, it must have retained the original meanings, *viz.*, 'wise,' 'learned,' 'great,' though slightly altered in its form as कवि *kavi*. The word is used in Sanskrit in those very meanings, and the degeneration of it in the Zend must therefore be of a subsequent date and was only in its application to the priests of the Deva religion (Hindu religion).

The Sans. कव *kava* taking the suffix य *y* becomes कव्य *kavya*, meaning 'wise,' 'learned,' and is applied also to the Manes, a class of celestials who preside over the spirits of deceased persons, and then to the oblations offered to them in contrast to what is given to the Deities (हव्य *havya*.) I would connect with कव *kava*, कायस्थ *kāyastha*, 'accountant.'

Even in the word गय *gaya*, I see some alliance to the Sans. कव *kava*, and it is in its form similar to Gr. Κοιος and to Sans. कव *kava*. गय *gaya* means 'goods,' 'chattels,' (cf. गौस् *gaus*), for in primitive times the property of men consisted in the cattle they possessed. The next meaning is 'house,' 'household,' and 'family.' As a proper name it is applied to several persons and among others to a giant who was killed at the holy place called *Gayā* by the Gods.

39. The word द्यौस् *dyaus* is modified as द्यस् *dyas* as in सद्यस् *sadyas*, then ग्यस् *gyas* by the change of द् *d* into ग *g* and then ख्यस् *khyas*. This form is modified as Χαος in Greek, which means 'space,' personified by Hesiod. The wife of Χαος is Γαια or Γη (Sans. ज्या *jyā*). As द्यौस् *dyaus* and पृथिवी *pṛthivī*, 'Heaven and Earth,' are always associated as husband and wife in the Rig Veda, so are Χαος and Γαια in the Greek mythology. The Latin expression '*Ubi tu Caius, ego Caia*' may be explained best by reference to Sans. द्यौस् *dyaus* and ज्या *jyā*, 'Heaven and Earth,' and Ζευς and Δα. A similar expression occurs in a Vedic passage which is to be repeated by the bridegroom in the marriage of the Yajur Vedi Brahmins :—

सात्वमस्यमूहममूहमस्मिसात्वम् द्यौरहंपृथिवीत्वम्[1] ॥

Sātvamasyamūhamamūhamasmisātvaṁdyaurahampṛthivītvam.

Tait. Mantrapraśna, 3.

---

[1] The same passage occurs in the Atharva Veda. Commenting on the above passage, Haradatta says :—

सेत्यृगभिधानम् अमेतिसाम्नः । सैवनामऋगासीत्अमोसा

Sētyṛgabhidhānam amētisāmnah | *Saivanāmaṛgāsīt amōsā*

मेतिबह्वृचब्राह्मणेदर्शनात् । त्वंसासिअमोहं । संहिताकाले

mētibahvṛcabrāhmaṇē darśanāt | *Tvaṁsāsi amōhaṁ* | *Saṁhitākālē*

ओकारस्यऊकारः। बह्वृचानांत्वमोहमितिपाठः। एषएवार्थः

ōkārasyaūkārah | *Bahvṛcānāntvamōhamiti pāṭhah* | *Eṣaēvārthah*

पुनरुच्यतेअमूहमस्मिसात्वम्। यथाऋक्सामेपरस्परंसंब

punarucyatē·amūhamasmisātvam | *Yathāṛksāmēparasparaṁsambad*

द्धे एवमावामपीत्यर्थः । द्यौरहंपृथिवीत्वं । औराधर्यं

dhē ēvamāvāmapītyarthah | *Dyaurahaṁpṛthivītvaṁ* | *Aurādharyaṁ*

(धौरंधर्यम्?) अत्रविवक्षितम् ॥

(dhauraṁdharyam ?) atravivakṣitam.

'सा *sā* is the name of the Rig Veda, and अम *ama*, that of Sāman, (for) "(the name) सा *sā* itself was Ṛk and अमो *amo*, Sāman," thus is said in the Brāhmaṇa of the Rig Veda. You are सा *sā* (that is Ṛk) and I am अमो *amō* (that is, Sāman). In the Sandhi *ō* becomes *ū*. The Rig V dis, however, read it as अमोहम् *amōham*. The same meaning is repeated. I am '*amō*' and thou art '*sā*.' "Just as the Ṛk and Sāman are united with each other, so are we also," is the purport. I am द्यौस् *Dyaus* (Heaven) and thou art पृथिवी *Pṛthivī* (Earth). Here it is desired to say that one bears the burden of the other.' Regarding अमो *amō*, vide § 65.

The same expression occurs also in the corresponding Vedic passage which is to be recited by the bridegroom in the marriage ceremony of the Rig Vedi Brahmins. As the passage does not occur in the Rig Veda, Āśvalāyana quotes it *in extenso* in his Gṛhya Sūtra.

अमोहमस्मिसात्वंसात्वमस्यमोहंद्यौरहंपृथिवीत्वम्. 1. 7.

Amōhamasmisātvaṁsātvamasyamōhaṁdyaurahaṁpṛthivītvam.

The above passage means "I am he, thou art she; thou art she, I am he. I am *Dyaus* (Heaven) and thou art *Pṛthivī* (Earth)." The same is the meaning of the passage quoted from the Yajur Veda. But the Latin extract means 'wherever thou art Caius, I am Caia.' We can, however, see the agreement of the meanings of those passages easily by comparing Caius with Sans. द्यौस् *Dyaus* and Caia with ज्या *Jyā*,[1] and interpret them by Heaven and Earth respectively. But the Romans who used to repeat the passage never knew the meanings of the words Caius and Caia and thought that they were meaningless words. In his *Roman Antiquities*, p. 404, Mr. Adam, speaking of the marriage of the ancient Romans, says: "A new married woman was called Caia from Caia Cæcilia, or Tanaquil, the wife of Tarquinius Priscus, who is said to have been an excellent spinster and housewife."[2]

40. स्वस् *svas* is modified into स्पश् *spaś*, Gr. *σκοπεω*, Lat. *specio* and means 'to see.' In the Dhātupāṭha this root is mentioned, but the above meaning is not given, though in the words स्पष्ट *spaṣta*, 'well seen,' 'clear' and स्पश *spaśa*, 'a spy,' the meaning is clearly seen. The

---

[1] Cf. Gr. Κοιος, Sans. कव *kava* and कवि *kavi* and गय *gaya* which have already been mentioned.

[2] Vide Smith's Antiquities, and Cox's Introduction to Mythology.

Vedic word स्पश् *spaś* used in the following passage must be connected with the above root.

बिभ्रंद्रापिंहिरण्ययंवरुणोबस्तनिर्णिजम् ।

Bibhraddhrāpimhiraṇyayaṁvaruṇōbastanirṇijam

परिस्पशोनिषेदिरे ॥ Rig Veda, I. 25, 13.

Parispaśōniṣēdirē.

'Varuṇa holding a clean golden armour wore it, and (from the armour) rays were issued on all sides.'

In his Commentary on the above passage, Sāyana says:

स्पशःहिरण्यस्पर्शिनोरश्मयः ॥ - - - - स्पशः स्पशबाधन

Spaśah hiraṇyasparśinō raśmayah - - - - - Spaśah spaśabādhana

स्पर्शनयोः । क्विप्चेतिक्विप् ॥

sparśanayōh | kvip cēti kvip.

'स्पशः *spaśah* means rays which *touch* (are issued from) gold. The root स्पश् *spaś* means 'to teaze,' 'to touch.' (The suffix) क्विप् *kvip* (is added to the root स्पश् *spaś*) according to the sūtra (of Pāṇini), क्विप्च *kvipca* (III. 2, 76).' He takes the word स्पशः *spaśah* to mean 'those which touch' (*sc.* golden armour) radically and thence from the context 'rays or light issued from it.' The difficulty which Sāyana thus felt in explaining the meaning of स्पश् *spaś*, was surely owing to Pāṇini's not mentioning 'to see' or 'to shew' as one of the meanings of the root स्पश् *spaś*. I would, therefore, take the word स्पश् *spaś* to mean 'light,' and derive it directly from the root स्पश् *spaś*, 'to see.'[1]

---

[1] Cf. पस्पशे *paspaśē*, 'showed' or 'explained,' as in Rig Veda, I. 22, 19 and अस्पष्ट *aspaṣṭa*, 'saw,' as in I. 10, 2, idem.

41. The root स्पश् *spaś* is modified as पश् *paś* and means 'to see,' and is substituted for दृश् *dṛś* in the conjugational tenses; and also as Sans. भास् *bhās*, भा *bhā*, 'to shine' and भी *bhī*, 'to fear,' भीष् *bhīṣ*, 'to cause to fear,' भाष् *bhāṣ*, 'to speak,' and the allied Greek and Latin words.

The Gr. φημι and Lat. *for*, 'to speak,' proceed from the Sans. भा *bhā*, 'to shine,' which is a contraction of भास् *bhās*, 'to shine,' and the idea of speaking originates from that of shining or causing to shine, as in भाष् *bhāṣ*, 'to speak,' as also in भ्राज् *bhrāj*, 'to shine,' Gr. φραζω, 'to speak,' Gr. φραδης, Lat. *fraus*, 'cunning,' Sans. भारती *bhāratī*, 'speech,' Lat. *pres*, 'speaker,' as in *interpres*, 'translator,' Ang.-Sax. *specan*, Ger. *sprechen*.

Similarly originates from the same idea of shining that of fear. Compare भर्त्सयति *bhartsayati* (§ 45). The Gr. φοβος, 'fear,' and φοβεω are reduplicated forms of भी *bhī* as Sans. पिब् *pib*, 'to drink,' पा *pā*, 'to drink.' The Sans. भ्यस् *bhyas*, 'to fear,' is traceable to the same source.

42. स्पश् *spaś* produces also क्वथ् *kvath*, 'to boil,' by changing the initial स *s* into क *k*, the following प *p* into व *v* and the final श *ś* into थ *th*; and also स्विद् *svid*, 'to perspire'—an idea which originated from the radical one of 'to be hot;' and the corresponding words, Gr. ἱδροω, 'to perspire,' ἱδος, 'sweat,' Lat. *sudo*, 'to sweat,' and *sudor*, 'sweat.' By the elision of the initial स् *s*, स्पश् *spaś* is modified as पच् *pac*, Lat. *coquo*, and Gr. πεσσω, 'to bake.' Lat. *focus* corresponds to Sans. पाक *pāka*; and Lat. *fecudus* which was wrongly spelt as *foecudus*, is in form allied.

to Sans. पचत् *pacat*, as *secundus*, 'second,' to Sans. सचत् *sacat*, सच् *sac*, 'to follow.' (Vide *Note* 1, p. 11, and § 65.)

43. From स्वर् *svar* can be derived, also, स्फुर् *sphur*, 'to shine,' स्फुट् *sphuṭ*, 'to become plain or visible,' hence 'to burst out,' मिष् *miṣ*, 'to keep awake,' विष् *viṣ*,[1] 'to be seen' (as in वेष *vēṣa*, 'appearance'), मील् *mīl*, स्मील् *smīl*, क्ष्मील् *kṣmīl*, श्मील् *śmīl*, 'to close as a flower.' मिष् *miṣ* is modified in Latin as *vigeo*, 'to be lively,' *mico*, 'to shine,' *nico*, 'to beckon,' *niteo*, 'to shine,' *nicto*, 'to wink.' In the last word *nicto*, Sans. मिष् *miṣ* is changed into *niko*, and *t* is added as in Gr. σκηπτω, Sans. क्षिप् *kṣip*, 'to throw,' Gr. χαλαπτω poetic for χαλαπαινω, 'to deal hardly,' from χαλαπος, 'rough.'[2] Gr. φυλασσω is allied to Sans. विष् *viṣ* of which the initial व *v* is changed into φ and the final ष *ṣ* into λ. The Gr. ειρων, 'dissembler,' comes from विष्मन् *viṣman*, 'shiner.'

From स्फुर् *sphur* is derived Sans. फुल् *phul*, 'to burst as a flower.'

---

[1] This root is not given in the Dhātupāṭha, and वेष *vēṣa* and its modification वेश *vēśa* are usually derived from विश् *viś*, 'to enter.' I think, however, that वेश *vēśa* and वेष *vēṣa* are allied to the Vedic पेशस् *pēśas*, 'form' and मिष *miṣa*, 'pretext,' Gr. ειρων, 'a hypocrite,' and are traceable to the root विष् *viṣ*, 'to be seen' or 'to shine,' which appears in वेष्टि *vēṣṭi*, 'light,' given in the Nirukta, II. 6.

[2] Or, we may suppose that the final ष *ṣ* of मिष् *miṣ* is changed into *ks* and *s* is hardened into *t* in Lat. *nicto*, as in निश् *niś*, Gr. νυκτ, 'night.' (Vide § 26.)

44. From द्यस् *dyas* we get दस् *daś* and then लस् *las*, 'to shine,' Gr. λυκη and Lat. *lux*, 'light,' लच् *lakṣ*, 'to see;' the proper names Λυκος, Λυκτος and Δικτη; and ऋच *ṛkṣa*, 'star,' Sans. निश् *niś*, Gr. νυξ, Lat. *nox*, 'night,' रात्र *rāṭra* modified as रात्रि *rātri*, 'night' (p. 68), which is a corruption of लस्त्र *lastra*, 'brightness.' From लस् *las* we may derive लसित्रम् *lasitram*, 'brightness,' converted into लचत्रम् *lakṣatram* by the change of स *s* into क्ष *ks*,[1] as in लच *lakṣa*, लस *lasa*, and then नचत्रम् *nakṣatram* by the change of ल *l* into न *n* as in नग्न *nagna*, 'naked,' लज्ज् *lajj*, 'to be ashamed,' a word which will be shown presently.

From लस् *las* I would derive लज् *laj* and लाज् *lāj*, 'to menace,' लज्ज् *lajj*, 'to be ashamed,' from the last of which comes नग्न *nagna*, 'naked.' In the first two words the original idea seems to be 'to shine,' 'to be brilliant,' which produces the secondary one of 'to menace.'[2] Compare, Sans. भी *bhī*, 'to fear,' भा *bhā*, 'to shine.'

---

[1] Vide § 26.

[2] भर्त्सयतितर्जयतेसंतर्जतिलजतिलाजतिच।
Bhartsayatitarjayatēsantarjatilajatilājatica,
लंजतिलांजतितुल्यास्तर्जयतिचदृश्यतेकविभिः॥
Lanjatilānjatitulyāstarjayaticadṛśyatēk wibhih.
Ākhyātacandrikā.

In भर्त्सयति *bhartsayati* which is equal to भ्रासयति *bhrāsayati* modified as भार्सयति *bhārsayati*, the *t* is inserted euphonically between *r* and *s* as in Gr. εσθλος, εσλος, 'good,' in which θ is inserted between σ and λ and as in Lat. *tonstrix* = *tonsor* + *ix*.

Sans. भीषयति *bhīṣayati*
,, भेषति *bhēṣati*
,, भेषते *bhēṣatē*
} भासते *bhāsatē*, भास् *bhās*, 'to shine.'

,, भर्त्सयति *bhartsayati* { भ्रासयति *bhrāsayati*, भ्रास् *bhrās*, 'to shine.'
भ्राजते *bhrājatē*, भ्राज् *bhrāj*, 'to shine.'

Gr. Οκνος, 'cowardice.'
,, Οκνεω, 'to shrink.'
} अनक्ति *anakti* { अंज् *anj*, 'to be visible.'

As too much brightness dazzles the spectator, and produces fear in him, so it exposes also the person who is seen, to the view of the spectator and makes him shy or ashamed; so that the word 'to shine' comes to mean 'to menace,' 'to fear,' and 'to shrink.' The Sans. नग्न *nagna* exactly corresponds to the Eng. *naked* which is traced to the Ang.-Sax. *nacod*, the root of which is found in the M. E *naken*, 'to lay bear.' This root is evidently connected with Sans. लस् *las* both in form and meaning and the alliance of the roots is settled when we consider that लस् *las* yields the radical part नग् *nag*[1] of नग्न *nagna* in Sanskrit itself. Similarly is derived from लस् *las* Tam. நகு *nagu*, 'to laugh,' நகை *nagai*, 'ornament;' Kan. ನಾಚಿಗೆ *nācige*, and Tel. సిగ్గు *siggu*, 'shame,' लड् *laḍ*, Lat. *ludo*, 'to be merry,' Lat. *rideo*, Gr. γελαω and Sans. हस् *has*, 'to laugh.'[2]

---

[1] Compare Pers. نور *nūr*, 'light'; also Tam. எலுமிஞ்சை *eluminjai*, 'lemon;' Kan. ನಿಂಬೆ *nimbe;* Sans. लवण *lavaṇa*, Arab. نمک *namak*, Hind. नोन् *nōn*, 'salt'; Gr. λιτρον, a kind of orange, Sans. नारङ्ग *nāraṅga*.

[2] The idea of shining produces that of laughing.

45. स्वस् *svas*, 'happiness,' may be modified as स्वद् *svad*, 'to taste,' स्वादु *svādu*, Gr. ἡδυς, Lat. *suavis*, 'sweet,' in which last the final द् *d* of Sanskrit is changed into व *v*, a change which has taken place in many instances, such as दिवस् *divas*, वियस् *viyas*, 'sky,' and especially in the Latin past tenses; e.g.

Lat. *amavi*, 'I have loved,' from *amo*, 'to love,' which corresponds to Sans. कमितोस्मि *kamitōsmi*, taking कमित *kamita* as an active participial adjective meaning 'having loved.' कमितोस्मि *kamitōsmi* would, therefore, mean 'I have loved.' If कमितोस्मि *kamitōsmi* is changed in Prakrit into कमिद्दोम्मि *kamidōmmi*, and the last part ओम्मि *ōmmi* undergoes the same change as the last part of भवामि *bhavāmi* undergoes in Greek, that is, being reduced to a mere long syllable as ω as in φυω, we shall have कमिदेा *kamidō* for कमितेास्मि *kamitōsmi*. Again, the final द् *d* is changed into य *y* and then also into व *v*, as in

Sans. चलितस् *calitas* }
Prak. चलिदो *calidō* } Prak. चलियो *caliyō*.

Prak. गदो *gadō* }
Sans. गतस् *gatas* } Hind. गया *gayā*, 'he went.'

Prak. दिदो *didō* }
Sans. दत्तस् *dattas* } „ दिया *diyā*.

Prak. भूदो *bhūdō* }
Sans. भूतस् *bhūtas* } „ हुवा *huvā*, 'he became.'

In these instances त *t* is changed into द *d* and then into य *y* or व *v*.

We have similarly कमिवो *kamivō* for कमितोस्मि *kamitōsmi,* a form which is almost identical with Lat. *amavi* in which the root *am* answers to Sans. कम् *kam* and the final *i* to *ō*. In this way, I think, most of the past tense forms in Latin ending in *vi* can be accounted for.

I would observe here that this theory accounts for all perfect forms in Latin except those which are reduplicated. Thus *avi* in *amavi*, which is, as shown above, a corruption of Sans. इतोस्मि *itōsmi*, appears, also, in the following forms :

Cupivi, 'I have desired,'	*cupio*, 'to desire,'	*ivi.*
Sapivi, 'I have been wise,'	*sapio*, 'to be wise,'	
Vetui, 'I have forbidden,'	*veto*, 'to forbid,'	*ui.*
Micui, 'I have glittered,'	*mico*, 'to glitter,'	

When the past participial termination त *t* is added without the augment इ *i*, we have instead of इतोस्मि *itōsmi* तोस्मि *tōsmi* which is shortened into *do* and then *di* ; and this *di* is modified as follows :—

Pluvi, 'I have rained' = *plu* + *di* (Sans. प्लुत *pluta*, 'floated'). Compare हुवा *huvā* mentioned above.

Stravi, 'I have spread,' (Sans. स्तीर्ण *stīrṇa* for स्तीर्त *stīrta*, Gr. στρωτος) = *stern* + *di* = *stren* + *di* wherein *stern* becomes *stren* by metathesis = *stre* + *di*, by the elision of the final *n* from *stern*, Gr. στορυν and Sans. स्तृण् *stṛṇ*.[1]

[1] According to Pāṇini's enunciation the roots of स्तीर्ण *stīrṇa*, वृत *vṛta*, लीन *līna*, हित *hita* and स्पृत *spṛta* are स्तृ *stṛ*, वृ *vṛ*, ली *lī*, हि *hi* and स्पृ *spṛ*, but for a scientific comparison I have given them as स्तृण् *stṛṇ*, वृण् *vṛṇ*, लीन् *līn*, हिन् *hin* and स्पृण् *spṛṇ*. (Vide Conjugation.)

Crevi, 'I have separated,' Sans. वृत *vṛta*, Gr. κριτος = *cern* + *di* = *cren* + *di* = *crevi* as in the preceding, *cern*, 'to separate,' Sans. वृण् *vṛṇ*, Gr. κριν.

Livi or *lēvi*, 'I have besmeared' = *lin* + *di*, *lin*, 'to besmear,' Sans. लीन् *līn*, 'to be absorbed.'

Sivi (Sans. हित *hita*), 'I have allowed' = *sin* + *di*, *sin*, 'to allow,' Sans. हिन् *hin*, 'to send.'

Sprevi (Sans. स्पृत *spṛta*), 'I have despised' = *spern* + *di* = *spren* + *di* by metathesis, *spern*, 'to despise,' Sans. स्पृण् *spṛṇ*, 'to love.'

In the above instances *di* is changed into *vi*.

Auxi, 'I have increased' = *aug* + *di* = *auk* + *si*, *augeo*, 'to increase.'

Vixi, 'I have lived' = *viv* + *di* = *vig* + *si* = *vik* + *si*, *vivo*, 'to live.'

Struxi, 'I have built' = *struv* (Sans. दृभ् *dṛbh*) + *si*, *struo*, 'to build,' in which root the final *v* of the root *struv*, answering to Sans. दृभ् *dṛbh*, 'to compose,' and Gr. τρεφω, 'to make firm,' is elided; and the same *v* reappears in *struxi* and is then changed into *k*.

Clausi, 'I have shut' = *claud* + *di*, *claudo*, 'to shut' = *claus* + *si*, in which the final *d* of the root and the initial *d* of the termination are changed into *s*'s and the first *s* is elided.

Divīsi, 'I have divided' = *devĭd* + *di*, *divĭdo*, 'to divide.' The processes of change are the same as in the preceding, the only difference being the lengthening of the vowel *ĭ* into *ī* owing to the elision of *s*.

Vīdi = *vĭd* + *di*, *vĭdeo*, 'to see' the *d* of *vĭd* being elided, the preceding vowel is lengthened as in the previous example.

Compare Lat. *vīde* (the singular of the imperative second person of *vĭdeo*, 'to see') = *vĭd* + *de*, Sans. विद्धि *viddhi*,

Gr. ἰσθι, the final *d* of *vid* being elided, the preceding vowel is lengthened; as in Sans. एधि *ēdhi* (Gr. ἰσθι) = अस् *as* + धि *dhi* = अध् *adh* + धि *dhi*, in which the final ध *dh* of the radical part अध् *adh* being cut off, the preceding vowel अ *a* is lengthened into ए *ē*.

The explanation of the perfect form in Latin, *Amavi* above given, is followed by the corollary that *amavĕram*, the indicative pluperfect of *amo*, 'to love,' should be = *amavus* + *ĕram*, the past tense of the root *esse*, 'to be;' *amavĕro*, the second future, = *amavus* + *ĕro*, the future tense of *esse*, 'to be;' *amavissem*, subjunctive pluperfect, = *amavus* + *essem*, the subjunctive imperfect of *esse*; *amavĕrim*, the perfect subjunctive = *amavus* + *erim*; *amavisse*, the perfect infinitive = *amavus* + *esse*. More will be said on the subject in my Comparative Grammar of Sanskrit, Greek and Latin, which is under preparation.

46. The Lat. *sapio*,[1] 'to taste,' and the noun *sapor*, 'taste,' are connected with *suavis*, 'sweet.' The Sans. शीधु *sīdhu*, 'wine,' (Gr. ἡδυς), comes from स्वादु *svādu*.

47. To the same source स्वद् *svad* are traceable Sans. मधु *madhu*, Gr. μελι (τ), Lat. *mel*, 'honey,' मिलिन्द *milinda*, Gr. μελιττα, 'a bee,' मधु *madhu*, Gr. μεθυ, Lat. *merum*, 'wine,' Sans. मैरेयम् *mairēyam*, 'toddy,' मरन्द *maranda*, 'honey of flowers,' Gr. μαλθα and μαλθη, 'a mixture of wax and pitch for calking ships,' 'a wax laid over writing tablets.' मरन्द *maranda* is modified by the addition of क *k* between म *m* and र *r* as मकरन्द *makaranda*. This law of syllabic development will account for the changes

[1] Or, it may be connected with कवि *kavi* and Gr. σοφος (q. v.).

undergone by several words in Sanskrit and Dravidian languages; e. g.,—

Sans. मूल *mūla*, 'root,'	Sans. मुकुल *mukula*, 'a bud.'
" मूर्द्धन् *mūrddhan*, 'head,'	" { मकुट *makuṭa*, / मुकुट *mukuṭa*, } 'a crown or coronet.'
" तूल *tūla*, 'cotton,'	" दुकूल *dukūla*, 'cloth.'
" नारङ्ग *nāraṅga*, 'a kind of orange,'	" नागरङ्ग *nāgaraṅga*, 'a kind of orange called *citrus aurantium*.'
" गौर *gaura*, 'red,'	" { कावेरी *kāvēri*, the Kavery (cf. पीतकावेर *pītakāvēra*, 'saffron.') }
" { कुण्ड *kuṇḍa*, कुट *kuṭa*, 'pot,' (Gr. *κυαθος*, a cup for drawing wine) }	" कमण्डलु *kamaṇḍalu*, 'a small vessel.'
Sans. वृष *vṛṣa* / Hind. भैस् *bhais* / " बैल् *bail* } 'a bull,'	" महिष *mahiṣa*, 'a buffalo.'
Hind. चार् *cār* / Sans. चत्वार् *catvār* } 'four,'	Pers. { چهار *cahār* as in چهارشنبه *cahārṣamba*, 'the fourth day,' (i.e. Wednesday.) }

This law will be illustrated in Vol. II, with reference to the Dravidian languages.

48. मधु *madhu* is modified as Lat. *vitis*, *vinum* and Gr. *οινη* and *οινος*, and मृद्वीका *mṛdvīkā*, 'grapes,' wherein the vowel ऋ *ṛ* is an inorganic addition.[1] वन *vana*, Gr. Πav, 'god

---

[1] Vide दृश् *dṛś* and the rule given under it, p. 96.

of woods,' Πενελοπη, the wife of Ulysses, whom Jupiter, charmed in the form of a goat and became by her the father of Παν. The word Πενελοπη seems to be a corruption of Παν, 'wood,' and εριφος, 'a young goat' (Sans. वनोरभ्र *vanōrabhra*, 'wild goat.')

49. From मधु *madhu* we next proceed to मद् *mad*, मुद् *mud*, 'to rejoice,' मद *mada*, 'joy,' 'intoxication,' पित्त *pitta*, 'bile' or 'madness,' वंद् *vand*, 'praise,' 'to bow to,' मंड् *maṇḍ*, 'to adore.' By the addition of the termination र *r* we get मद्र *madra*, 'happiness,' modified also as भद्र *bhadra*, and by that of the termination इका *ikā* to मद्र *madra*, मद्रिका *madrikā*, and at last मतल्लिका *matallikā*, 'the most excellent.' Compare पुत्र *putra*, 'son,' पुत्तल *puttala*, 'a puppet,' Gr. κολοσσος, 'statue,' पोतलिका *pōtalikā*, 'calf.' This last मतल्लिका *matallikā* is again modified as मचर्चिका *macarcikā* by the palatalization of त *t* and ल्ल *ll* into च *c* and the addition of an inorganic र *r* to the beginning of the second च *c*. From भद्र *bhadra* may be derived Gr. εσθλος which, like the Sanskrit original, is not only used in the sense of good in general, but is also used of persons indicating bravery, stoutness and the like. The original form of the word seems to be Fεςλος with an initial digamma, and without θ (as in Doric εσλος), which is inserted for euphony between σ and λ.

To this Sanskrit word भद्र *bhadra* I would trace the Gr. αθλον, 'the prize of contest,' generally a gift or reward. Αθλον is contracted from the Epic form αεθλον in which the vowel ε is owing to the elision of σ before θ; so that the original form seems to be Fασθλον with an initial digamma which must have been lost. It is very interesting to see the alliance of the Gr. αθλος, 'a contest between prizefighters' and the Sans. मल्ल *malla,* which also is traceable to the same root भद्र *bhadra* and which means 'an athlete.'

50. To the same source I would trace Sans. मृड् *mṛḍ,* 'to be happy,' मंद् *mand,* 'to praise,' 'to be happy,' भंड् *bhaṇḍ* and भंद् *bhand,* 'to be happy,' 'to rejoice,' मंदार *mandāra,* 'the celestial tree which is a source of happiness,' मंदर *mandara,* 'slow,' which quality is the result of *happiness,* and बृंद *bṛnda* and बृंदारक *bṛndāraka,* 'good,' 'beautiful.' From मंद् *mand* comes मृदु *mṛdu* which means 'soft,' physically or mentally. As happiness produces the softness of the mind, the word applied to the former was transferred to the latter. From mental softness the word extended its meaning to physical softness. By the change of *m* into *b, rd* into *ll,* and *r* into *l,* मृदु *mṛdu* becomes *βραδυς* in Greek, *mollis* in Latin, and *milde* in Anglo-Saxon. The letter ऋ *ṛ* in मृदु *mṛdu* may perhaps be inorganic as in बृहस्पति *Bṛhaspati* (q.v.) and have disappeared in Lat. *mitis,* 'soft.' To the same source भद्र *bhadra* are traceable the comparative degrees, Lat. *melior* and Gr. *βελτιων,* in which latter λ answers to the *r* in Sans. भद्र *bhadra,* and the superlative *βελτιστος.* The Eng. *good* and Ang.-Sax. *god* and their comparative and superlative degrees exactly correspond to the Greek and Sanskrit, as shown in the following table :—

	POSITIVE.	COMPARATIVE.	SUPERLATIVE.
ENG.	good[1]	better	best.
A.-S.	god	bettera	betest, betst.
GR.	*αγαθος*	*βελτιων*	*βελτιστος.*
SANS.	साधु *sādhu* or बृंद *bṛnda*	बृंदीयस् *bṛndīyas*	बृंदिष्ठ *bṛndiṣṭha.*

[1] Regarding साधु *sādhu, αγαθος* and A.-S. *god,* vide आकाश *ākāśa.*

The anusvāra in वृन्द *brnda* is non-radical; and Pāṇini takes वृंदिष्ठ *brndiṣṭha* as the superlative degree of वृंदारक *brndāraka*.[1] We can therefore infer that the positive form वृंद *brnda* is not used and in its stead is used the derivative adjective वृंदारक *brndāraka* = वृंद *brnda* + आरक *āraka*, वृन्द *brnda*, 'excellence,' and आर *āra*, a suffix meaning 'having,' and क *ka*, an enclitical suffix.

51. From दिवस् *divas* may be derived the form युवस् *yuvas*, and from this, the Vedic युवश *yuvaśu*, 'youthful,' 'bright,' युवन् *yuvan*, 'young,' युवाकु *yuvāku*, 'bright,' 'hot,' and यवागू *yavāgū*, 'the hot water taken from boiled rice,' called also उष्णिका *uṣṇikā* in Sanskrit. Compare Gr. Ιοκαστη, 'the wife of Laios,' which I have explained already (p. 51). The word युवस् *yuvas* occurs in the following passage:—

> यार्जरन्ता युवशाता कृणोतन. Rig Veda, I. 161-7.
>
> *Yājarantā yuvaśātā krṇōtana.*
>
> 'You have made those who were old young.'

युवस् *yuvas* is contracted into यूस् *yūs* and is applied to rice gruel, because it is hot, being taken from boiled rice. यूस् *yūs* is modified also as यूषन् *yuṣan* and यूषम् *yūṣam*, by the addition of अन् *an* and अम् *am*. यूस् *yūs* is a Vedic word.

> रसोवा एष पशूनां यद्यूः. Tait. Sam. VI. 3.
>
> *Rasōvā ēṣa paśūnām yadyūh.*
>
> 'Rice gruel is delicious to cattle.'

---

[1] प्रियस्थिरस्फिरोरुबहुलगुरुवृद्धतृप्रदीर्घवृंदारकाणाम्प्र *Priyasthirasphirōrubahulaguruvrddhatrpradīrghabrndārakāṇāmpra* स्थस्फवर्बंहिगर्वर्षित्रब्द्राघिवृंदाः ॥ Pāṇini, VI. 4, 157. *sthasphavarbaṁhigarvarṣitrabdrāghibrndāh.*

The Vedic युवाकु *yuvāku,* variously interpreted by Sāyana in his commentary of the Rig Veda, may be derived from युवस् *yuvas* by the change of स *s* into क *k* and taken to mean 'bright,' 'hot,' &c.

दस्रायुवाकवस्सुतानासत्यावृक्तबर्हिषः ।

Dasrāyuvākavassutā nāsatyāvṛktabarhiṣah

आयातंरुद्रवर्तनी ॥ Rig Veda, I. 3, 3.

Āyātaṁrudravartanī.

'O truthful Aswins, whose ways are full of awe, bright or fresh (soma juice) has been distilled, come and occupy the trimmed darbha grass.'

यवागू *yuvāgū,* 'rice water,' is so called on account of its heat as it is taken from boiled rice.

52. I shall next proceed to the Sanskrit word युवन् *yuvan,* 'youthful,' 'young,' and the corresponding Lat. *juvenis* and Gr. ἥβη.[1] While the Lat. *juvenis* is closely connected with युवन् *yuvan,* the Gr. ἥβη seems to be rather remote; for the connection of य *y* and ज *j* is very frequent and apparent, but that of य *v* and ह *h* is not easily seen. In many Greek words, however, the change of य *y* into ह *h* has taken place; and the word under discussion is one of them.

Compare the following :—

Sans. याज्य *yājya,* 'belonging to sacrifice' (यज् *yaj*), Gr. ἅγιος.

,, याग *yāga,* 'sacrifice,' ,, ἄγος, 'any matter of religious awe.'

---

[1] We may perhaps trace to युवस् *yuvas,* Lat. *jubar,* 'light,' *juba,* 'mane of a horse,' *puber,* 'adult,' in which last the य *y* of युवस् *yuvas* is changed into *p.*

Sans. यकृत् *yakṛt* Gr. ἧπαρ (τος), liver, Lat. *jecur.*

„ यद् *yad* „ ὁς, relative pronoun '*what.*'

„ या *yā* „ ἱημι, 'to go.'

„ युध्वन् *yudhvan* „ ὑσμινι, 'battle.'

(Vide Bopp's Comp. Gram. Vol. II, p. 538.)

„ युवस् *yuvas* Gr. ὑβρις, 'strong.'

In ἡβος which means 'young,' the final न् *n* of युवन् *yuvan* is elided. The feminine form of युवन् *yuvan,* viz. युवति *yuvati,* is allied to Ιας (δος), the feminine form of Ιον (q. v.), 'an Ionian woman,' just as युवन् *yuvan* to Ιον. युवस् *yuvas* being changed into युबर् *yubar* by the insertion of र् *r* for स *s,* and ब *b* for व *v,* and shortened into युब्र *yubra,* may produce the Gr. ὑβρις, 'strong,' ἁβρος, 'delicate,' 'soft,' οβρια, 'strength,' and οβριμος, 'strong,' in the last two of which the aspirate sound of the initial vowel of ὑβρις is lost.

As छाया *chāyā,* that is 'light,' is the wife of the sun अहस्कर *ahaskara* (अहस् *ahas,* 'day,' and कार *kara,* 'producing'), so Ἡβη is the wife of Ἡρακλεης, which word seems to be a contraction of अहस्कर *ahaskara* by the elision of the initial अ *a* and the change of स *s* into र् *r* as in अहर्पति *aharpati,* 'lord of the day,' i. e., 'the sun.' (Vide p. 61.)

53. From ὑβρις we get βριαρος, 'strong,' and also the proper name βριαρεως, applied to a hundred-handed giant, who is called so by the gods, and Ægion by men, and who assisted Zeus. He was the son-in-law of Poseidon and with his brothers Cottus and Gyas assisted the gods against the Titans. Allied to ὑβρις we have in Sanskrit कुमार *kumāra*, 'young' and 'soft,' as in सुकुमार *sukumāra*. It is applied to 'the war god,' who was a son of Śiva and assisted the gods and whose name गुह *Guha* resembles that of *Gyas* (Γυγης), brother of βριαρεως. In वीरभद्र *Vīrabhadra*, a son of Śiva who destroyed the sacrifice of Dakṣa who had insulted Śiva, we see a likeness to βριαρεως, and also in कार्तवीर्य *Kārtavīrya*, 'a prince of the Hehayas,' who had a thousand arms and was defeated by Paraśurāma. The names βριαρεως and Κοττυς seem to have been coined from कार्तवीर्य *Kārtavīrya*, Κοττος answering to कार्त *kārta* and βριαρεως to वीर्य *vīrya*. कोमल *kōmala*, 'soft,' is a modification of कुमार *kumāra*. βρι is a contraction of ὑβρις and is used as a prefix to intensify the meaning of an adjective.

Ὑβρισ may be modified as वीर *vīra* and ἡρως and Lat. *vis*, pl. *vires*, and Gr. ις (ινος), 'strength.'

54. The word यवन *yavana* is, I think, converted into Ιω (ν) and was applied to Ion, the son of Xuthus (Apollo) and Creusa, who is said to be the ancestor of the Ionian race. But it is applied to many nations in Sanskrit such as Persians, Greeks, Jews, Arabians, Mahomedans and so on. The Heb. יָוָן, 'Javan,' was the name of the fourth son of Japhet, whom the Jews supposed to have been the ancestor of all the Grecians or Ionians. The word is, therefore, applied in the Old Testament to Greece or an inhabitant of Greece. There can be no doubt about the identity of this word Javan, יֶפֶת, 'Japheth,' the Gr. Ιαπητος, Ιω (ν) and Sans. यवन *yavana* and युवन् *yuvan*. (Vide Rajendra Lal Mitra's Article on the 'Yavanas' in the *Bengal Asiatic Society's Journal*, 1874, No. III, pp. 246-279; and Dr. Oppert's Śukra., pp. ix–xi.)

The following Hebrew words, notwithstanding the different origins assigned to them, must be connected, I think, with the Sanskrit and Greek words mentioned here:— יְהוֹשֻׁעַ, 'Jehoshua,' the son of Nun; יְהוּדָה, 'Judah,' the fourth son of Jacob; יְהוּד, 'the land of Judah.' The Sans. युवस् *yuvas* modified as यहुस *yahusa* by the change of व *v* into ह *h*, and यहुद *yahuda* by the change of स *s* into द *d*, has produced all the Hebrew words mentioned here. (Vide Semitic Analogy.)

55. Allied to the Gr. Ιω and Sans. यवन *yavana* is Gr. Ιαπητος, son of Cœlus or Titan by Terra or, according to Hesiod, son of Ουρανος and Γαια, who married Asia, or according to others, Clymene, who bore to him Atlas, Menœtius, Prometheus and Epimetheus. The Heb. יֶפֶת, 'Japheth,' is identical with the Gr. Ιαπητος and Sans. यवन *yavana*. Japheth was the eldest son of Noah whose descendants occupy the whole of Europe. To यवन *yavana* is to be traced the Egyp. *Hauvanu* mentioned in Mr. Gladstone's Hom. Syn., p. 267. From the Sans. युवन् *yuvan* must be derived the Pers. جوان *javān*, 'youth,' and then, 'a servant,' for a youth is engaged as a servant,—a change of meaning, which has taken place in the Eng. *boy*, and Hind. چھوکرا *chōkrā*, which was borrowed either from Kan. ಚಿಕ್ಕನು *cikkanu* or Sans. किशोर *kiśōra*, 'a boy,' and is now applied by the European residents of Madras to 'a (young) servant.'

56. The Sans. युवस् *yuvas* may next be changed into युसव *yusava*, युहव *yuhava* and at last into यह्व *yahva*, meaning 'bright,' 'young,' 'great,' 'mighty,' &c., but the radical meaning is, I think, 'bright,' to which the other meanings may be traced; e.g.

आभंदमाने उपाके नक्तोषासा सुपेशसा

Ābhandamānē upākē naktōṣāsā supēśasā

यह्वीऋतस्य मातरा सीदतां बर्हिरा सुमत्॥

Yahvīrṛtasya mātarāsīdantām barhirāsumat.—Rig Veda, I. 142, 7.

'Let Night and Dawn who are cheerful, living together, of beautiful forms, bright or young, and are mothers of sacrifice, approach (sit on) the darbha grass happily.'

यह्व *yahva* is contracted into यह्व *yahu* and means 'young,' hence 'a son,' as in the Rig Veda, I. 26, 10.

चनोधास्सहसोयहो *Canōdhāssahasōyahō.*

'O son of strength, give us food.'

The word यह्वत् *yahvat* is a modification of यह्व *yahva*, and means 'bright,' as in the following passage:—

सुपर्णा एत आसते मध्य आरोधने दिवः

Suparṇā ēta āsatē madhya ārōdhanēdivaḥ

ते सेधन्ति पथो वृकं तरन्तं यह्वतीरपो वित्तं मे अस्य रोदसी॥

Tesedhanti pathōvṛkam tarantam yahvatīrapō vittam mē asya rōdasī.

Rig Veda, I. 105, 11.

'These rays of the sun spread in the all-covering centre of the sky. They prevent the wolf from crossing the bright waters on its way. O, Heaven and Earth, hear this praise of mine.'

To this root यह्व *yahva* I would trace some Semitic words which, like those already referred to, are derived in a peculiar and different way by the lexicographers and scholars; such as,

Heb. יַעֲקֹב, 'Jacob,' (Arab. يعقوب *Yākūb*), the younger twin son of Isaac;

" יוֹסֵף, 'Joseph,' (Arab. يوسف *Yūsuf*), the first-born son of Rachel;

Heb. יֵהוּא, 'Jehu,' a prophet and the son of Hanani, and also the grandson of Jehoshaphat;

,, יְבוּס, 'Jebus,' the ancient name of Jerusalem, so called after the third son of Canaan;

,, יְהוָֹה, 'Jehovah,' God;

and many other words which will be mentioned in the Semitic Analogy.

57. From स्व *sva*, 'possession,' we can derive सव *sava*, which form is changed into सह *saha*, 'with,' and सख *sakha*, 'a friend,' by inserting *kh* for *v* as in सुख *sukha*, स्वस् *svas*, 'happiness.' सह *saha* is contracted into स *sa*. Again, the form सव *sava* is changed into सम *sama*, 'equal,' 'with,' and सिम *sima*, 'all,' of which अमा *amā*, 'near,' Gr. *ἅμα*, 'at the same time,' and *ὁμος*, 'common,' are modifications. Sans. समान *samāna*, 'equal,' 'common,' Gr. *ὁμαλος*, 'of equal degree,' and Lat. *similis* are formed from the above words. सम *sama* is contracted into सम् *sam*, and Gr. *συν* and *ξυν*, the latter being used in Old Attic for the later and more common *συν*. The corresponding form in Latin is *con* in which the initial *c* stands for the initial स *s* of Sans. सम् *sam*.[1] सम *sama* is also modified as समया *samayā*, 'near,' and सह *saha*, as साकम् *sākam*, सत्रा *satrā* and सार्धम् *sārdham*, 'with.' सत्रा *satrā* is formed from स *sa* which is a shortened form of सह *saha* as shown above, by the addition of the terminations तर *tara* and आ *ā*; and सार्धम् *sārdham*, from सह *saha* by the addition of तर *tara* and

---

[1] Vide p. 114.

अम् *am.* The last word सार्धम् *sārdham* is, however, formed somewhat peculiarly; for, the final aspirate of सह *saha* is blended with the following त *t* which letter is thereby changed into ध *dh* as in सध्र्यंच् *sadhryañc* = सह *saha* + तर् *tar* + अंच् *añc*, as I have already shown (vide p. 18); and the *r* of तर् *tar* is transposed to the middle of the word.

सह *saha* is modified also as सघ *sagha* and सच *saca* by the change of ह *h* into घ *gh* and च *c*, and from the latter of them is derived सचिव *saciva*, 'a minister.' सच *saca* produces the roots सच् *sac*, 'to join,' सज् *saj*, 'to come in contact,' and लग् *lag*, 'to adhere,' Gr. θιγγανω, Lat. *tango*, 'to touch,' and Gr. τυγχανω, 'to happen.'

Corresponding to Sans. स *sa*, 'with,' 'equal,' which I have shown above to be a contraction of सह *saha*, we have in Greek ἁ which is changed into *a* by the loss of the aspirate sound. Like its original स *s*, *a* is used as the first member of a compound as in αδελφος', Sans. सगर्भस् *sagarbhas*, in which *a* and स *s* mean 'the same' and δελφος and गर्भस् *garbhas*, 'womb.' Αδελφος and सगर्भस् *sagarbhas* mean, therefore, 'of the same womb,' that is, brother and sister; similarly, Gr. αταλαντον, Sans. सधरित्रम् *sadharitram*, 'of equal scales.' (Compare αλιγκιος, p. 98.)

The Sans. सम् *sam* and Gr. ξυν have respectively produced सेन *sēna* and ξενος, the radical sense of which is 'who is with another,' that is, 'attendant.' In Sanskrit सेना *sēnā* means 'an army,' and ξενος in Greek, 'a guest' or 'the friend with whom one is bound in a treaty of hospitality.' The Gr. ευξενος or ευξεινος meaning 'kind to strangers,' and 'hospitable,' corresponds exactly to the Sans. सुषेण *suṣēṇa* which may mean either 'very hospitable' or 'having good attendants.'

58. From द्यौस् *dyaus* we can derive ग्यौस् *gyaus* and गौस् *gaus* by the elision of य *y*, and the word has several meanings, such as 'heaven,' 'earth,' 'rays,' 'eye,' 'sight,' 'horizon,' 'arrow,' &c.,[1] which are all traceable to the original meaning of the word 'heaven or light.' गौस् *gaus* becomes 'βους' in Greek by the change of ग *g* into β. This change occurs frequently in Greek as shown in the following examples :—

Sans. गुरु *guru*,	Gr. βαρυς, 'heavy' (Lat. *gravis*, 'heavy')
,, गल् *gal*, 'to fall,'	,, βαλλω, 'to throw.'
,, गम् *gam*,	,, βαινω, 'to go.'
,, गाध *gātha*, 'bottom,'	,, βαθυς, 'deep.'
,, ग्राभ् *grābh* (the causal form of Vedic गृभ् *gṛbh*, 'to take')	,, βλαπτω, 'to stop,' 'to arrest,' 'to catch.'
,, गा *gā*,	,, βοαω, 'to cry.'

---

[1] गौःस्वर्गेचवलीवर्दे रश्मौचकुलिशेपुमान् ।
Gauhsvargēcavalīvārdēraśmaucakuliśēpumān,
स्त्रीसौरभेयीदृग्बाणदिग्वाग्भूष्वप्सुभूम्निच ।
Strīsaurabhēyīdṛgbāṇadigvāgbhūṣvapsubhūmnica,
गायत्र्यामपिगम्भीरेजगत्यांभुवनेजने ॥ *Mēdinī.*
Gāyatryāmapigambhīrējagatyāmbhuvanējanē.

Sans. गर्भ *garbha*, (κορπος.) Gr. βρεφος, 'the child unborn.'
,, गोल *gōla*, ,, βωλος, 'a ball.'
,, गुहा *guhā*, 'a cave," ,, βυθος, 'deep sea,' 'depth.'
,, गर्जितम् *garjitam*, 'roaring,' ,, βαρβιτον, 'a musical instrument of many strings.'
,, गव *gava*, as in अजगव *ajagava*, 'Siva's bow.' ,, βιος, 'a bow.'

Compare the corresponding change of क *k* into π in Greek, which will be illustrated lower down.

गौस् *gaus*, 'light,' is contracted into गुस् *gus* and modified as गुष् *guṣ* by the change of स् *s* into ष् *ṣ* as in द्युस् *dyus*, त्विष् *tviṣ*, and then शुष् *śuṣ*,[1] 'to burn,' by the change of ग *g* into श *ś*. From शुष् *śuṣ* we can derive उष् *uṣ*, 'to burn,' by the elision of the initial consonant, and सूच् *sūc*,[2] 'to point out,' by changing श *ś* into स *s* and lengthening the vowel *u* as in दूष् *dūṣ*, 'to abuse,' the causal of दुष् *duṣ*, 'to become corrupt,' and as in गूह् *gūh*, 'to cause to enter,' the causal of गुह् *guh*, 'to enter.'

From शुच् *śuc* comes रुच् *ruc*, 'to shine,' and this is modified as लोक् *lōk*, लोच् *lōc*, 'to see,' Gr. δοκεω, 'to seem,' Lat. *luceo*, 'to shine.'

59. रुच् *ruc*,[3] 'to see,' assumes the form of दृश् *dṛś* (Gr.

---

[1] Tam. சுடு *suḍu*, Kan. ಸುಡು *suḍu*.

[2] Tel. చూడు *cūḍu*, Kan. ನೋಡು *nōḍu*, Tam. நோக்கு *nōkku*, சூழ் *sūḷ*.

[3] I would trace रोदस् *rōdas* and रोदसी *rōdasī*, 'Heaven and Earth,' to द्युस् *dyus* through the form रुस् *rus* which with the final

δερκομαι) by a peculiar change of र *r* into दृ *dṛ* wherein द *d* may stand for *r* as in गुड *guḍa*, Gr. γυρος,[1] and ऋ *ṛ* may be a strengthening letter, or *vice versâ.*

I give here below some instances to illustrate the law according to which the vowel ऋ *ṛ* is added to strengthen a consonant.

Sans. कृसर *kṛsara*, originally किसर *kisara* as mentioned by Pāṇini in sutra IV. 4, 53, wherein किसर *kisara* is mentioned as a saleable article and appears to be allied to Lat. *cicer*, 'chick-pea.'

„ यकृत् *yakṛt*, यकन् *yakan* in the oblique cases, Gr. ἡπαρ (ηπατος) wherein π answers to the क *k* of यकृत् *yakṛt*. The ऋ *ṛ* of यकृत् *yakṛt* is, therefore, non-radical.

„ शकृत् *śakṛt*, शकन् *śakan* in the oblique cases, Gr. σκωρ (σκατος), 'dung.'

„ असृक् *asṛk*, असन् *asan* in the oblique cases, Gr. αἱμα (ατος), Lat. *sanguis* in which the initial अ *a* of असन् *asan* is elided.

„ सृगाल *sṛgala*, छगल *chagala*, 'a goat,' Eng. *jackal*, Gr. σισυρος, 'a shaggy goat skin,' σατυρος, a

---

म् s changed into द् *d* and by the addition of the termination अस् *as* becomes रुदस् *rudas*, and, when *u* is gunated, assumes the form रोदस् *rodas*. रोदस् *rodas* is modified further as रोदसी *rodasī* by the addition of the feminine suffix ई *ī*. The words are always used in the dual number and mean 'Heaven and Earth.' To the same root द्युस् *dyus* is traceable Pers. روز *rōz*, 'a day.'

[1] Vide p. 51.

monster 'satyr' partly a goat and partly a man, Sans. किशोर *kiśora*, 'a foal;' नक्र *nakra*, 'alligator,' नकुल *nakula*, 'mungoose;' and other allied words, which will be mentioned in the *Śiras* Group, and in which the first consonant is not strengthened by ऋ *ṛ* as in the Sans. सृगाल *sṛgāla*.

Sans. सृमर *sṛmara*, 'a quadruped like the deer,' चमर *camara*, चमूरु *camūru*, 'bos grunniens,' कमल *kamala*, 'a kind of deer.'

,, सृक्वन् *sṛkvan*, 'the corner of the lips,' Gr. *σιαγων*, (*σιηγων*,) 'jaw,' 'jaw-bone.'

,, मृद्विका *mṛdvikā*, मृद्वीका *mṛdvīkā*, 'grapes,' मधु *madhu*, Lat. *vitis*, 'vine.'

,, मृदु *mṛdu*, 'soft,' मद् *mad*, 'to rejoice.'

,, बृहस्पति *Bṛhaspati*, 'the priest of the Deities,' वियस्पति *Viyaspati* (q.v.).

,, कुंडृणाची *kuṇḍṛṇācī*,[1] 'going crookedly,' कुटिल *kuṭila*, 'crooked.'

The insertion of the vowel ऋ *ṛ* in the above instances comes under a general law that ऋ *ṛ* is used to strengthen a consonant. It is treated as a vowel owing to the metrical necessity of considering as short the quantity of a vowel which is followed by two consonants one of which is र *r*. Thus, if, in सुध्रट् *sudhraṭ* (सुधृट् *sudhṛṭ*), Gr. *ευθραξ*, the vowel सु *su* is to be considered short, we ought to treat ध्र

---

[1] पतातिकुंडृणाच्यांदूरंवातोवनादधि. Rig Veda, I. 29, 6.
Patātikūṇḍṛṇācyādūraṁvātōvanādadhi.
'The wind blows far from the grove in a crooked way.'

dhra as a single and not a compound consonant; and this can be done only by treating the र *r* as a vowel. At first the necessity for such treatment of the letter was very limited, and in consequence the grammarians very easily inserted for र *r* in such cases the letter ऋ *ṛ* which is only a modification of र *r* both in sound and character; but, when subsequently the use of the compound consonants as क्र *kra*, प्र *pra* after short vowels was very frequent, there arose a metrical rule to the effect that short vowels followed by compound consonants of which र *r* is the second may optionally be treated as short.

दृश् *dṛś*, coming at the end of compounds with pronouns, assumes the force of 'like' or 'similar.' Thus in Sanskrit, यादृश् *yādṛś*, तादृश् *tādṛś* and कीदृश् *kīdṛś* mean respectively, 'like what,' 'like that,' and 'like what' (interrog.), the word conveying the idea of 'like,' viz. इव *iva*, being really understood. The above Sanskrit words are modified as ἡλικος, τηλικος (Doric ταλικος), and πηλικος in Greek, and *qualis*,[1] *talis* and *qualis* in Latin. In Eng. '*which*' and '*such*' we can trace the corresponding Anglo-Saxon forms,

[1] Latin has the same form *qua* corresponding to Sans. क *ka*, 'who' (interrog.), and य *y*, 'who' (rel.), which seems to be older than the latter क *ka* and य *y* and the allied Greek words. Hence *qualis* is interrogative, and also relative as the correlative to *talis*. (Vide p. 134).

The stems *tali* and *quali* are formed exactly alike, and consist of *ta* (Sans. त *ta* and स *sa*) and *li* and *qua* (Sans. य *ya* and क *ka*) and *li*. The latter part of the compounds, *li*, is a contraction of Sans. दृश् *dṛś* which is changed in Prakrit into रिस *risa* as in सरिस *sarisa* for Sans. सदृश *sadṛśa*, 'equal,' ईरिस *īrisa* for Sans. ईदृश *īdṛśa*, and into रिख *rikha* and रख *rakha* as in Pali सरिखो *sarikhō* and Gaud. सारख *sārakha*. Just as Sans. दृश् *dṛś* is modified as रिस *risa*

hwaleik and *swaleik*. The English word *like* and the Ang.-Sax. *lic*, 'similar,' are taken from the compound words such as *hwa-leik, swa-leik, god-leik* and the like, where *leik* is a corruption of the root '*look*.' They must, therefore, mean radically 'to look,' 'to be seen,' as the verb 'look' itself does not convey and can not convey the idea of 'similar' originally. But coming as the latter parts of the compounds, such as *hwaleik* and *swaleik*, they mean there only 'to be seen,' the word conveying the idea of similarity being omitted; but the idea of similarity was, in course of time, attached to the word *leik* itself. The word then came to mean 'to look similarly' and at last 'to be similar,' the idea of 'being seen' having been omitted altogether. The word *like*, 'similar,' is, therefore, to be connected with the latter part of the above compounds and has no direct connection with the word '*like*' which means 'to desire' and which I derive from Sans. तृष *tṛṣ*, 'thirst,' corresponding to Lat. *lis* (*tis*), 'strife,' and the old form of the word *stlis*.

The Gr. *αλιγκιος*, meaning 'similar,' 'resembling,' is to be connected with the Sans. सदृश *sadṛś*, स *sa*[1] (सह *saha*), 'equal,' and दृश् *dṛś*, 'to look,' and means 'looking like.' The difference between this word and *τηλικος*, *πηλικος*, *&c.*, is simply the insertion of a nasal before *κ* in *αλιγκιος*[2] and the termination *ιο*, that is, Sans. य *y*, which are not found in *τηλικος* and *πηλικος*, *&c.*

> Πεῖδ' ἐπὶ κόλπον ἔχουσ' ἀταλόφρονα νήπιον αὔτως
> Ἑκτορίδην ἀγαπητὸν ἀλίγκιον ἀστέρι καλῷ.
>
> Il. vi. 400, 401.

---

and then is contracted into रि *ri* in the Dravidian Vernaculars as in Tel. సరి *sari*, and Tam. சரி *sari*, 'equal,' so is it modified as λικα in Greek and *li* in Latin.

[1] Vide p. 92.

[2] The *γ* in *αλγκιος* is sounded like Sans. ङ *ṅ*.

'Carrying in her bosom the only child of Hector lovely, tender-minded, very young and resembling a beautiful star.'

In this passage αλιγκιον αστερι καλω is exactly equal to Sans. सदृशंताराया: कलाया: (चारो:) *sadṛśaṁtārāyāh kalāyāh* (*cārōh*), αλιγκιον and सदृशम् *sadṛśam* governing similar cases. 'Ηλιξ, in the sense of 'equal age,' may be a modification of सदृश् *sadṛś*, ή standing for स *s* and λικ for दृश् *dṛś*.

From दृश् *dṛś* may be derived the modified forms तर्क् *tark*, 'to conjecture,' and चर्च् *carc*, 'to discuss.'

60. From श्वस् *śvas* may be derived Gr. σπαιρω, ασπαιρω, 'to pant,' Lat. *spero*, and Gr. ελπω, 'to hope,' ελπις (ιδος), and Lat. *spes*, 'hope.' This last word (pl. *speres*) originally ended in *r*, but, losing the final *r* in some cases, it is declined partly as a vowel stem. Perhaps Gr. οφελλω, 'to help,' 'to be obliged,' οφειλω, 'to be indebted,' and their derivatives, (Eng. *help*, Ang.-Sax. *helpan*, Goth. *hilpan*, Ice. *hialpa*, and Germ. *helfen*), may be traced to the Gr. ελπις. If so, the aspirate sound of the initial vowels in the above Teutonic words must be non-radical. The Ang.-Sax. *ulph*, 'help,' also, is very closely allied to the Gr. οφελλω.

61. स्वर् *svar* is modified as स्वृ *svṛ*, 'to heat' or 'to sound,' ज्वर् *jvar*, 'to be hot,' by inserting ज *j* for स *s*, and ज्वल् *jval*, 'to burn,' by inserting ल *l* for र *r*. The word स्वस् *svas* may give us, also, तपस् *tapas*, 'heat,' 'penitence,' through the forms सवस् *savas* and तवस् *tavas*. From this तपस् *tapas* we have the ve तप् *tap* (*tepio*), 'to be warm,' 'to be hot' and 'to make penance.' तपस् *tapas* is changed into तस्प *taspa*, by the transfer of the final स *s* between त *t* and प *p* as in जल्प् *jalp* from स्वर् *svar*, 'to sound,' सर्व *sarva* from स्वर् *svar*, 'happiness,'[1] and θαλπω by the change of *s* into *l*. As स्वर् *svar* means 'heaven,' 'the region of wind,' it passes to the meaning of 'sound,' and in this meaning it is modified as जल्प् *jalp*, and assumes the form of σαλπ in Greek and produces the verb σαλπιζω (Sans. जल्पयामि *jalpayāmi*), from which is derived the noun σαλπιγξ (ιγγος), 'a war trumpet.' The Sans. शब्द *śabda* and Gr. ψεφος, 'sound,' are modifications of जल्प् *jalp*. स्वर् *svar* (स्वृ *svṛ*), 'to sound,' is changed into स्वन् *svan*, ध्वन् *dhvan*, Lat. *sono* (*tono*, स्तन् *stan*, 'to thunder'), Sans. वन् *van*, (वाणी *vāṇī*, Gr. φωνη), पन् *pan*, पण् *paṇ*, फण् *phaṇ*, भण् *bhaṇ*, पठ् *paṭh*, वद् *vad*, and वच् *vac*, 'to speak.'

62. दिवस् *divas* is shortened into दिव् *div* and means 'to shine,' 'to rejoice,' and, by substituting ज *j* for द *d* and by lengthening the vowel इ *i*, we have जीव् *jīv*, 'to live,' Gr. βιοω, ζαω, and Lat. *vivo*. दिव् *div* gives us दीप् *dīp* by the change of व *v* into प *p* and the lengthening of the vowel इ *i*. दीप् *dīp* is modified as Gr. λαμπω, 'to shine,' and Lat. *limpo*, the obsolete root of *limpidus*, by the change of *d* into *l*.[2]

---

[1] Vide p. 15.

[2] Compare the following words :—

Sans.	द्वार *dvāra*, 'gate,'	Gr. λαυρα, 'an alley,' (*q.v.*)
"	द्यौस् *dyaus*, 'Heaven,'	" Λαιος, 'a king of Thebes,' (*q.v.*)

जीव् *jīv*, 'to live,' produces the word जेम् *jēm*, चम् *cam*, जम् *jam*, 'to eat,' तीव् *tīv*, दृप् *dṛp*, 'to be fat,' Gr. λιπας, 'fat,' and Sans. तृप् *tṛp*, 'to be satisfied.' The Gr. δαπτω, 'to devour,' is nearer to दीव् *dīv* than to जीव् *jīv*. The Gr. δειπνον,[1] 'meal or meal-time,' is a contraction of जेमनम् *jēmanam*, 'eating,' or तेवनम् *tēvanam*, 'pastime,' to which Gr. δαπανος, 'extravagant,' δαπανη, 'expenditure,' Lat. *daps*, 'a stately feast,' and Gr. δαις (τος), 'a meal,' are allied. Gr. Δαις is a contraction of δαπετος or δαπτος.

In the Greek ειλαπανη, 'a banquet given by a single host,' opposed to ερανος, the vowels ει are added to the beginning for euphony as η in ηλιβατος and O in Ολυμπος.

63. I have already shown how शुभ् *śubh*, 'to shine,' is derived from स्वर् *svar*, 'heaven,' (p. 13); and I may now proceed from शुभ् *śubh* to स्तुभ् *stubh*, 'to praise,' by the change of श *ś* into स्त *st*.[2] From स्तुभ् *stubh* is derived

Sans.	दृषद् *dṛṣad*,	Gr. λιθος, 'stone'.
,,	देवनम् *dēvanam*, 'to be pleased'	,, ειλαπανη, 'feast,' 'banquet,' (*q.v.*)
,,	जेमनम् *jēmanam*, 'to eat'	
Gr.	Οδυσσευς,	Lat. *Ulyxes* or *Ulysses* (q.v.)
Sans.	दहन *dahana*,	Gr. λιγνυς, 'smoke mixed with flame.'
,,	दर्प *darpa*, 'pride,'	,, λιπας, 'fat' ,, λιπος, 'grease'
,,	हृद्य *hṛdya*,	,, ἱλαος, 'propitious,' 'gracious.'

[1] Compare Mod. Tam. சாப்பாடு *śāppāḍu*, Arab. ضيافت *ziāphat*, 'a feast, banquet,' ضيف *zaif*, 'a guest,' دعا *daʿā* and دعوت *daʿvat*, 'invitation,'

[2] Vide p. 28, Note 3.

स्तुप् *stup*, 'eulogist,' and the word occurs in the Rig Veda and is mentioned by Yaska among the synonyms of स्तोता *stōtā*, 'eulogist;' as,

अभ्यनूषतस्तुभः *Abhyanūṣatastubhah*,

'The eulogists praised.' Rig Veda, IX. 68, 8.

The corresponding Greek word θωψ has degenerated in its meaning and is applied to 'a flatterer.' The word स्तोभ *stōbha*, which is a verbal noun from स्तुभ् *stubh*, 'to praise,' and means 'praise,' is modified as स्तोम *stōma*,[1] 'a hymn,' 'sacrifice' and 'multitude,' by the change of भ *bh* into म *m*. As शुभ् *śubh*, 'good,' is contracted into सु *su*,[2] meaning 'good,' so is स्तुभ् *stubh* contracted into स्तु *stu*, 'to praise,' Gr. θυω, 'to offer sacrifice,' and is modified as दुव *duva* meaning 'to serve' as in दुवस्यति *duvasyati*. From स्तुभ् *stubh* we can derive लुभ् *lubh*, 'to covet' (Ang.-Sax. *lufian*, 'to love'); or it may better be referred to वृक *vṛka* of the Third Group.

64. I have hitherto spoken of the modifications undergone by the original word स्वस् *svas* and स्वर् *svar* in their monosyllabic forms, and now I shall take up a dissyllabic form अस्वर् *asvar*, which leads us to आत्मन् *ātman*, a word from which स्वस् *svas* and स्वर् *svar* seem to have

[1] As स्तोभ *stōbha*, changed into स्तोम *stōma*, originally means 'a praise' or 'collection of praises' and then comes to mean 'any collection;' similarly perhaps स्तव *stava*, 'a praise' from स्तु *stu*, 'to praise,' becomes स्तवक *stavaka* by the addition of the termination क *ka* and means 'a praise' or 'a collection of praises' and from this meaning passes also to that of 'a collection as of flowers.'

[2] Vide p. 14.

been derived, and which I have taken as the representative of this Group. आत्मन् *ātman* means in Sanskrit 'life,' 'soul,' 'breath,' &c., of which meanings the most original seems to be 'breath' and 'life,' each of which is a concomitant of the other (p. 14). To it are traceable Gr. *αυτος*, 'self,' *ατμος*, *ατμις* (*ιδος*), 'vapour,' *ατμη*, 'smoke,' 'heat,' *ανεμος*, 'wind,' *ασθμα* (*τος*), 'hard-drawn breath,' Lat. *animus*, 'the spiritual principle of life in man,' *anima*, 'air, breeze, wind.' The Lat. *elementum* and Eng. *element* are to be derived from the Sans. आत्मन् *ātman*, the final *n* of which is doubled by the addition of अम् *am*, and then the second *n* is hardened into त *t* as in *mentes* = *men* + *es*, plural of the Latin word *mens*, 'intellect.' आत्मन् *ātman* is shortened into त्मन् *tman* which also means 'self.'

A similar elision has taken place in Gr. *ασθμα* and has given us *θυμος* which means 'the soul,' 'life,' 'breath,' and corresponds to Sans. धूम *dhūma* and धूप *dhūpa*, 'smoke.'

Sans. बाष्प *bāṣpa* which means 'vapour,' and Lat. *vapor*, 'steam,' 'exhalation,' and 'vapour,' are modifications of आत्मन् *ātman* which, being changed into आस्म *āsma* by the elision of the final *n* and आस्प *āspa* by the change of म *m* into प *p*, assumes the form of बाष्प *bāṣpa* by the initial addition of ब *b* (as व *v* in वानर *vānara*, 'monkey,' Gr *ανηρ*, and Sans. वासर *vāsara*, अतस *atasa*, 'light'). बाष्प *bāṣpa* is changed into वाप्स *vāpsa* by the interchange of the consonants स *s* and प *p*, *vāposa* by the insertion of the vowel *o* between प *p* and स *s*, and *vapor* by the elision of the final vowel अ *a* and the change of *s* into *r*. The form said to be used by Lucretus, viz., *vapos*, must be a contraction of *vapor*.[1] The connection of αυτος, 'self,' with आत्मन् *ātman*, seems to be a remote one, but if we consider a peculiar orthographical law prevailing in Sanskrit, Greek, Latin and other Aryan languages, the difference can be easily accounted for. The *m* of आत्मन् *ātman* being elided, the preceding vowel is lengthened, as in

Gr. Κειvος 'empty,'	Sans. शून्य *śūnya* corresponding to the Epic form κενεος in which εο stands for य *y* of the Sans. शून्य *śūnya*.
,, Καινος, 'new,'	,, कन्या *kanyā*,[2] 'a young girl.'
,, Ταπαινος,	,, दमनीय *damanīya*, 'which can be subdued,' from दम् *dam*, 'to subdue.'
,, Κενταυρος, 'a Centaur'	,, गंधर्व *gandharva*, a kind of celestial beings (Vide the *Śiras* Group.)

---

[1] Compare Tam. ஆவி *āvi* which is derived from आत्मन् *ātman* by the elision of त *t* and न *n*, and the change of *m* into *v*, and does not contain the initial *v* which is found in *vapos*.

[2] कन्या *kanyā* is allied to Gr. Εννεα, Sans. नवन् *navan*, 'nine,' in the former of which I see the full word for new and which is to be connected with Gr. καινος. From Gr. εννεος is derived by contraction νεος, Sans. नव *nava*, 'new,' and also Sans. नवन् *navan* and Gr. εννεα. It is very interesting to see that the Tam. புது *pudu*, Tel. కొత్త *kotta* (*kutu*+*a*), Kan. ಪೊಸ *posa* and ಹೊಸ *hosa*, meaning 'new,' are more closely allied to the Gr. καινος and εννεος than to the Sans. नव *nava*. All these words are traceable to the root कन् *kan*, Gr. γαναω, 'to shine,' the idea of brightness producing that of freshness.

Answering to the contracted form of आत्मन् *ātman*, viz., त्मन् *tman*, we see in Latin *pse* and *pte*,[1] in which the initial *ā* of आत्मन् *ātman* is elided, and the letters त *t* and म *m* are transposed, so that त्म *tma* becomes म्त *mta*, and प्त *pta*, by the change of म *m* into प *p* as in धूप *dhūpa*, धूम *dhūma*, 'smoke.' These contracted forms come at the end of the pronoun *is* and its casal forms; as, *ipse*, 'the very same' = *is* + *pse*, the final *s* of *is* being elided in the compound; *eapse*, *eampse*, and so on; the other form *pte* occurs in such words as *suopte*, *meopte*, *eopte*, *mepte*, *suumpte*, and the like.

The Sans. त्मन् *tman* is used similarly; e.g.,

इहत्वाभूर्याचरेदुपत्मन् दोषावस्तर्दीदिवांसमनुद्यून् ॥

IV. 4, 9.

Ihatvābhūryācaredupatman dōṣāvastardīdivāṁsamanudyūn.

'O God of fire, thee, shining day and night, man should much serve himself here every day.'

Here त्मन् *tman* is used as an adverb and corresponds to Lat. *pte* which is, however, united with the pronoun to which it refers in the sentence. Corresponding to the Sans. त्मन् *tman* and Lat. *pte*, I see in Greek *θην*,[2] *δε* and *δι*, which suffixed to pronouns give them greater force just as Sans. त्मन् *tman* and Lat. *pte* do. But they are added to nouns also without conveying any particular meaning, and in that case are merely enclitical. The two particles *δε* and

---

[1] In *ipse*, the final *us* used in the ancient form *ipsus* is shortened into *e* as in *iste* and *ille* which ought to be *istus* and *illus*. (Vide Zumpt's Latin Grammar, p. 107.)

[2] Compare the Dravidian *tān* which is a corruption of Sans. त्मन् *tman* and agrees with the Gr. *θην*, both in form and meaning.

δι, I think, are contractions of त्मन् *tman*, modified as तन् *tan*, दन् *dan*[1] and then shortened into δε and δι. The Eng. *soul*, Ang.-Sax. *sawol*, Icel. *sal*, Goth. *sawala* are connected with Sans. त्मन् *tman* and आत्मन् *ātman*, the त *t* of which is changed into *s* in the above words. But in Eng. *self*, Ang.-Sax. *self*, *silf*, Germ. *selbe*, and Goth. *selba* there is a further modification, viz., the transfer of the final *l* which represents the final *n* of Sans. त्मन् *tman* between the preceding *s* and *f* which answer to the त *t* and म *m* respectively. I may mention here also the Eng. *smell* which is derived from the Low Germ. *smellen*, 'to smoke.' I think that it is connected with the Teutonic words above mentioned and Sans. ध्मा *dhmā*, 'to blow,' Lat. *sibilus*, 'hissing,' and is traceable to Sans. त्मन् *tman*.

65. I shall now take the contracted form of आत्मन् *ātman*, viz., त्मन् *tman*, and show how this prolific small word gave rise to a great number of suffixes, the alliance of which to the original word is very clearly seen in Sanskrit, though not in the allied languages so clearly. The original meaning of the radical word is, as shown already, 'the soul,' 'spirit,' and, when the word is metamorphosed into various forms, each of which serves the purpose of a suffix, these derivatives pass from that original meaning to new meanings. Thus when त्मन् *tman* and its derivatives are added to a noun, they refer to the condition or the state of a thing or a person, and so on; when added to an adjective, they convey the state of being so and so; and, when added to verbs, they indicate the act of doing an action, the object affected by the action, the place where

[1] Compare the suffix *don*, as in *formidon*, which I derive from the suffix त्मन् *tman*. (Vide § 65).

the action takes place, and so on. त्मन् *tman* is modified as त्वन् *tvan* by the change of म *m* into व *v* and also as त्वता *tvatā* and त्वनम् *tvanam*. त्वन् *tvan* corresponds to the Lat. *tion*, and त्वनम् *tvanam*, to the Gr. σvνη and to the Lat. *tura*; and त्वन *tvana* is changed into त्वर *tvara* by the insertion of र *r* for न *n*; e. g.,

Sans. कवित्वनम् *kavitvanam*, 'the state of a kavi or pandit.'

„ महित्वनम् *mahitvanam*, 'the state of being great.'

„ पूरुषत्वता *pūruṣatvatā*, 'the state of a man.'

„ इषित्वता *iṣitvatā*, 'the state of being excited.'

„ जित्वन् *jitvan*, 'one who has conquered.'

„ सत्वन् *satvan*[1] } 'that which exists.'
Gr. ετυμον }

Gr. δικαιοσυνη, 'righteousness.'

„ ἱεροσυνη, 'holiness.'

„ τεκτοσυνη, 'the art of a carpenter,' (τεκτον + συνη, in which the final ν of τκτον is elided before the suffix συνη).

„ ἡγεμοσυνος, 'belonging to ἡγεμον, a leader.'

---

[1] सत्वन् *satvan*, properly असत्वन् *asatvan* from अस् *as* + अ *a* + त्वन् *tvan* in which अस् *as*, 'to be,' is the root, अ *a*, a connecting particle, त्वन् *tvan*, suffix, corresponds to Gr. ἑτυμο, from εσετυμο = εσ + ε + τυμο, in which the suffix τυμο is a modification of the Sans. त्वन् *tvan*; εσετυμο = σετυμο by the elision of the initial vowel as in सत्वन् *satvan*, = ἑτυμο and ετυμο by the elision of the aspirate sound of the initial vowel. (Cf. सत्यस् *satyas*, ετεος.)

Gr. *γειτοσυνος*, 'belonging to a *γειτον*, a neighbour.'
Lat. *picura*, 'the art of painting.'
" *cultura*, 'the art of cultivation.'
" *mercatura*, 'trade,' 'commerce.'
" *dictatura*, 'the office of a dictator.'
" *censura*, 'the office of a censor.'

Sans. इत्वर *itvara* (Lat. *iturus*), 'going.'
" गत्वर *gatvara*, 'going.'

Lat. *futurus* (Sans. भूत्वर *bhūtvara*), 'which will be or come.'
" *maturus* (Sans. गत्वर *gatvara*, Gr. *βασυνος*), 'going,' 'speedy,' 'early,' thence 'ripe.'

The suffixes त्वनम् *tvanam*, त्वन् *tvan*, and त्वना *tvanā* are used only in Vedas and are modified as त्वम् *tvam* in the classical Sanskrit. The Prakritic and the vernacular तनम् *tanam* is to be traced to the above त्वनम् *tvanam* and not to the classical त्वम् *tvam*. त्वन् *tvan* is simplified as तन् *tan* and is changed into तात् *tāt* and ताति *tāti* by the change of न *n* into त *t* as seen in Gr. *τατος*, a suffix of the superlative degree of adjectives, which is a corruption of the Sans. तन *tana* as will be shown hereafter. The Sans. तात् *tāt* corresponds to the Gr. *τητ* and Lat. *tat*.

The suffix त्वन् *tvan* is further developed into two syllables as *tuvan* by the insertion of *u* between *t* and *v* and *tudon* by the change of *v* into *d* as in अंडम् *aṇḍam* (अंदम् *andam*), 'egg,' which is a modification of Lat. *ovum* and Gr. *ωον*, originally *ωFον*, by the change of *v* into *d* and the insertion of a nasal before *d*. Compare the Sanskrit suffix एयस् *ēyas*, Gr. *ιδης*, pp. 119-120.

त्वन् *tvan* is contracted into *don* in Latin by the elision of व *v* and is suffixed to verbs as in *formidon* = *form* + *i* + *don*, the root *form* meaning 'to fear,' and connected with Sans. ब्रह्मन् *brahman*, 'great,' and Gr. μορμω, 'a bugbear' (vide p. 33); *cupidon* = *cup* + *i* + *don*, from *cupio*, 'to desire.' It may, otherwise, be derived from वन् *van* by the change of *v* into *d* and may be ultimately traced to त्वन् *tvan* as is the case with *gon* (as in *robigon*, q. v.)

त्वन् *tvan* is shortened into वन् *van* and मन् *man* and added to verbs as धन्वन् *dhanvan*, 'a bow,' कर्मन् *karman*, 'an action.' वन् *van* is modified as वत् *vat* and उस् *us* and added to simple and reduplicated roots to form present and past participial adjectives, as, विद्वान् *vidvān*, 'knowing,' and शुश्रुवान् *śuśruvān*, 'having heard.' Before the suffixes of the nominative dual and plural and accusative singular and dual, the suffix वन् *van* is modified as वन्न् *vann* by the doubling of the final न् *n*, वन्त् *vant* by the hardening of the second न *n* into त *t*, and at last वान्स् *vāns* by the change of त *t* into स *s* and the lengthening of the previous vowel *a*. In the accusative plural and in the singular of other cases वस् *vas* is changed into उस् *us*.

Thus we have,—

	SINGULAR.	DUAL.	PLURAL.
Nom.	विद्वान् *vidvān*	विद्वांसौ *vidvāṁsau*	विद्वांसस् *vidvāṁsas*
Accus.	विद्वांसम् *vidvāṁsam*	विद्वांसौ *vidvāṁsau*	विदुषस् *viduṣas*
Instr.	विदुषा *viduṣā*	विद्वद्भ्याम् *vidvadbhyām*	विद्वद्भिस् *vidvadbhis*

Compare the suffix ईयस् *īyas*, which will be presently mentioned.

It is the same suffix वन् *van*, I think, which, taking the augment ई *ī*, becomes ईवन् *īvan* and then ईयन् *īyan* (cf. इयत् *iyat* for इवत् *ivat*, Gr. *ἴσος*), and also ईयस् *īyas*. The last change takes place in the accusative plural and the following cases; and, in the nominative case and in the accusative singular and dual, ईयन् *īyan* follows the analogy of वन् *van* (as in विद्वन् *vidvan*). Thus we have,—

	SINGULAR.	DUAL.	PLURAL.
Nom.	गरीयान् *garīyān*	गरीयांसौ *garīyāṁsau*	गरीयांसस् *garīyāṁsas*
Accus.	गरीयांसम् *garīyāṁsam*	गरीयांसौ *garīyāṁsau*	गरीयसस् *garīyasas*

But in the corresponding Gr. *ιων*, the final *n* of the original वन् *van* remains unchanged, and in the Lat. *ior* it is changed into *r*.

It is to be remarked here that in the suffixes अत् *at*, मत् *mat*, वत् *vat*, वस् *vas*, ईयस् *īyas* (radically अन् *an*, मन् *man*, वन् *van*, वन् *van*, and ईयन् *īyan*), Lat. *en* and *men*, and Gr. *αν*, *ον* and *εν*, which are modified as अंत् *ant*, मंत् *mant*, वंत् *vant*, वंस् *vaṁs*, and ईयंस् *īyaṁs*, Lat. *ent* and *ment*, Gr. *αντ*, *οντ* and *εντ* respectively, the final न् *n* of the suffixes which appears in the form of त् *t* in some cases, is doubled, the second *n* is hardened into *t*, and in वस् *vas* and ईयस् *īyas*, the त *t* is changed into स *s*, and the previous vowel is lengthened or the first *n* is elided. The same remark applies to the final न *n* of मान *māna* and आन *āna* which are modified as *bundus* and *endus* through the forms *bunnus* and *ennus*, in each of which *n* is doubled and the second *n* is changed into *d*.

Even the corresponding superlative suffix इष्ठ *iṣṭha* seems to be a modification of वस् *vas* which, taking the augment ई *ī*, becomes ईवस् *īvas* and then ईयस् *īyas*, as shown before; and this ईयस् *īyas* is shortened into इस् *is* and, taking the termination *a*, becomes इस्स *issa* and, with the second स *s* hardened into त *t*, इस्त *ista*, Gr. ιστος. But in Sanskrit, इस्त *ista* is modified as इष्ठ *iṣṭha* by the aspiration of *t*. This suffix is found in Latin only in *magister*, *minister* and *sinister*. *Magister*, I think, is composed of *magnus* + *ist* + *ter*, corresponding to Sans. महत् *mahat* + इष्ठ *iṣṭha* + तर *tara* and Gr. μεγαλ + ιστ + τερος, so that *magister* would be exactly equal to Sans. महिष्ठतर *mahiṣṭhatara* and Gr. μεγιστοτερος. The word, then, must contain two suffixes, the first, *istus*, superlative, and the next, *ter*, comparative, as we have in Sans. श्रेष्ठ *śrēṣṭha*, 'excellent,' श्रेष्ठतर '*śrēṣṭhatara*, 'more excellent,' श्रेष्ठतम *śrēṣṭhatama*, 'most excellent,' taking the superlative श्रेष्ठ *śrēṣṭha* itself as positive. Similarly, *minister* = *minus* + *ist* + *ter*. The word *sinister* may be distributed in the same way, e. g., *sinus* (crooked) + *ist* + *tor*, *sinus* being closely allied to Sans. जिह्म *jihma*, 'crooked,' the idea of the left side originating from the fact of a man's inability to do a work directly with the left hand, that is, his doing the work crookedly with the left hand.

I cannot, with some philologists, consider *magister* and *minister* as composed of the comparative degrees of *magnus*, that is, *major* and *minor*, in which case the words *magister* and *minister* must be spelt *majoster* and *minoster* respectively, even if we suppose that the final *r* of *major* and *minor* is changed into *s* before the suffix *ter*.

मन् *man* is added to the Ātmanēpadi roots to indicate the agency of a present action and is modified as मान *māna* by the addition of अ *a*, and the lengthening of the preceding vowel अ *a*, but in Gr. μενος the vowel is not lengthened. In Latin, in addition to such modifications as *mnus*, *minus* and the like, which are found in Greek also, it has undergone a transformation which has thoroughly concealed its alliance to the original Sans. मन् *man* and baffled the investigation of the greatest scholars. The Sans. मानस् *mānas* becomes मन्नस् *mannas* by shortening the vowel आ *ā* of मा *mā* and doubling, in consequence, the following consonant न *n*; then बन्नस् *bannas* by the change of म *m* into ब *b*; and at last *bundus* by inserting द् *d* instead of the second न *n*, which process serves the purpose of strengthening the first.[1] This termination is added to roots of the first conjugation chiefly with the signification of the present participle and with a reference to the fulness of the action, as *cogitabundus* from *cogito*, *gratulabundus* from *gratulare*, *errabundus* from *errare*; and also to some roots of the third conjugation, as *fremebundus*, *gemebundus*, *furibundus*, *nitibundus*. But when the root does not take any augments as अ *a*, य *y* and अय *aya* (that is शप् *śap* and श *śa*, श्यन् *śyan* and णिच् *ṇic* respectively), the initial म *m* of मान *māna* is elided, as बिभ्राण *bibhrāṇa*, 'bearing,' कुर्वाण *kurvāṇa*, 'doing.' The termination आन *āna* is shortened into *andus*, *endus* and *undus* in Latin as मान *māna* into *bundus*. Thus we have *amandus*, *scribendus*, *potiundus*, *audiundus*.

---

[1] Vide my remark on the suffixes अत् *at*, वत् *vat*, मत् *mat*, &c., p. 110.

From the same root मन् *man* and वन् *van* I would derive the participial suffix अत् *at*,[1] Gr. *ον* and Lat. *en*, which are added to the simple root to convey the present tense and to the root modified by the addition of the augments स्य *sya* and स *sa*, to convey the future and past tenses respectively; as,

Sans. द्रवत् *dravat*, Gr. *λυον*, 'dissolving.'
" द्रोष्यत् *drōṣyat*, " *λυσον*, 'about to dissolve.'
" द्रुसत् *drusat*, " *λυσαν*, 'that has dissolved.'

The suffix आन *āna* is added to the Ātmanēpadi roots with the temporal augment स *sa* which is a sign of the past tense; as,

मंदसान *mandasāna*, 'having joyed or having been happy.'
धियसान *dhiyasāna*, 'having thought or contemplated.'
सहसाम *sahasāma*, 'having born,' by the change of *n* into *m*.[2]

The temporal augment स *sa* is changed in Latin into *c* (*k*) in the corresponding forms, and आन *āna*, into *undus*.

Thus the part सान *sāna* in the above forms appears in Latin as *cundus* = *c* (*k*) + *undus*, as in

Lat. *facundus* (Sans. भासान *bhāsāna*), 'eloquent,' radically 'having spoken.'
" *iracundus*, 'irascible,' radically 'having been angry.'
" *verecundus*, 'full of bashfulness,' radically 'having felt shame.'

In the above forms the Sanskrit particle स *s* is changed into *c* (*κ*) as in the following list :—

Sans. सूर *sūra*, 'powerful,' Gr. *κυρος*, 'power.'
" युवस् *yuvas*, Sans. युवाकु *yuvāku*, 'bright.'

[1] Vide my remark on it, p. 110. [2] Vide p. 129

Sans. ईषत् *īṣat*, a corruption of एतत् *ētat*, ‘this,’	Gr. *ηκα*, ‘little;’ *ησσων*, (*ηκιων*), *εσσων* (*εκιων*), ‘less.’
,, स्पश् *spaś*, ‘to shine,’	Sans. क्वथ् *kvath*, ‘to boil.’
,, सम् *sam*,	Lat. *con*, ‘with.’
,, एष *ēṣa*, ‘this,’	Sans. एक *ēka*, ‘one,’ the words for ‘one’ in the Aryan languages being traceable to the pronoun ‘this.’
,, साम् *sām*, the gen. pl. suffix of pronouns, which, as well as the gen. sing. suffix of nouns and pronouns स्य *sya*, I hold to be a corruption of स्वम् *svam*, ‘possession’ and which is changed into नाम् *nām* as in रामाणाम् *Rāmāṇām*, ‘of Ramas.’	,, कम् *kam*, the genitive plural suffix as in युष्माकम् *yuṣmākam*, ‘of you,’ अस्माकम् *asmākam*, ‘of me.’
Gr. Ισος, ‘equal,’ which is a modification of इयत् *iyat*, (q.v.)	Lat. *equus* in which *q* (*k*) stands for the *σ* of Ισος.
Sans. श्वशुर *śvaśura*, originally स्वसुर *svasura*, from स्वसृ *svasṛ*, ‘daughter.’	Gr. ἑκυρος.

Compare also the Table given further on, in which the change of श *ś* into क *k* has been illustrated.

The same change appears to have taken place in the temporal augment of the perfect and pluperfect participial adjectives in Greek.

The suffix अत् *at* with the temporal augment स *s* seems to have been changed into *κοτ* by the change of स *s* into *κ*. *κοτ* is added to the reduplicated roots to form perfect participial adjectives. Thus we have λελυκως (stem λελυκοτ) answering to a Sanskrit form such as दुद्रुसत् *dudrusat* = λελυκοτς where the final *τ* of the stem λελυκοτ is cut off before *s*.

If this view be correct, we may, in conformity to the grammatical construction, designate those forms 'aorist participial adjectives' instead of 'perfect participial adjectives.'

But a better explanation of the form λελυκοτ is found in comparing it with Sans. दुद्रुवस् *dudruvas*, the past participial adjective of द्रु *dru*, of which the final स *s* corresponds to the final *τ* of λελυκοτ and the penultimate syllable व *va*, to the corresponding syllable *κο*, the root द्रु *dru*, to λυ, and दु *du*, to λε. From this it would follow that the forms दुद्रुवस् *dudruvas* and λελυκοτ are identical and that the syllables व *v* and *κο* are allied. The question then would be, which of them is original and which, derived? The solution is not difficult. The form दुद्रुवस् *dudruvas* is satisfactorily accounted for by distributing it as दु *du* + द्रु *dru* + वस् *vas*, दु *du* being the reduplication, द्रु *dru*, root, and वस् *vas*, the termination; and as the forms दुद्रुवस् *dudruvas* and λελυκοτ are constructed on the same principle and are identical, the syllable *κο* which corresponds to व *va* must be a corruption of the latter.

If this theory be right, it may be applied to many of the perfect forms in Greek ending in *κα*; such as,

Gr. *πεπλυκα*, Sans. पुप्लाव *puplāva*, *πλυ*, 'to wash,' प्लु *plu*, 'to float.'

,, *λελυκα*, Sans. दुद्राव *dudrāva*, *λυ*, द्रु *dru*, 'to dissolve.'

,, *πεφυκα*, Sans. बभूव *babhūva*, *φυ*, भू *bhū*, 'to be.'

,, *εκτακα*, Sans. चिक्षाय *cikṣāya*, *κτειν*, क्षिण् *kṣiṇ*,[1] 'to kill.'

,, *τετακα*, (Sans. तिताय *titāya*), *τειν*, तन् *tan*, 'to extend.'

,, *εσβηκα*, (Sans. शिश्माय *śiśmāya*), *σβε*, शम् *śam*, 'to quench,' appearing in *Σβεννυμι*, शम्नामि *śamnāmi* as given in Yaska's Nirukta, II. 19.

,, *ἑστηκα*, Sans. तस्थौ *tasthau*, *στο*, स्था *sthā*, 'to stand.'

,, *δεδωκα*, Sans. ददौ *dadau*, *δο*, दा *dā*, 'to give'

In *πεπλυκα*, *λελυκα* and *πεφυκα* we clearly see that the *κα* must be a modification of the corresponding part व *va* of the Sanskrit forms. In *εκτακα*, the part *κτει* of *κτειν* is to be taken as the radical part;[2] so that *κτει* + *κτει* becomes *κτεκτει*, *κεκτει* and at last *ἑκτει* by the change of the initial *κ* into *h*. From this we obtain *εκτει* by the loss of the aspirate sound. By the addition of the first person singular suffix *a*, *εκτει* becomes *εκτειya*, by the insertion of

---

[1] Compare स्तृण् *stṛṇ*, वृण् *vṛṇ*, लीन् *līn*, हिन् *hin*, and स्पृण् *spṛṇ*, Note 1, p. 79.

[2] In that case, the *ν* of *κτεινω*, which appears before the first pers. sing. suffix *ω*, must be treated like the *n* of *no* of क्षिणोमि *kṣiṇōmi* which will be taken as the angment नु *nu* (that is श्नु *śnu* according to Pāṇini), if it disappears in the other tenses as चिक्षाय *cikṣāya*; and, if not as in चिक्षेण *cikṣēṇa*, क्षिण् *kṣiṇ*, 'to kill,' it will be treated as the radical part.

y to fill up the hiatus between the vowels *ει* and *a*, and it is modified as *εκτακα* by the change of *y* into *k*. Similarly in *τετακα* and *εσβηκα*,[1] *τει* and *σβε* are the radical parts of the verbs *τεινω* and *σβεννυμι*, and *κα*, a modification of *y* which occurs in the bracketed Sanskrit forms which are conceivable, if we have such verbs as तैनोमि *tainōmi* and श्मिनामि *śmināmi* instead of तनोमि *tanōmi* and शम्नामि *śamnāmi*, and if we take तै *tai* of तैनोमि *tainōmi* and श्मि *śmi* of श्मिनामि *śmināmi* as the radical parts.

In the remaining forms *ἑστηκα* and *δεδωκα*, the final *κα* must also be a corruption of *ya*; e. g.,

$$\sigma\tau o + \sigma\tau o + a = \sigma\tau\epsilon\sigma\tau\eta ya = \sigma\epsilon\sigma\tau\eta ya = \acute{\epsilon}\sigma\tau\eta\kappa a.$$

In support of this theory, I may adduce the fact that य *y* is changed into स *s* in a similar way in the following grammatical forms, such as दासीष्ट *dāsīṣṭa*, 'may he give' = दा *dā* + ईस्त *īsta*, wherein दा *dā* is the root, ईस् *īs*, optative augment before the Ātmanēpadi terminations, (the corresponding augment before the Parasmaipadi terminations being आस् *ās*), becomes दायीष्ट *dāyīṣṭa* and then दासीष्ट *dāsīṣṭa* by the change of य *y* into स *s*.[2] Similarly अधासीत् *adhāsīt*, 'he drank' = अ *a* + धा *dhā* + इ *i* + स् *s* + त् *t*, wherein इ *i* is a connective augment, स् *s* the

---

[1] The aspirate sound of the initial ε is lost.

[2] In the dual दासीयास्ताम् *dāsīyāstām*, there is a peculiar metathesis, as दासीयास्ताम् *dāsīyāstām* = दा *dā* + ईस् *īs* + आताम् *ātām* = दा *dā* + ई *ī* + आ *ā* + स् *s* + ताम् *tām*, by the transposition of the initial vowel आ *ā* of the suffix आताम् *ātām* between ई *ī* and स् *s*, = दायीयास्ताम् *dāyīyāstām* = दासीयास्ताम् *dāsīyāstām*.

temporal augment, and त् *t*, personal suffix, becomes अधासिस्त् *adhāsist*; and as two consonants स्त् *st* cannot remain at the end of the word, the first consonant स् *s* is elided and the previous vowel is lengthened. (Compare πᾶς = πὰν + ς, 'all,' διδους = διδον + ς, 'giving'). Similarly springs from य *y* and व *v* θ in some forms, such as λυθησομαι लविष्ये *laviṣyē*, ἑθησομαι यायिष्ये *yāyiṣyē*, δοθησομαι दायिष्ये *dāiṣyē*. But in δειχθησομαι which ought to be properly δειξομαι corresponding to Sans. द्रक्ष्ये *drakṣyē*, 'I shall be seen,' θ is inorganically inserted as in अरम्सीत् *aramsīt*. (Vide, p. 119.)

In the following κα is inserted by wrong analogy:—

Gr. ἑσταλκα, तस्थाल *tasthāla*, στελλω, 'to set,' स्थल् *sthal*, 'to be.'

„ εσπαρκα, चकार *cakāra*, (σ) περω, 'to sow,' Sans. किर् *kir* (कृ *kṛ*), 'to scatter.'

„ πεπεικα, बुबोध *bubōdha*, πειθω, बोध् *bōdh*, 'to advise,' πεπειθκα becoming πεπεικα by the elision of θ.

„ εσπεικα, शश्वास *śaśvāsa*, σπευδω, 'to offer an oblation,' श्वस् *śvas*, 'hope,' εσπευδκα becoming εσπεικα, by the elision of νδ.[1]

Similar to this is the use of र् *r* which is derived from

---

[1] I see a similar usage in the Dravidian languages, in which the change of *y* and *v* into *k* takes place in many grammatical forms and the *k* so derived is inorganically inserted in other forms not requiring it; thus, in Tam. நடக்க *naḍakka*, உரைக்க *uraikka*, which are respectively modified from நடவ *naḍava* = நட *naḍa* + அ *a*, 'to walk,' and உரைய *uraiya* = உரை *urai* + அ *a*, 'to say,' in which நட *naḍa* and உரை *urai* are roots and அ *a* infinitive suffix. From the analogy of such wrong forms we get கற்க *kaṟka*, 'to learn,' which stands for கல்ல *kalla*, and நிற்க *niṟka*, 'to stand,' for நில்ல *nilla*, from the roots கல் *kal*, 'to learn,' and நில் *nil*, 'to stand.' (Vide Vol. II.)

य *y* and स *s* as in एधेरन् *ēdhēran* = एधेयन् *ēdhēyan*, 'they may grow' = एध् *ēdh* + ईय् *īy* + अन् *an*; एधिषीरन् *ēdhiṣīran*, 'may they grow' = एध् *ēdh* + ईस् *īs* + अन् *an* = एधियीसन् *ēdhiyīsan* = एधिषीसन् *ēdhiṣīsan* by the change of य *y* into स *s* = एधिषीरन् *ēdhiṣīran* by the change of the second स *s* into र *r*; शेरते *śēratē* = शेयते *śēyatē* = शे *śē* + अते *atē*. The र *r* which is so derived from य *y* and स *s* and the स *s* derived from य *y* as in अधासीत् *adhāsīt* as shown above, are inserted in forms which do not require them, as संविद्रते *saṁvidratē*, 'they feel,' for संविदते *saṁvidatē*, अगृभ्रन् *agṛbhran*, 'they took,' for अगृभन् *agṛbhan*, अरंसीत् *aramsīt*, 'he played,' for अरमीत् *aramīt*. (Vide Note 1, p 27.)

It is worth notice here that, as व *v* is changed into क *k*, and य *y* into क *k*, स *s* and र *r*, य *y* is changed also into δ. Thus, the final δ in the feminine nouns and adjectives ending in ι in Greek is traceable to the Sans. य *y*, as in πατρις (ιδ), 'native land,' φροντις (ιδ), 'thought,' 'care,' πεντηκονταετις (ιδ), feminine form of πεντηκονταετης, 'lasting fifty years,' θερμαστρις (ιδ), 'fire tongs,' (θερμαστρα, 'oven, furnace,') θερμαστις (ιδ), 'boiling kettle,' (θερμανσις (εως), 'heating,') Θετις (ιδ), सिंधु *sindhu*. The δ in these and other nouns and adjectives similarly declined cannot belong to the stems as these end in vowels only; for Gr. πατρις must be equal to Sans. पितृ *pitṛ* + ई *ī* = पित्री *pitrī*, the final ई *ī* of which being shortened in πατρις, the word should be considered as an इकारांत *ikārānta*, that is, a stem ending in इ *i*, and declined like Sans. मति *mati*. Compare πατρα, another form used instead of πατρις. The same remark applies to Gr. θερμαστρις, for it is the feminine form of θερμαστωρ and, consequently, in analogy of the Sans. कर्तर् *kartar*, mas., कर्त्री *kartrī*, fem., 'doer,' should be *θέρμαστρη* (cf. *θερμαστρα*), but the final vowel being shortened, it becomes *θερμαστρις* in the nominative singular. The words *θερμαστις* and *θερμαντις* are identical forms, being nonns formed from the verb *θερμαινω*, 'to heat,' by the addition of the suffixes *τι* and *ςι*, the only difference being the insertion of the augment *ν* before *τι* in *θερμαντις*. *ςι* and *τι* are identical with Sanskrit verbal nonn suffix ति *ti*.

As for Θετις[1] which is applied to one of the Nereids, who was the wife of Pelens and mother of Achilles, I think it corresponds to, and is a modification of, Sans. सिंधु *sindhu*, 'a river,' the final उ *u* of which is changed into *ι* in Θετις. The word, therefore, mnst be a vowel stem and be declined like मति *mati*. From this it would follow that the *δ* appearing in the declension of the above nonns cannot be a part of the stem, bnt mnst be an ontgrowth of the orthographical changes which take place when the casal suffixes are affixed to the stem; thus,

SINGULAR.	DUAL.	PLURAL.	
Θετις	Θετιδε	Θετιδες	*Nom.*
——*δα*	——*δοιν*	——*δας*	*Acc.*
——*δος*[2]	——*δοιν*	——*δων*	*Gen.*

[1] Θετις seems to be identical with Θητυς, differing only in form slightly. I have shown in the *Salila* Group the alliance of these two words to the Sans. सिंधु *sindhu*, 'a river,' 'ocean,' and through it have traced them to the word सलिल *salila*, so that the radical meaning of those words is 'water.' The above etymology receives support from a remark of Mr. Gladstone made in his Juv. Mun., p. 343. He says: 'With reference to the etymology of this name, it is perhaps worthy of remark that the only office of mediation at all resembling hers is ascribed to Tethus who with her husband Okeanos gives shelter and nurture to Here, at the great crisis when Zeus was thrusting his father Cronos down to the under world.'

[2] In some nouns the *δ* declension alternates with the *ι* declension, as in Ιβιος and Ιβιδος, the gen. sing. of Ιβις, 'the ibis.'

Now comparing the above declensional forms with the corresponding ones of मति *mati*, we can easily see that the δ is referrible to the *y* which makes its appearance in some forms such as मतयस् *matayas* and मतये *matayē*. But this *y* appears uniformly in all casal forms in the declension of such nouns as धी *dhī* with which, therefore, we may compare the declension of Θετις better.

SINGULAR.	DUAL.	PLURAL.	
धीस् *dhīs*	धियौ *dhiyau*	धियस् *dhiyas*	*Nom.*
धियम् *dhiyam*	धियौ *dhiyau*	धियस *dhiyas*	*Accus.*
धियस् *dhiyas*	धियोस् *dhiyōs*	धियाम् *dhiyām.*	*Gen.*

Now, if we call Θετις a consonant stem, we may with equal propriety call धी *dhī* also the same. But धी *dhī* is only a vowel stem and the य *y* appearing in its declension is only an offshoot of the rules of Sandhi, and the declension of धी *dhī* and Θετις are very similar, the only difference being that the former is a long vowel and the latter a short vowel stem. From this it follows that धियस् *dhiyas*, &c., and Θετιδες, &c., being equal, part to part, the letter δ must be a modification of *y*.[1]

Compare also the Greek and Sanskrit patronymics in which the δ of Greek answers to the य *y* of Sanskrit;—

Sans. आत्रेय *Ātrēya*, descending from अत्रि *Atri*, Gr. Ατριδης.

---

[1] Prof. Bopp says: "The Greek termination ιδ, the δ of which is undoubtedly an inorganic affix, is, however, in so far ambiguous, that its ι is frequently the abbreviation of a Sans. ī, ... so we might also regard the said Greek formations in ιδ as corresponding to the Sanskrit formations in ī and therefore derive, e. g., γραφιδ from a to-be-presupposed masculine base γράφο or γραφὸ in the same way as, e. g., στρατηγ'-ίδ, 'female leader of an army,' comes from στρατηγό; κορων'-ίδ from κορωνο." (Comparative Grammar, Vol. III, p. 1313).

Sans. आश्वपतेय *Āśvapatēya*, descending from अश्वपति *Aśvapati*, Gr. Ἱπποταδης, from ἱπποτης = ἱππο + ποτης. (ποσις, पति *pati.)*

Sans. नादेय *nādēya*, 'sprung from a river,' नदी *nadī*, 'a river,' Gr. Ναιας.[1]

I may mention here a similar change of य *y* into other consonants such as *ss*, *z*, and *t*; as,

GREEK	SANSKRIT
φυλασσω, 'I watch,'	मीलयामि *mīlayāmi*, 'I shut'
αλλασσω, 'I change,'	अन्ययामि *anyayāmi*.
αφασσω, ἁφαω } 'I handle,'	ग्राभयामि *grābhayāmi*.
πατασσω, 'I beat,'	पाटयामि *pāṭayāmi*.
δοξαζω, 'I believe,'	दीक्षयामि *dīkṣayāmi*.
θοαζω, 'I move,'	जावयामि *jāvayāmi*.
κραυγαζω, 'I scream,'	क्रोशयामि *krōśayāmi*.
σχεδιαζω, 'I do off-hand,'	क्षण्ययामि *kṣaṇyayāmi* (from क्षण *kṣaṇa*, 'a moment' + य *y* = क्षण्य *kṣaṇya*, 'momentary'.)
ιαπτω, 'I send,'	यापयामि *yāpayāmi*.
καλυπτω, 'I conceal,'	गर्भयामि *garbhayāmi*.
κολαπτω, 'I hew,' allied to γλυφω and γραφω	ग्रावयामि *grāvayāmi* (from ग्रावन् *grāvan*, 'stone.')
δαπτω, 'to devour,'	जेमयामि *jēmayāmi*. / तेवयामि *tēvayāmi*.

[1] The Sans. नद *nada*, 'a river,' is softened into Gr. ναιος which, taking the suffix αδης, becomes ναιαδης and then shortened into ναιας (stem ναιαδ).

In the above examples σσ and ζ and τ are inserted for the य *y* of the Sanskrit words. The change of *y* into *t* does not take place directly, but through *s*; as यापयामि *yāpayāmi* = ιαπαγω = ιαπγω, by the elision of the *a* preceding *y* = ιαπσω, by the change of *y* into σ and ιαπτω by the hardening of σ into τ.

I may mention here a similar change of *y* into *g* which I suppose to have taken place in the following verbs :—

Lat. *mitigo*, Sans. म्रदयामि *mradayāmi*, 'I soften,' मृदु *mṛdu*, Lat. *mitis*, 'soft.'

" *castigo*, " शुद्धयामि *śuddhayāmi*, 'I purify,' शुद्ध *śuddha*, Lat. *castus*, 'pure.'

" *fumigo*, " धूपयामि *dhūpayāmi*, 'I cause to smoke,' धूप *dhūpa*, Lat. *fumus*, 'smoke.'

The latter parts in the above Latin verbs are considered as a contraction of *ago*, 'to make.'[1]

From the above examples it is clear that in λελυκοτ, the termination वस् *vas* is changed irto κοτ by the insertion of κ for व *v*. We may therefore lay down a general rule that वस् *vas* is changed into κοτ after roots ending in vowels, and, after those ending in consonants, the initial *v* is elided. But in the irregular form λελειχμοτες (लेलिह्वतस् *lēlihvatas*) the original fo m of वस् *vas*, viz. मत् *mat*, appears as suffix, as λελειχμοτ = λειχ + λειχ + μοτ, λειχω, 'to lick.'

The aorist participial adjective λυσασ (stem λυσαντ) has

---

[1] In the Dravidian languages also the change of *y* and *v* into *s*, *t*, *g*, *d*, *l*, *r* and other letters frequently occurs and has been illustrated in Volume II.

already been compared with द्रुसत् *drusat,* the past participial adjective from द्रु *dru,* 'to dissolve.' (p. 113.)

Next वन् *van* and मन् *man* used to indicate possession are changed in Latin and Greek as follows :—

Lat. *formōsus,* 'beautiful' = *forma* + *vat* + *us.*

,, *formidōlosus,* 'dreadful' = *formidon* + *vat* + *us,* in which the final *n* of *formidon* is changed into *l.*

,, *dives*[1] (*itis*), Sans. रैवत् *raivat* (p. 51) = Sans. रैस् *rais* (Lat. *res*) + वत् *vat.*

,, *opulus* (*entes*), Sans. अपसवत् *apasavat,* 'rich,' Lat. *oper* (Sans. अपस *apasa*) + *vat.*

,, *Neptunus,* 'Neptune,' is a contraction of Sans. नभस्वत् *nabhasvat* meaning 'having नभस् *nabhas,* water,' and so applied to the God of ocean, + अस् *as* = नभस्वंतस् *nabhasvantas* = Nepsantus = Neptunus, wherein the *a* of भ *bha* is elided and भ् *bh* is changed into *p, s* is changed into *t,* and the part *antus,* into *ūnus.*

Gr. μελιτοεις,—εσσα-εν, Sans. मधुमत् *madhumat,* Gr. μελιτ + ο + Fες, wherein the ο is a nexus ; Gr. τυροεισ, 'like cheese,' from τυρο + Fες.

,, Διονυσος, 'Bacchus, the god of wine, vineyards and dramatic poetry' = दिवस् *divas* + वत् *vat* + अस् *as* = Διον + υς + ος by the change of दिवस् *divas* into दियस् *diyas* and then into Διον. Compare the Latin suffix *osus.*

,, Τριτων, 'Triton, a sea god, son of Poseidon,' (प्रचेतस् *Pracētas*) and Amphitrite' = सरस् *saras* + वन् *van*

---

[1] Also shortened into *dis* (*ditis*).

(सरस् *saras*, 'water') = τριτ + ων, where सरस् *saras* is contracted into τριτ.[1] Similarly,

Gr. Ανδρων, 'men's apartment' = ανηρ + *van* = ανδρ + ων.

,, Ιππων, 'a stable' = ἱππο + *van*.

,, Τιταν, 'A Titan, applied to a race of gods placed beneath Tartarus, or, according to the Hesiodic Theogony, to the six sons and six daughters of Uranus and Gaia; laterly applied to the sun; = दिवस् *divas* + वन् *van* = तित् *tit* + वन् *van* by the contraction of दिवस् *divas* into दिस् *dis* and then into τιτ (cf. दिति *diti*) and then = Τιταν.

,, Τιθωνος,[2] 'Tithonos, brother of Priam and husband of Aurora and father of Memnon'; = सिंधु *sindhu* + मन् *man* + अस् *as* in which मन् *man* is changed into ων.

---

[1] The same word सरस् *saras*, 'water,' is shortened into त्रित *trita*, Gr. τριτος. त्रित *trita* in the Vedas is 'the god of water and air,' and we can infer the same of the Gr. τριτος from the epithet of *Athênê*, τριτογενεια, 'the child of τριτος' (vide the *Salila* Group). We must give up the idea of deriving the word त्रित *trita* from त्रि *tri*, 'three,' or from the alleged Eeḥi word for head, though the word त्रित *trita* is as close to the Sans. शिरस् *śiras*, 'head' as it is to सरस *saras*, 'water.' (Cox's Mythology, Vol. I, p. 440.)

[2] Similarly the suffix वन् *van* added to मघ *magha* in मघवन् *maghavan* is optionally changed into वान् *vān* and ओन् *ōn* as in मघवानौ *maghavānau*, nom., accus., voc. dual, मघोना *maghōnā* instr. sing., मघोने *maghōnē*, dat. sing.

Gr. Αξον, 'axle,' अक्ष *akṣa* + वन् *van* = Αξ + ον.

Next वन् *van* and मन् *man* are affixed to verbal roots to indicate *nomen agentis*, the action of the verb, its object and so on, and correspond to Gr. *μων, μον, μεν*, Lat. *men* and *mentum* and so on. They are changed into उस् *us* as वस् *vas* (originally वन् *van*) is in some oblique cases, as विदुषा *viduṣā*, 'by the sage,' विदुषे *viduṣē*, 'to the sage,' विदुषः *viduṣaḥ*, 'of a sage'; as also वन् *van*, the possessive suffix, is changed in the Vedic language in the vocative singular, as भगवस् *bhagavas*, भगोस् *bhagōs*, भवस् *bhavas*, and भोस् *bhōs*, 'o lord,' भगवन् *bhagavan*, 'lord.'

Sans. यज्वन् *yajvan*, 'a sacrificer,' यज् *yaj*, 'to sacrifice.'

,, धीवन् *dhīvan*,[1] (Gr. *θαομων*), 'a thinker,' ध्यै *dhyai*, 'to think.'

,, पीवन् *pīvan*, 'one who has become fat,' प्यै *pyai*, 'to swell.'

,, यजुस् *yajus*, (यज्वन् *yajvan*), 'the Yajur Vēda,' यज् *yaj*, 'to sacrifice'

,, धनुस् *dhanus*, (हन्वन् *hanvan*), 'a bow,' हन् *han*, 'to kill.'

,, परुष् *paruṣ*, (पर्वन् *parvan*, 'a knot,' परि *pari*, 'end.'

,, जनुष् *januṣ* (जन्मन् *janman*), 'birth,' जन् *jan*, 'to be born.'

,, चक्षुस् *cakṣus*, (चक्ष्मन् *cakṣman*), 'eye,' चक्ष् *cakṣ*, 'to say,' 'to proclaim.'

Gr. *ἡγεμων*, 'a leader.'

,, *θεομων*, 'a spectator.'

---

[1] Unādi Sūtra, IV. 114.

Lat. *sermo(n)*, 'a speech,' literally any thing connected, *sero*, 'to connect.'

,, *termo(n)*, 'a boundary,' *tero* (Sans. तर् *tar*), 'to cross.'

Gr. ποιμην (μεν), 'a herdsman,' ποι, 'grass.'

,, πυθμην (μεν), 'bottom,' from an obsolete root πυθαω, 'to be deep.'

Lat. *segmen* (*ĕnis*), 'that which is cut off,' from *seco*, 'to cut.'

,, *certamen* (*ĕnis*), 'a contest or struggle,' from *certo*, 'to contend,' *cerno*, 'to separate.'

,, *velamen* (*ĕnis*), 'a cover,' from *velo*, 'to cover.'

This suffix *men* is modified as *mentum* by the addition of the suffix *um*, as *men* + *um* = *mennum* by the doubling of *n*, and *mentum* by the hardening of the second *n*[1]; as in *velamentum, velamen*, 'cover'; *segmentum, segmen*,' 'segment;' *argumentum, argumen*, 'argument.'

In *velamen* and *certamen*, the augment *ā* preceding the suffix *men* and also the *ĭ* as in *specimen*, and *ŭ* in *tegumen* are like *ē*, *ĭ*, *ī* in पचेलिम *pacēlima*, 'ripe,' गरिमन् *gariman*, 'greatness,' and भरीमन् *bharīman*, 'wealth.'

त्वन् *tvan* is shortened into त्वम् *tvam* and is suffixed to nouns, adjectives and, in the Vedic language, to verbs also; as,

जनित्व *janitva*, 'parent,' जन् *jan*, 'to be born,' (Uṇādi Sūtra, V. 104, 105).

पेत्वम् *pētvam*, 'nectar,' पा *pā*, 'to drink.'

सोत्व *sōtva*, 'which is to be poured,' सु *su*, 'to pour,' (Rig Veda, X. 160, 2.)

कर्त्वम् *kartvam*, 'action,' कृ *kṛ*, 'to do.'

---

[1] Compare *elementum* = *elemen* (आत्मन् *ātman*) + *um*.

We may next proceed to स्म *sma*, Gr. σμος, which are directly derived from त्मन् *tman* by the change of the initial त *t* into स *s* and the elision of the final *n*. Like त्व *tva*, σμος is used both as an adjective and a noun suffix; as,

Sans. सूक्ष्म *sūkṣma*, 'small,' सूच् *sūc*, 'to point.'
Gr. εγκελευσμος, 'encouragement.'
,, βαπτισμος, 'a dipping in water.'
,, κατευθυσμος, 'direction.'

The Latin suffix corresponding to त्वम् *tvam* is *tium*. Compare *tion*, त्वन् *tvan*, in which the letter व *va* is changed into two syllables as *io* in *tio* (*n*), Sans. त्वन् *tvan*; e. g.,

Pretium, 'price' = *pre* + *tium*, in which *pre* is an obsolete root connected with Sans. क्री *krī*, and Gr. πρε, which becomes περ by metathesis as in περναμαι, and πρα as in πρατηρ, Sans. क्रेतृ *krētṛ*, 'a seller,' πρατος क्रीत *krīta*, 'sold.'

Initium, 'a going in or entrance' = *in* + *i* + *tium*, *i*, 'to go.'
Exitium, 'a going out' = *ex* + *i* + *tium*.

त्वम् *tvam* is changed in Sanskrit into त्य *tya* corresponding to Lat. *tiu* and forms adjectives as कृत्य *kṛtya*, and into ष्य *ṣya* (स्य *sya*) as रुचिष्य *ruciṣya*, 'agreeable,' 'desirable,' रुच् *ruc*, 'to like;' भुजिष्य *bhujiṣya*, 'serving,' भुज् *bhuj*, 'to enjoy.'

In धेनुष्या *dhēnuṣyā*, 'a cow tied up for milking,' the suffix is used with a diminutive force, like the corresponding Greek suffix διον as in βοηδιον.

Corresponding to the Sans. स्य *sya* we have in Greek σιο, as in θυσια, 'sacrifice,' from θυω, 'to sacrifice;' ετησιος, 'a year long,' ετος, 'a year;' Ιθακησιος, 'belonging to Ithaca;' Φλιασιος, 'belonging to the town of Phlius.'

त्वन् *tvan* is modified as तन *tana* and is used as an adjectival suffix corresponding to Lat. *tinu*; as Sans. श्वस्तनस् *śvastanas*, Lat. *crastinus*, 'of to-morrow;' दिवातनस् *divātanas*, 'belonging to the day,' Lat. *diutinus*, 'lasting long' (radically, 'belonging to day.')

It is from this suffix तन *tana* that one set of comparative and superlative suffixes are derived in the Aryan languages, while the other set is produced by the suffix वत् *vat* as already shown (pp. 110-111). तन *tana* is modified as तर *tara* by the change of न *n* into र *r* as in तृ *tṛ*, Gr. τορ, and Lat. *tor*, suffixes of agency; त्र *tra*, an adverbial suffix of place; and त्रम् *tram*, Gr. τρον, Lat. *trum*, suffixes indicating instrumentality, and the like. These suffixes are derived from तन *tana* as will be shown hereafter. The suffix तर *tara* so formed is used to form comparative degrees of adjectives.

तन *tana* produces also the superlative suffix तम *tama* in Sanskrit by the change of न *n* into म *m* as in स्यून *syūna*, स्यूम *syūma* (§ 22), सहसान *sahasāna*, 'having born,' that is, 'able to bear,' changed into सहसाम *sahasāma*.[1] The change occurs in the following pronominal stems also and deserves notice here. एष *ēṣa*, एत *ēta*, एन *ēna* and अन *ana* are all identical forms composed of इ *i*, 'this,' and स *sa*, त *ta*, and न *na*, modifications of the demonstrative pronoun 'he,' and they appear also in the form of अम *ama* and इम *ima*.[2] अनस् *anas* is changed into अनो *anō* by the

[1] Tait. Mantra Praśna, I. 11.

[2] Corresponding to इम *ima* (इन *ina*), there must be a form एम *ēma* (एन *ēna*); and the indeclinable particles इव *iva*, 'like,'

Prakritic method of changing अस् *as* into ओ *ō*, and अमो *amō*[1] by the change of न *n* into म *m* and then modified as अमु *amu*, अमू *amū* and अमी *amī*, which are substituted for the declensional forms of अदस् *adas*.

Compare अमो *amō* occurring in the passage quoted in p. 72, अमोहमस्मिसात्वम्सात्वमस्यमोहम् *amōhamasmisātvam sātvamasyamōham*, where I divide अमोहस् *amōhas* into अमो *amō* + अहम् *aham*; for it answers to the word अमू *amū* occurring in a corresponding passage quoted in the previous page, अमूहमस्मिसात्वम्सात्वमस्यमूहम् *amūhamasmisātvam sātvamasyamūham*. (Vide Note 1, p. 71).

As Sans. तनस् *tanas* becomes *tinu* in Latin, so does Sans. तम *tama* become *timu, simu, rimu*, of which *tumu, sumu, rumu*, &c., are original forms (Zumpt's Latin Grammar, p. 85). But in Greek, the final न *n* of the Sans. तन *tana* is changed into *t* and produces the superlative suffix τατο. To illustrate this change of *n* on the one side into *m* and on the other into *t*, I shall give one example.

---

and एव *ēva*, 'thus,' in the earlier language, 'only,' 'certainly,' and एवम् *ēvam*, 'thus,' and 'like,' are modifications of इम *ima* and एम *ēma* respectively. This change of म *m* into व *v* has taken place in अवोस् *avōs*, the genitive of अमु *amu*, used in the Rig Veda, X. 132. 5.

[1] Similarly the nominative singular masculine and feminine form असौ *asau* is to be derived from असो *asō* which is a modification of असस् *asas*, as अनो *anō* is of अनस् *anas*, the other form of असस् *asas*.

The masculine suffix अस् *as,* Gr. and Lat. *os,* is changed into अन् *an,* Gr. *ον,* and this अन् *an* is modified as अम् *am* in Sanskrit as in ज्ञानम् *jñānam.* But the न *n* of the same अन् *an* is hardened into त *t* in pronouns as in तत् *tat,* 'that,' यत् *yat,* इतरत् *itarat* (Gr. ἑτερον), wherein the final *t* corresponds to the *ν* of Gr. ἑτερον and *d* of the Lat. *istud, illud.*

From तम *tama* is derived Sans. लिम *lima* as in पचेलिम *pacēlima* and भिदेलिम *bhidēlima,* Gr. σιμος and σινος as in κρισιμος, 'decisive,' βασιμος, 'accessible' (p. 6), and γελασινος, 'laughter;' Lat. *tivus* as in *dativus,* 'giving,' *optativus,* 'wishing.'

In the Gr. Οφθαλμος, the suffix लिम *lima* seems to be shortened into λμο, thus Οφθαλμος = Οπτ + α + λμος, *a* being the connecting vowel, from οπτω, 'to see' (Sans. अक्ष् *akṣ*). The word, therefore, means 'that which sees,' that is 'the eye.'

तन *tana* yields तर् *tar,* Gr. τωρ and Lat. *tor,* is shortened into त्न *tna* and then modified into त्नु *tnu* and also स्नु *snu.* तर *tara* is shortened into त्र *tra,* Lat. *tru* and *tra* and assumes in Greek the forms or θρο, θρα, τλο, τλα, θλο and θλη, and also of δνο as in λεπαδνον, 'a broad leather strap,' from λεπω, 'to strip off the husks;' εχιδνα, 'a viper,' 'a monster having the upper part of the body of a woman and the lower part of that of a serpent,' from εχις, 'a viper;' Αριαδνη, from αρειος, 'warlike,' originally 'good,' Sans. अर्ह *arha;* and Ευαδνη, from ευ, 'good,' Sans. सु *su.* Evadne[1] was the daughter of Iphicles of Argos, of whom

---

[1] The Sans. सुंदरी *sundarī* is closely allied to Gr. Ευαδνη, सु *su* answering to ευ and तरी *tarī* to δνη. Radically the word must be सुतरी *sutarī* and then modified as सुंदरी *sundarī.*

Apollo was enamoured. But she rejected his love and married one of the seven chiefs who went against Thebes. Her husband was killed by Jupiter with thunder stroke for his blasphemy, and she perished with him.

Ariadne was the daughter of Minor II, king of Crete, by Pasiphae. She loved Theseus and was married by him. But when she was pregnant she was forsaken by him in the island of Naxos.

In these words the suffixes *δνα* and *δνη* are added to *εχις* and *αρειος* and *εν*.

From तर् *tara* is derived the adverbial suffix त्र *tra* and from तन *tana*, तस् *tas* (Gr. *θεν*) and तात् *tāt*.

There are many more suffixes which may be included in the list; but as I have to treat of the subject at full length in my Comparative Grammar of Sanskrit, Greek and Latin, I content myself with what I have said.

66. I have to observe here that if the above genealogy of the Sanskrit, Greek and Latin suffixes be correct, it would follow as a corollary that most of the personal pronouns in the above languages which are allied to them both in form and meaning are traceable to the same sources त्मन् *tman*, and आत्मन् *ātman*; for त्मन् *tman* is modified, as shown above, into त्मत् *tmat*, त्वत् *tvat*, त्वनम् *tvanam*, त्वता *tvatā*, त्वत *tvata*, त्य *tya*, स्य *sya*, तन *tana*, तम *tama*, तात् *tāt*, Lat. *don*, *gon*, Sans. मान *māna*, Gr. *μενο*, Sans. मन् *man*, वन् *van*, म *ma*, व *va*, Lat. *ion* (य *ya*), &c.

Similarly आत्मन् *ātman* may be modified in the first person as अस्मन् *asman*, अस्म *asma*, अहम् *aham*, आव *āva* by the change of अस्म *asma* into आम *āma* and by the insertion of व *v* for म *m*; वयम् *vayam* properly अवम् *avam* which, by the initial addition of व *v*, becomes ववम् *vavam* and then वयम् *vayam* (Comp. यूयम् *yūyam*); मा *mā* a shortened form of आम *āma* and न *na* which is to be derived directly from म *ma*. In these forms the general meaning of आत्मन् *ātman*, viz., 'a soul' or 'spirit,' is modified by reference to the speaking 'soul,' that is, the person who speaks, or, in one word, 'I.' In the second person the same radical word आत्मन् *ātman* is modified as उस्मन् *usman*, युष्म *yuṣma* (properly उस्म *usma*), युव *yuva* (उस्म *usma* being changed into उम *uma* and उव *uva* by the change of म *m* into व *v* as in आव *āva*, and at last युव *yuva* by the initial addition of य *y*), यूयम् *yūyam*, उवम् *uvam* modified as युवम् *yuvam* and यूयम् *yūyam* by the change of व *v* into य *y*, त्वत् *tvat*, त्व *tva* (Gr. σφεις, you, *pl.*) and व *va* which is a contraction of उव *uva*. In these forms, आत्मन् *ātman* restricts its meaning to the hearing soul, that is, the person that hears, in one word, 'thou.' Just as आत्मन् *ātman* modified as अस्मन् *asman* and उस्मन् *usman* came to mean 'I' and 'thou' respectively, so did it come to mean 'he' under the form त्व *tva*, Gr. σφεις, 'they' (masc. pl.), σφεα (neut. pl.), σφων (gen. pl.). This त्व *tva* is modified as त्य *tya* and स्य *sya* by the change of व *v* into य *y* and also into त *ta* and स *sa* by the elision of य *y*. The same त्व *tva* passes from the meaning of 'he' to that of 'who,' both inter. and rel., under the modified forms क्व *kva*, Lat. *qua*, and Teut. *hva*, wherein the त *t* of त्व *tva* is changed into क *k*, and ह *h*. This क्व *kva* is developed into two syllables as कव *kava*,

कय *kaya* and किय *kiya,* and shortened into क *k* and य *y*. कव *kava* is changed in Greek into ὁπο as in ὁποσος in which the initial क *k* is changed into ह *h,* and व *v* into π, and corresponding to which we may conceive such a form as कवावत् *kavāvat* (that is कियत् *kiyat*); and as in also ὁποιος which is shortened from ὁποσος as ποιος and κοιος from ποσος and κοσος (p. 138). The Sans. क *ka,* inter. 'who,' becomes in Greek πο, and य *ya,* rel. 'who,' ὁ. In Latin and the Teutonic languages, *kva* and *hva* remain unchanged and are used for the rel. and the inter. pronoun. (Vide p. 97.)

To the different forms which the word आत्मन् *ātman* assumes in the pronouns may be added the following forms which are the remnants of abraded pronominal forms amalgamated with roots: FIRST PERSON, मस् *mas,* मसि *masi,* μεθα, μεθον, वस् *vas,* व *va,* वहे *vahē,* वहै *vahai,* वहि *vahi,* वसि *vasi,* मा *mā,* मस् *mas* and μεν, &c.; SECOND PERSON, तन *tana,* थन *thana,* स्यन *syana,* तात् *tāt* (sing. & pl.), ध्वात् *dhvāt,* ध्वैनम् *dhvainam,* ध्वा *dhvā,* ध्वे *dhvē,* ध्वम् *dhvam,* स्व *sva,* स्वा *svā,* Lat. *mini,* तम् *tam,* τον, थास् *thās,* थाम् *thām,* से *sē,* थे *thē,* थस् *thas,* σθον, &c.; THIRD PERSON, तात् *tāt,* Lat. *tote,* τωσαν, σθωσαν, την, των, τον, σθην, σθων, σθον, ति *ti,* ते *tē,* ται, त *ta,* ताम् *tām* and तस् *tas,* &c.

67. From the same word आत्मन् *ātman* is contracted त्मन् *tman* as already noticed, which is modified as स्वन्नम् *svannam* by the addition of the suffix अम् *am* and by the change of त *t* into स *s* and म *m* into व *v,* and स्वांतम्

svāntam[1] by the hardening of the second न *n* into त *t*, and the lengthening of the first vowel अ *a*. आत्मन् *ātman* is contracted into मन् *man*, 'to think,' from which come the words मनस् *manas*, Gr. μενος, Lat. *mens*, and मा *mā*, 'to think,' Gr. μναομαι, 'to remember,' 'to court.' म्ना *mnā*, 'to think repeatedly' Gr. μανθανω, 'to learn,' Lat. *men* as in *mimini*, 'to think,' and *moneo*, 'to remember.' The word स्वांतम् *svāntam* corresponds to the Lat. *spons*, 'self,' or 'accord,' a word which occurs only in the ablative and genitive cases, as *sponte* and *spontis*, and to Gr. σπενδω, 'to pour out or offer a drink-offering to a god,' and to Lat. *spondeo*, 'to promise legally,' 'to betroth.' In the ideas conveyed by the above Latin and Greek words a free will or vow to act is necessarily involved. In the Gr. θυμος the final consonant of त्मन् *tman* is cut off and the initial consonants त्म *tma* are developed into two syllables. Gr. θυμος is allied to Sans. धूम *dhūma*, 'smoke,' and धूप *dhūpa*, 'the smoke arising from a fragrant substance.' As the म *m* of धूम *dhūma* is changed into प *p*, there is no difficulty in changing the प *p* into क *k* in Greek, a change which takes place in that language very often. So we have from धूप *dhūpa* Gr. συκη which, by the addition of an initial π, assumes the form of ψυκη, 'soul,' ψυχω, 'to breathe.' Compare ψυχρος = π + συχρος, Sans. तुषार *tuṣāra*, तुग्र *tugra* of which δροσος and Lat. *ros* are modifications.[2] Gr. συχη seems to be allied to Arab. روح *rūh*, 'soul,' ريح *rīh*, 'wind,' and Heb. רוּחַ, 'breath,' in which *r* stands for *s*.

---

[1] Cf. ध्वांत *dhvānta* which I have derived from तमस् *tamas* shortened into त्मस् *tmas* (p. 137).

[2] Vide the *Salila* Group.

68. आत्मन् *ātman* may be metamorphosed into आन्मन् *ānman*, आन्मर् *ānmar*, आन्वर् *āvnar* and, at last, by the addition of अ *a* at the end, अम्बर *ambara* which means 'heaven,' and when modified as अमर *amara* is used in the sense of a deity. अंबर *ambara* is shortened into अभ्र *abhra*, Gr. ομβρος, αφρος, Lat. *imbra*, 'a shower of rain,' *imber*, 'clouds,' and *umbra*, 'shade,' and also into अंबु *ambu*, and अंभस् *ambhas*, 'water,' which last is derived from अंबर *ambara*, by the loss of the final अ *a* and the aspiration of the letter ब *b* and the change of र् *r* into स *s*. From अंभस् *ambhas* has been evolved a form of three syllables अनभस् *anabhas* by the insertion of the vowel अ *a* between the anusvāra and the following भ *bha*. It is shortened into नभस् *nabhas*. नभस् *nabhas* means 'water' and in this sense is changed into νυμφη, 'a water nymph,' and subsequently was transferred to the nymphs of other elements; thus came into existence the nymphs of trees, mountains, &c. Ναιδες were spring nymps; Νηρηιδες, sea nymphs; Ορεστιαδες or Ορεαδες, mountain nymphs; Δρυαδες, 'Αμαδρυαδες, Αδρυάδς, tree nymphs, and, similarly, other nymphs. In Sanskrit the word νυμφη is modified as रंभा *Rambhā* by the change of न *n* into र *r*. Compare सरस्वती *Sarasvatī* which originally meant 'water nymph' and subsequently was applied to the goddess of speech. (Vide p. 32.)

In Sanskrit the word रंभा *Rambhā* is a proper name and is applied to one of the celestial damsels. The word then passes to another meaning; the plantain tree is also called रंभा *rambhā* for the tree with its tender and green foliage bears a striking contrast to the hardy and gigantic pippal and other trees which are personified as males. The plantain tree is therefore personified as a female. This deification is clearly seen in a ceremony which is called कदलीविवाह *kadalīvivāha*, 'the marriage of the plantain tree,' and which is performed when a widower marries a fourth time.

In the third marriage, the widower should marry the arka plant, '*Calotropis gigantea*,' and in the fifth the galūcī creeper, '*Menispermum cordifolium.*'

The Sans. निंब *nimba* is applied to the tree *Azadiracta Indica*, commonly called neem. This tree is worshipped as the wife of the pippal and is often grown with the latter. When the ceremony called अश्वत्थविवाह *aśvattha-vivāha*, 'the marriage of the pippal tree,' takes place, both the trees are planted together on a raised pial and are often worshipped. निंब *nimba* is also applied to one of the celestial trees, पारिजात *pārijāta*.

नभस् *nabhas* is modified as तमस् *tamas* by the change of न *n* into त *t* and भ *bha* into म *ma* and is also shortened into ध्वांतम् *dhvāntam* (p. 135), तमस् *tamas* and ध्वांतम् *dhvāntam* meaning 'darkness.'

From नभस् *nabhas* can be derived नभसस् *nabhasas* by the addition of the suffix अस् *as*. It is modified as नवतस् *navatas* by the change of भ *bh* into व *v* and स *s* into त *t*. नवतस् *navatas* is contracted into Gr. Νοτος, 'south-west wind,' by the shortening of the two syllables नव *nava* into No, a change which is referrible to a general law, that weak consonants after a vowel are often elided and the vowel preceding is lengthened. According to this law many Sanskrit words have undergone a process of contraction in Greek and Latin, which often conceals the alliance of the originals and their derivatives: Thus,

SANSKRIT.	GREEK.	LATIN.
तावत् *tāvat*	τοσος	*tantus*, 'that much,' *totus*, 'whole,' *tot*, 'so much.'
यावत् *yāvat*	ὁσος	*quantus* and *quotus*, 'how many,' *quot*, 'how much.'
कियत् *kiyat* for कावत् *kāvat*	{ κοσος, ποσος }	*quantus* } Do., (interrog.)
कवावत् *kavāvat*	{ ὁποσος, ὁκοσος }	*quantus* } Do., (interrog.)
इयत् *iyat* for इवत् *ivat*	ισος	*aequus*, 'this much.'

In the above Greek and Latin words *y* and *v* following vowels are elided. For the same reason, the central *s* of the Greek words are elided; e. g.,

τοςος is shortened into τοιος; οσος, οιος; κοςος, κοιος; ποσος, ποιος; ὁποςος, ὁποιος and ὁκοσος, ὁκοιος. Compare एषस् *ēṣas* shortened into ιος, 'one,' which is the Epic form of ειν, 'one,' and also into οιος, 'alone.'

The Latin word *aequus*, meaning 'this much,' gives *aequam*, the feminine accusative case, which is shortened into *iam* according to the above law, owing to the weakness of the sound of *q*, and then modified as *jam* and means 'at this time' or 'now.'

From नभस् *nabhas* we get Gr. νεφελ.., 'a mass of clouds;' Lat. *nebula* 'mist,' 'vapour' and 'smoke;' Gr. νεφος, Lat. *nubes*, 'a cloud;' Gr. νεφρος, 'kidney,' because it contains water (urine), Lat. *nervus*; and Gr. νευρον in which last the भ *bh* of नभस् *nabhas* is changed into υ as in Gr. βασελευς, Sans. वृषभ *vṛṣabha*, 'chief,' and Gr. ορευς, 'a mule,'

Sans. उरभ्र *urabhra*, 'a kind of sheep.' The nerves were so called because they were considered as the channels of animal fluid, blood, &c. The word नमुचि *namuci* applied to a giant whom Indra killed, may be traced to the same word नभस् *nabhas*, as well as the Lat. *lemures*, 'the manes,' and *larva*, 'a ghost' or 'spectre,' by the change of *n* into *l*. In *larva*, the *v* (*u*) which represents the भ *bh* of नभस् *nabhas* is transposed after *r* as in *nervus*. To the same root are traceable Gr. *νιπτω*, 'to wash,' *ναω*, 'to flow,' *νεω*, 'to swim,' Lat. *nix* (*vis*), 'snow,' *nimbus*, 'rain storm,' Gr. *νιφω*, 'to snow,' *νιφας* (*αδος*), 'storm of snow,' and *ναφθα*, 'a clear combustible petroleum.' The word नभस् *nabhas* is modified as नाभ *nābha* and नाभि *nābhi*, 'navel,' the former of which is the original form, and the latter a modified one as shown already (p. 68). The corresponding Greek and Latin words are *ομφαλος*, *umbilicus*, and Lat. *umbo* (*nis*), 'centre,' all contracted from a form *ονυφος* allied to अंभस् *ambhas* mentioned above.

From this meaning, viz., 'navel,' the word passes to that of 'a child,' and in this meaning is modified as नपात् *napāt*, Gr. *νεπους*(*δες*). नपात् *napāt*, modified as नप्तृ *naptṛ*, and Lat. *nepos* (*otes*), is applied to a grandson. In the Gr. *ανεψιος*, 'a cousin,' of which the original is *ανεπτιος*, the initial *a* and the suffix *io* are peculiar.

A similar contraction of the word नभस् *nabhas* has taken place in the Lat. *neptune* which comes from Sans. नभस्वत् *nabhasvat*, 'having clouds or water.' (Vide p. 124).

I trace the same word नभस् *nabhas* in the latter part of तनूनपात् *tanūnapāt* which is applied to 'the God of fire.' The former part of it, तनू *tanū*, I would connect with दनु *danu*, Gr. *Δαναιος*, and Egyp. *tanau*, mentioned by Mr.

Gladstone in his Hom. Syn., p. 267.[1] तनूनपात् *tanūnapāt* comes from the original form दनुनपात् *danunapāt*, by the hardening of द *d* and the lengthening of the vowel उ *u*. Agni is called तनूनपात् *tanūnapāt*, because of his birth from Heaven. I have already spoken of this relationship of the God of fire to Heaven. (p. 53).

From नभस् *nabhas* is contracted Sans. नौस् *naus*, Gr. *ναυς* and Lat. *navis*, of which the latter is more closely allied to the original as it retains the *v* which represents the भ *bh* of the Sans. नभस् *nabhas*. The Heb. נֹחַ, 'Noah,' seems to be allied to Sans. नौस् *naus* and to be a corruption of नभस् *nabhas* and refers to the ark which served the purpose of a ship and saved him and his family. (*Vide* Introduction and Semitic Analogy).

The above evolutions and contractions of अंभस् *ambhas* (p. 136) are very like what have taken place in अंगु *aṅgu*, Lat. *unquis*, अंगुल *aṅgula*, नखर *nakhara*, and Gr. *ονυξ*, in which the two combined consonants न *n* and ग *g* of the Latin and Sanskrit words *unquis* and अंगु *aṅgu* are developed into a syllable as, *ονυξ* and नख *nakha*. (Vide अग्र *agra* mentioned further on).

69. I may next proceed from आत्मन् *ātman* modified as अस्मन् *asman* in the sense of 'light' and 'fire,' to अश्मन्तम् *aśmantam*,[1] 'a hearth,' so called because it contains fire

---

[1] In अश्मंतम् *aśmantam* the final न *n* of अस्मन् *asman* is doubled by the addition of the suffix अम् *am* and the second *n* is hardened into *t* as in Lat. *elementum* (vide pp. 103 and 110), and in the Gr. *ασαμινθος*, the *t* so derived is aspirated as in *ξανθος* = *ξαννος*, Sans. शोण *śona*, 'red.' (q. v.)

or is like heaven. अश्मंतम् *aśmantam* assumes the form of *καπνος*, 'smoke,' *καμινος*, Lat. *caminus*, 'an oven or furnace,' by the elision of the initial vowel, the change of श *ś* into क *k* and the insertion of the vowel *a* between क *k* and म *m*. Gr. *καμινος* is contracted into *καπνος*[1] and is modified as *ιπνος*, 'furnace,' in which the initial *ka* was changed into *ki*, then *hi* and at last *ι*. From अश्मंत *aśmanta* we may proceed to Gr. *ωον*, originally written as *ωFον* which form corresponds to *οβεον* quoted by Hesychius and to Lat. *ovum*, Sans. अंडम् *aṇḍam*, 'egg,' and Eng. *oven* and Ang.-Sax. *ofen*. I would mention here the Gr. *ασαμινθος*[2] which is applied to a tub or vessel in which the bather sat to have hot water poured on him. Water was heated in a caldron or tripod with fire below it. When sufficiently hot, the water was taken out in a separate vessel and poured on the person who was sitting in the *ασαμινθος*.[3] I think that the name was given to the bathing vessel with reference to the heat of the water with which the bath was performed in the *ασαμινθος*. As the hearth was called in Sanskrit अश्मंतम् *aśmantam* on account of fire used for cooking, so the allied name *ασαμινθος* was first applied perhaps to the bath-room where fire was kindled to heat water for bath, and from the room the name was transferred to the vessel in which a hot bath was performed.[4] Just as we get from अश्मंतम् *aśmantam*, *καπνος* and *καμινος*, so do we get from it

---

[1] Regarding the change of *μ* into *π*, compare Sans. धूम *dhūma* and धूप *dhūpa*.

[2] Vide the Note in the preceding page.

[3] Smith's Greek and Roman Antiquities.

[4] Cf. Tam. அசம்ந்தம் *aśaṁdam*, from Sans. अजमोदा *ajamōdā* in the following page.

also Κυμινον and Lat. *cuminum*, 'the cummin seed,' so called on account of its burning the food or digesting it as is seen in some of its synonyms, जीरक *jīraka*, जीरण *jīraṇa*, and जीर *jīra* which are derived from जॄ *jṝ*, 'to digest.' But where is the Sanskrit word corresponding to κυμινον? It does not occur in any form among the words which are applied to cummin seeds, viz., जीरक *jīraka*, जीरण *jīraṇa*, जीर *jīra*, अजाजी *ajājī*, and कणा *kaṇā*. A minute investigation, however, has led me to the word अजमोदा *ajamōdā* which means 'Bishop's weed,' the seeds of which are often kept and sold by merchants with cummin seeds. अश्मन् *aśman* is modified as अजमोदा *ajamōdā*, by changing श *ś* into ज *j*, the addition of आ *ā*, the doubling of the final न *n*, the change of the second न *n* into द *d*, the elision of the first न *n* and the lengthening of the preceding अ *a* into ओ *ō*.

70. The Lat. *camera* applied to a 'chamber,' literally means a 'vault' and is traceable, I think, to Gr. καμινος and ultimately to Sans. आत्मन् *ātman* and originally signified 'heaven,' or 'concave of heaven.' The Pers. كمان *kamān*, 'an arch,' Gr. γεφυρα, 'a bridge,' *azimuth*, an astronomical term, borrowed from the Arabs and used in the sense of the arc of the horizon between the meridian of a place and a vertical circle passing through any celestial body, *zenith*[1] applied to 'the point of the heavens

[1] The word *zenith* is generally considered to be a shortened form of the Arab. سمت الرّاس *samturrās*, literally, 'way of the head.' I think, however, that the word سمت *samt* seems to be allied to the Arab. سما *samā*, 'heaven,' 'sky,' and Pers. آسمان *āsmān*, 'heaven,' and to convey the same meaning. If so the expression سمت الرّاس *samturrās* may mean the heaven or that part of heaven which is over the head.

directly above the head,' Arab. سما samā, 'heaven,' and Pers. آسمان āsmān, seem to be allied to the Sans. आत्मन् ātman, 'heaven.' Sans. कर्पूर karpūra, 'camphor,' Lat. *camphora,* so called on account of the smoke issuing from it, and कपिश kapiśa, 'smoke-colored,' may be connected with Gr. καμινος, 'oven.' In जीमूत jīmūta, meaning 'clouds,' the initial κ of καμινος is changed into ज j, and the last ν into त t.

71. Allied to Gr. γεφυρα is Sans. गवीनि *gavīni*, 'thigh,' from which comes Tam. கவான் *kavān* and it occurs in a Vedic passage quoted in the St. Petersburg Dictionary.

अस्यानार्यागवीन्योः पुत्रमाधेहि

Asyānāryāgavīnyōh putram ādhēhi.

'Create a son in her womb (*lit.* 'thighs.')

The thigh is so called because it is bent and inclined with the body.

From γεφυρα we can derive κυβερνη, 'the helm of a ship,' from which is derived the verb κυβερναω, (Lat. *guberno*), 'to steer or hold the helm of a ship' and thence metaphorically 'to govern a kingdom.' The Sanskrit word कैवर्त *kaivarta*[1] seems to be a modification of κυβερνητης and means 'a fisherman,' because of his knowledge of steering a ship. केनिपातक *kēnipātaka*, which is used in the sense of a helm in Sanskrit, must be a corruption of κυβερνητικος, 'skilled in steering,' the word passing from its meaning of agency to that of instrumentality. The word κυβερνητικος is modified as κεπευητικος and then as κενιπατακος by the transfer of the syllable νη between κε and πα. From केनिपातक *kēnipātaka* is contracted into केनिप *kēnipa*, a word which is used in the Rig Veda in the sense

[1] Also केवर्त *kēvarta*.

of 'clever,' 'intelligent,' according to Sāyana and Yāska, but may be interpreted into 'sailor' as in the following passage :—

ओजः कृष्व सं गृभाय त्वे अप्यसो यथा केनिपानामिनो वृधे

Ōjahkr̥ṣvasaṅgr̥bhāyatvēapyasōyathākēnipānāminōvr̥dhē.

Rig Veda, X. 44. 4.

'Give us strength; keep us in thee; thou art for our prosperity like the headman of sailors.'[1]

72. From Gr. γεφυρα we may derive Lat. *curvus* by the transfer of the final ρ to the middle of the word, and the word is allied to Gr. καμπη, 'curve,' καμπυλος, 'curved,' and Sans. खर्व *kharva*, 'short.' Gr. γεφυρα passes from the meaning of a bridge to that of a town-gate, or an ornamented gate of the town, and is modified as गोपुर *gōpura*, and by metathesis as πυργος in which the initial ग *g* of गोपुर *gōpura* is transferred to the end. To this πυργος seem to correspond Sans. वलज *valaja*,[2] 'town-gate,' and the Lat. *fornix*, in which the central ρ of the Gr.

---

[1] This meaning is supported by the occurrence of the word नौस् *naus*, 'a ship,' in the third hymn following it, in which the sacrifice is compared to a ship and those who do not embark in it are said to go down. In this meaning is involved a comparison between Indra and the captain of a ship and the comparison is, I think, expressly stated in the stanza quoted above. In आकेनिप *ākēnipa* used in Rig Veda, IV. 43, 6, meaning 'wise,' the initial आ *ā* is an extraneous addition.

[2] वलजं गोपुरे क्षेत्रे सस्यसंगरयोरपि

Valajaṁgōpurēkṣētrēsasyasaṅgarayōrapi

वलजा वरयोषायां यूथ्यामपि॥ *Mēdini.*

Valajāvarayōṣāyāṁyūthyāmapi.

πυργος is probably strengthened by the addition of *n*. *Fornix* means 'vault or arch,' and by metonymy a 'brothel' from its being in subterraneous vaults. With γεφυρα may be connected Sans. कपोणि *kapōṇi*, and कूर्पर *kūrpara*, 'elbow,' in the latter of which an inorganic र *r* is inserted before प *p*. The Lat. *cumulus*, 'a heap,' seems to be traceable to the same source.

73. From Gr. γεφυρα may be contracted Sans. चक्र *cakra*,[1] Gr. κυκλος, Lat. *circus*, Gr. γογγυλος and γογγυλιος, 'round,' Sans. चंकुर *caṅkuru*, 'a car,' because it is moved by wheels (चक्र *cakra*). शकट *śakaṭa*,[2] 'cart, is a modification of चक्र *cakra*. The word चक्र *cakra* may, otherwise, be taken as a reduplicated form of गोल *gōla*, Gr. βωλος and Lat. *glebus*, which have been already traced to Sans. ग्लौ *glau*, 'moon.'

I think that, in Sans. शक्वरी *śakvarī*, 'a girdle,' 'a kind of metre so called perhaps on account of its resemblance to a circle,' and शष्कुली *śaṣkulī*, 'a round cake,' the word चक्र *cakra* (Gr. κυκλος) has undergone a thorough metamorphosis. A minute examination will, however, show the alliance clearly. चक्र *cakra* being modified as कक्र *kakra* by the restoration of the original क *k* instead of च *c*, ककुर *kakura* by the insertion of उ *u* between क *k* and र *r*, (compare चंकुर *caṅkuru*), कक्वर *kakvara* by the insertion of व *v* for उ *u*, and at last शक्वरी *śakvarī* by changing the ini-

[1] चक्र *cakra* is modified as திகிரி *tigiri* in Tamil. From திகிரி *tigiri* comes திங்கள் *tiṅgaḷ*, 'moon.'

[2] It is modified in Tamil as சகடு *śagaḍu* and சாகாடு *śāgāḍu*.

tial क *k* into श *ś* as in शूर *śūra*, Gr. κυρος (vide p. 151). By the same processes we can evolve शष्कुली *śaṣkulī* from चक्र *cakra*, but there is a peculiarity which needs explanation, that is, the appearance of स्क *sk* instead of the क *k* of चक्र *cakra*. It can however be accounted for by reference to other examples such as पुष्कर *puṣkara* where similar change has taken place. Proceeding from the form ककुर *kakura* which has been derived above from चक्र *cakra*, we get कक्कुर *kakkura* by doubling the second क *k* and then शक्कुल *śakkula* by changing the initial क *k* into श *ś* and the final र *r* into ल *l*, and inserting स्क *sk* for क्क *kk* and cerebralizing *s*, we get शष्कुल *śaṣkula*. Compare पुष्कर *puṣkara*, 'hollow,' which I derive from कुहर *kuhara* modified as कुहुर *kuhura*, कुह्वर *kuhvara*, कुक्कर *kukkara*, and कुष्कर *kuṣkara* as shown above, and at last पुष्कर *puṣkara* by inserting प *p* for क *k* as in पाप *pāpa*, Gr. κακος.

The interchange of *p* and *k* often occurs in the Aryan languages and deserves to be mentioned here :

Sans. अक्ष् *akṣ*,	Gr. οπτομαι (οπς), 'to see.'
,, अक्षर *akṣara*, 'sky,'	,, Ἑσπερος, 'evening,' (q. v.)
,, क्षु *kṣu*, 'to sneeze,'	,, πτυω.
,, क्षुद्रा *kṣuārā*,	,, ψυλλα in which क्ष *kṣ* is changed into πς and written as ψ and द्र *dra* is softened into λλ as in मल्ल *malla*, मद्र *madra*, 'an athelete.'
,, क्षपा *kṣapā*, 'night,'	,, ψεφος, 'darkness.'

Sans. कडार *kaḍāra*, कद्रु *kadru*, 'brown,' which are modified as कार्दूल *kārdūla* and then शार्दूल *śārdūla*	Gr. παρδος, ,, παρδαλις } 'leopard.'
,, पृ *pṛ*, 'to please,'	,, κορεννυμι, the radical part being κορς, from κρε.
Gr. κελλω,	Lat. *pello*, 'to drive.'
Sans. क्री *krī*, 'to purchase,'	Gr. παρναμαι for πρανὰμαι, the root being πρα, answering to Sans. क्री *krī*.
Lat. *coquo*, 'bake,'	,, πεσσω, Sans. पच् *pac* } 'to become ripe.'
Sans. वाक् *vāk*,	Gr. επος, 'a word.'
,, क *ka*, ,, कि *ki*, ,, कु *ku*	,, πο, ,, κο { relat. prons. 'who' and 'which.'
,, कव *kava*, ,, कय *kaya*, ,, किय *kiya*	,, ὁπος, ,, ὁκος { relat. prons. as in ὁποσος and ὁκοσος, contracted into ὁποιος and ὁκοιος.
Lat. *quinque*,	{ ,, πεντε, Sans. पंच *pañca* } 'five.'
Sans. यकृत् *yakṛt*,	Gr. ἡπαρ, 'liver.'

The above derivation explains clearly the several meanings which the word पुष्कर *puṣkara* has, such as 'sky,' 'the face of a drum,' 'the proboscis of an elephant,' 'the lotus flower,' 'an island,' 'water,' &c.

74. गवीनि *gavīni* is contracted into गोनि *gōni* and then modified as Gr. γονυ, Sans. जानु *jānu*, and Lat. *genu*, 'knee,' because it is bent, and, by the change of *g* into *s*, as सनु *sanu*, '*knee*,' as in सनुतः *sanutah* (p. 55), and सानु *sānu*, 'ridge of a mountain.' जानु *jānu* is shortened into ज्ञु *jñu* as in प्रज्ञु *prajñu*, 'bandy-legged,' as γονυ, into χνυ as in προχνυ in which γ is changed into κ before ν and then aspirated. A similar contraction takes place in सानु *sānu* which becomes स्नु *snu* in the oblique cases optionally. From गोनि *gōni* abovementioned we can derive कोण *kōṇa*, Gr. κωνος, Lat. *conus*, 'a cone,' and Gr. γωνια, 'an angle.'

The Sans. जघन *jaghana* and Gr. κοχωνη, 'the hams,' seem to be reduplicated forms of γονυ, 'knee.' From जघन *jaghana* may be derived the form जघ्न *jaghna* which is changed into दघ्न *daghna* and then into सक्थ *saktha*, 'thigh,' Gr. ιξυς, 'waist.' सक्थ *saktha* is modified as सक्थि *sakthi* (p. 68) and is used more commonly, while its original form occurs in compounds. With reference to the change of घ्न *ghna* into क्थ *ktha*, compare Gr. χθων (p. 39).

75. As the द्य *dy* of द्यौस् *dyaus* is changed into ग *g* in गौस् *gaus* and as the स *s* of द्यौस् *dyaus*, into न *n* in दिन *dina* and *Janus*, so does the word undergo both the changes mentioned, and thus is modified as गोन *gōna* and then as गान *gāna*. From this form we can obtain the words γανος[1], 'beauty,' 'brightness,' and γανυ as in γανυμηδης. The Sanskrit root कन् *kan*, 'to shine,' is traceable to γανος

[1] The verb γανυμαι, 'to brighten up,' must be distributed as

while the word कण्व *Kaṇva* used in the Rig Veda for a sage and कण्वतम *kaṇvatama,* the superlative form of कण्व *kaṇva,* intensifying the meaning of the word कण्व *kaṇva,* correspond to γαννος. I would therefore infer that the radical meaning of कण्व *kaṇva* is 'bright.' Compare अंगिरस् *Aṅgiras* and अंगिरस्तम *Aṅgirastama* which are used in the Vedas and whose radical meaning has already been shown to be 'bright' (p. 62).

The Sans. कन्या *kanyā,* 'a young girl,' Gr. νεος, Sans. नव *nava,* Gr. καινος, Lat. *novus,* 'new,' and Sans. नवन् *navan,* Gr. εννεα, Lat. *novem,* 'nine,' are traceable to the same source. The Sans. कम् *kam* and Lat. *amo,* 'to love,' seem to be a modification of कन् *kan* by the change of न *n* into म *m.* To the same source are referrible यम् *yam,* γαμεω, 'to marry,' and जामातर् *jāmātar,* γαμβρος, 'son-in-law.' The original form of जामातर् *jāmātar* is गामातर् *gāmātar* which is shortened into गामर् *gāmar* and assumes the form γαμβρο. The elision of the त *ta* of गामातर् *gāmātar* in γαμαρ is like that taking place in देवर् *dēvar,* Gr. δαηρ for देवितर् *devitar,* 'husband's brother;' स्वसर् *svasar,* Lat. *soror,* for स्वसितर् *svasitar,* श्वस् *śvas,* 'to hope,' and ननंदर् *nanandar* for ननंदितर् *nananditar,* 'sister-in-law.' गामातर् *gāmātar* is shortened into गातर् *gātar* by the elision of the nasal म *m* as in भ्रातर् *bhrātar* from भ्रामातर् *bhrāmātar*

γαν + υ + μαι so that the υ may be considered as the *u* of कुरुते *kurutē.* Compare δαινυμι, 'to give a banquet,' = δαιν + υ + μι, δαιν being a contraction of δαπν, δαπαν, δαπανη, 'expenditure'

from भ्रम् *bhram,* 'to love.' गातर् *gātar* becomes जातर् *jātar* as गामातर् *gāmātar,* जामातर् *jāmātar* and then यातर् *yātar* by the change of ज *j* into य *y.* But in Latin and Greek गातर् *gātar* is changed into गालर् *gālar* by inserting *l* for त *t* and then modified as ग्लार् *glār* and गलर् *galar* which forms produce respectively *glos (ris)* and γαλοως, 'husband's sister.'

76. I derive Gr. ξανθος from γανος, 'bright,' and the word means 'yellow,' and can be connected with the Sans. शोण *śoṇa,* though the latter means 'red.' As Ξανθος is a golden stream in Lykia, so is शोणा *śoṇā,* a river, which is a tributary of the Ganges and is modified as *Sone.*

The Sans. कोकनद *kōkanada,* 'red lotus,' and the corresponding Gr. ὑακινθος are, I think, modifications of शोण *śoṇa,* and the orthographical affinity between them can be seen in the identity and alliance of their consonants, viz. क *k* and ὑ, क *k* and κ, न *n* and ν, and द *d* and θ. In the Greek word, ν and θ are combined, whereas in Sanskrit the corresponding न *n* and द *d* are separated by the vowel अ *a.* There is alliance also in the meaning, Sans. कोकनद *kōkanada* meaning 'a red lily,' and the Gr. ὑακινθος being first used, as we learn from Liddell and Scott, for a 'Laconian youth beloved by Apollo who killed him by a cast of the discus,' and then a flower said to have sprung up from the blood of Hyacinthos, or, according to others, from that of Telamonian Ajax: and some botanists, as Sprengel, think they can decipher on the petals the initial letters of their names ΥΑ or ΑΙ or the interjection *αἰαῖ.*

The radical idea seems to be that of 'red,' and I conjecture that the words are reduplicated forms of the Sanskrit word शोण *śoṇa* (originally कोण *kōṇa*), 'red,' Gr. ξανθος, 'yellow,' in which latter *θ* is used to strengthen *n* which usage is common to Greek and Sanskrit and of which I have already spoken.

I am sure that Sans. जांबूनद *jāmbūnada,* 'gold,' notwithstanding its curious appearance, is allied to Gr. *ὑακινθος* and Sans. कोकनद *kōkanada,* the first two syllables कोक *kōka* being modified as कांबू *kāmbū* and then जांबू *jāmbū* by the palatalization of *k* as *j*. Compare कंबू *kambū,* a 'conch shell,' which is allied to Sans. शंख *śaṅkha,* Gr. *κογχος* and *κογχη,* Lat. *concha,* 'a conch shell.' If शंख *śaṅkha* and *κογχος* become कंबू *kambū,* the *kōka* of कोकनद *kōkanada* may also become कांबू *kāmbū* and then जांबू *jāmbū.* To the same root *ξανθος* are traceable the words चांपेय *cāmpēya,* चंपक *campaka,* 'a campaka flower,' and चामीकर *cāmīkara,* 'gold.' The first two syllables of these words are modifications of शोण *śōṇa* and *ξανθος,* the *n* of which is changed into *m* and then receives a strengthening *p*. In हेमन् *hēman,* 'gold,' also, I see a clear trace of Sans. शोण *śōṇa* and Gr. *ξανθος.*

The letter *ś* is not an original one, and it is traceable in form to *s*. It is found only in Sanskrit and often replaces an original *k* in words derived from Sanskrit or Greek; thus:—

SANSKRIT.	GREEK.
Sans. शूर *śūra,* 'brave,'	Gr. *κυρος,* 'power.'
,, शी *śī,*	,, *κιομαι,* 'to sleep.'
,, शून्य *śūnya,*	,, *κενεος,*[1] 'empty.'

[1] Vide p. 104.

SANSKRIT.	GREEK.
Sans. शूक *śūka*,	Gr. ακωκη, 'point.'
,, शम् *śam*,	,, καμνω,[1] 'to be weary.'
,, शूल *śūla*,	,, καυλος, 'shaft.'
,, शाला *śālā*, 'branch,'	,, καρα, 'head,' 'top.'
,, शिरस् *śiras*,	,, καρα, 'head.'
,, शृंग *sṛṅga*,	,, κερας, 'horn.'
,, शूर्प *śūrpa*, 'winnowing basket.'	Sans. कूर्म *kūrma*, 'tortoise,' कूर्पर *kūrpara*, 'elbow,' the original idea being 'hollow.'
,, शुंठ *śuṇṭha*, 'stupid'	,, कुंठ *kuṇṭha*, 'blunt.'
,, श्रीमन् *śrīman*, 'wealthy,'	Gr. κρειων, 'ruler,' χρεων, 'needful.'
,, श्री *śrī*, 'fortune,' 'wealth,' 'beauty'	,, χρη, 'use,' 'advantage.'
,, श्रु *śru*,	,, κλυ, 'to hear.'
,, श्याम *syāma*, 'black,'	,, κυανος, 'dark blue substance used in the Heroic age to adorn works in metals.'
,, आशु *āśu*,	,, ωκυς, 'quick.'
,, शस् *śas*, 'a suffix as in भूरिशस् *bhūriśas*.	,, κις, a suffix as in πολλακις, 'frequently.'

[1] Allied to σβεννυμι, 'to quench,' p. 116.

Sans. शरत् *śarat*,[1] 'autumn.' Gr. χορτος, 'a feeding place,' Sans. कृत्तिका *kṛttikā*, the constellation 'Pliades.'

---

[1] The name शरत् *śarat* is applied to the season in reference to growth of trees. कृत्तिका *kṛttikā*, applied to the Pliades, has reference to the same phenomenon, and the constellation is also called बहुला *Bahulā*, radically meaning 'plentiful.' From these names of the constellation are derived the names कार्त्तिकिक *Kārttikika* and बाहुल *Bāhula*, which are applied to the second of the two months that constitute the season called *śaradṛtu*. (Compare ऊर्ज *ūrja*, the same month, from ऊर्ज *ūrja*, 'strength'). The name इष *iṣa* which is used for the other month *Āśvayuja*, the first month of the season, is to be derived from इष *iṣa*, 'food.' To the same source कृत् *kṛt* are traceable कांतार *kāntāra*, 'wilderness,' कानन *kānana*, अरण्य *araṇya*, 'forest,' Lat. *hortus*, Eng. *garden* and *yard*. Compare the word Πλειαδες applied to the seven daughters of Ατλας and Πλειονη, which latter exactly corresponds to Sans. बहुला *Bahulā* except the fem. termination *ονι* (आनि *ānī*, the fem. suffix found in शिवानी *Śivānī*.) The son of बहुलास् *Bahulās* is बाहुलेय *Bāhulēya* and the term is used for the War-god, *Subrahmaṇya*, in reference to *Bahulas*' having nourished him in his childhood. I have already shown (p. 33) that the Gr. πολυ is a shortened form of बहुल *bahula*; and πλειος or πλεος, which is only a contraction of πολυ, must be a still more shortened form of बहुल *Bahula*. The suf. ιδης and एयस् *ēyas* have also been shown to be allied, (pp. 121-2). We can therefore clearly see that बाहुलेय *Bāhulēya* and Πλειαδες are allied patronymic forms. The only difference is that in Sanskrit बहुला *Bahulā* is the name of six stars and बाहुलेय *Bāhulēya*, that of their son, the War-god, while in Greek the corresponding Πλειονη (properly πλεια, बहुला *Bahulā*) is applied to the mother of the Constella-

77. आत्मन् *ātman* may be modified as अतन *atana* by the elision of म *m*, and अतस *atasa* by the change of न *n* into स *s*; अतस *atasa* means 'wind,' 'air,' 'water,' and perhaps 'tree.' Compare its derivatives which will be mentioned further on.

यथा चिद्वृद्धमतसमग्ने संजूर्वसि क्षमि. VIII. 60. 7.

Yathācidvṛddhamatasamagnē sanjūrvasikṣami.

'O god of fire, just as you heat water which is spread on the earth.'

The word may be applied to a tree as in the following passage :—

अग्निश्शोचिष्मा अतसान्युष्णन्. II. 4. 7.

Agniśśōciṣmā atasānyuṣṇan.

'The brilliant God of fire burning tree.'

But Sāyana understands by the word अतसानि *atasāni* dried sticks (शुष्ककाष्ठानि *śuṣkakāṣṭhāni*), but this meaning is not right; for the original meaning of अतस *atasa* is sky or anything connected with sky and is high, viz., a tree, a rock, or a mountain; and in fact these are the meanings of a list of words which will be mentioned lower down in this Group. (अद्रि *adri*, अजिर *ajira*, दारु *dāru*,

---

tion representing the seven stars and Πλειαδες to the seven daughters. The War-god is rightly called कार्त्तिकेय *Kārttikēya*, and बाहुलेय *Bāhulēya*, son of the Constellation of कृत्तिका *Kṛttikā*, that is, the son of plenty and strength. Observe also the fact that in India the autumnal season is considered as the best time for the warlike operations of kings. The above derivation of Πλειαδες from Πλεος, 'full,' of which the comparative and superlative degrees are πλεων and πλειστος, refutes the doubtful etymologies assigned to the word.

तरु *taru*, &c., traced to the same word अतस *atasa*). I would therefore take the word अतसानि *atasāni* to mean 'trees' in this passage.

अतसी *atasī* is used in the sense of a kind of hemp, and the name seems to have been applied to the plant on account of its flower which is blue like अतस *atasa*, 'the sky.' Compare Gr. *καννaβoς*, *καννaβις*, Lat. *cannabis* and *canabum*, from which the Eng. *convas* and *hemp*, Ang.-Sax. *haenep*, Sans. शण *śaṇa* are derived. They are applied to another kind of the plant and may be traced to *καπνος*, 'smoke,' and *καμινος*, 'oven,' and refer to the blue colour of its flowers.

78. अतस *atasa* may be modified as अथर *athara* by the change of स *s* into र *r* and then as Gr. *αιθρα*, 'clear sky,' *αιθηρ* and Lat. *æther*, 'upper air,' and *αιθαλος*, 'smoky flame.'

Αιθρα is used as a proper name by which the air is personified as a woman. Αιθρα had a son named Theseus by Ægeus. Theseus represents the sun who may be considered as the son of air by अहस् *ahas*, that is 'day,' which word is modified as Ægeus as shown lower down. Αιθρα was also the daughter of Tethus (सिंधु *Sindhu*) and Oceanus, a relationship which refers to the apparent rising of the sky from the ocean, and she was the wife of Ατλας, अतल *atala*, the nether world.

79. The Gr. *αιρ* is a contracted form of *αιθρα* by the elision of *θ*. It is a peculiarity of the Greek language that it often shortens or simplifies words by elision of an internal consonant, such as, *σ*, *θ*, *ξ*, *χ*, *π*, *β*, *δ*, *γ* and the like.

Compare the following :—

Cr. *μαια*,[1]	Sans. मातृ *mātṛ*, 'mother.'
,, *ην*,	,, आसीत् *āsīt*, 'he was.'
,, *εντι* for *εσεντι*,	,, संति *santi*, 'they are.'
,, *ου* as in *αγαθου* = *αγαθο* + *σya* = *αγαθο* + *ya*, then shortened into *αγαθου*.	,, स्य *sya*, the gen. sing. suf.
,, *ων* as in *ανδρων*, *ανηρ*, 'of men.'	,, साम् *sām*, नाम् *nām*, कम् *kam*, (as in युष्माकम् *yuṣmākam*, properly युष्मासाम् *yuṣmāsām* or युष्मानाम् (*yuṣmānām*), gen. plu. suffixes, answering to Lat. *rum*, in which the स *s* of साम् *sam* is changed into *r*.
,, *υια* as in *ειδυια*, fem. of *ειδως*, perfect participial adjective of *ειδω*, 'to see.'	,, उषी *uṣī* as in विदुषी *viduṣī*, fem. form of विद्वान् *vidvān*, 'learned.'
,, *τοιος*,[2] Gr̃. *τοσος*	,, तावत् *tāvat*, 'that much.'

---

[1] Compare the Hind. and Urdu माइ *mā-i*, 'mother,' which comes from the same root.

[2] In this and the following five examples, the words of the second column contain the elision of the *v* of the corresponding Sanskrit words and those of the first column contain the elision of the *s* of the corresponding Greek words.

Gr. ὁποιος, ,, ὁκοιος,	Gr. ὁποσος ,, ὁκοσος	Sans. कियत् *kiyat*, कवावत् *kavāvat*, 'how much.'
,, ποιος, ,, κοιος,	,, ποσος ,, κοσος	,, कियत् *kiyat*, कावत् *kāvat*; (interrog.)
,, οἱος,	,, ὁσος,	,, यावत् *yāvat*, 'how much;' (relat.)
,, ιος, 'one,'		,, एष *ēṣa*, 'this,' which pronoun gives the numeral एक *ēka*,[1] 'one,' in Sanskrit.
Lat. *amabo*,[2] 'I shall love,' = *am* + *a* + *sva* + *o* = *amasvo*, in which *s* is elided and *v* is changed into *b*.		,, कमिष्ये *kamiṣyē* = कम् *kam* + इ *i* + स्व *sva* + ए *ē* = कमिस्वे *kamisvē*, in which व *v* is changed into य *y*.

[1] The corresponding Greek εισ(εν) and Lat. *unus* are derived from एन *ēna*, another form of एष *ēṣa*. The fem. of εις, viz., μια, is a contraction of अम *ama*, which is also a modification of एन *ēna* and which assumes the forms of अमी *amī* and अमु *amu*.

[2] The particle स्व *sva*, which I hold to be the source of the temporal augment स्य *sya*, indicating future time, means possession and is identical with the gen. suffix. In Greek this स्य *sya* is simplified as σ in roots ending in vowels, and in consonants which can be readily blended with *s*, such as *g*, *k*, *p*, *b*, &c.; but in roots ending with λ, μ, ν and ρ, it is changed into σ and then elided. Thus, στελω, 'I shall put,' = στελλ + ε + σ*y* + ω = στελλεσ*y*ω = στελεσω = στελεω and στελω. (Buttman's Greek Grammar, pp. 135-36.)

Sans. आय *āya*, ए *ē*, &c., dat. and loc. terminations in Sanskrit.	Sans. स्य *sya*, the gen. sing. suf., of which the initial *s* being elided the previous vowel in *a* stem is lengthened, and which is modified as सु *su* in the loc. plu. in Sanskrit.
Gr. *μυια*,	„ मशक *maśaka*, मक्षिका *makṣikā*, 'fly.'
„ *οαρ*,	„ योषित् *yōṣit*, Latin *uxor*, 'wife.'
„ *Μωα*, Laconic form,	Gr. *Μαυσα*, 'the muse.'

In the above examples *s* is elided.

Gr. *υαλος*,	Sans. उपल *upala*, 'a stone.
„ *δαις*, 'banquet.'	Gr. *δαπτς*, *δαπατος* contracted into *δαπτ*.
„ *δαινυμι*, 'to give a banquet.'	„ *δαινος*, contracted from *δαπατος*, allied to Sans. तेवन *tēvana*.
„ *βουτης* = *βου* + *ποσις*, 'a herdsman.'	Sans. गोपति *gōpati*, 'a cowherd.'
„ *ἱπποτης* = *ἱππο* + *ποσις*.	„ अश्वपति *aśvapati*, 'a cavalier.'
„ *στρατιωτης* = *στρατια* + *ποσις*, 'a citizen on military service' or 'a soldier,' from *στρατια*, 'an army,' and *ποσις*, 'lord.'	Compare Sans. सेनापति *sēnāpati*, 'leader of an army.'

In the above examples *p* is elided.

Gr. πραος and Ionic πρηυς and πραυτης, modified forms of βραδυς and βραδυτης,	Sans. मृदु *mṛdu*, 'soft.'
„ μυελλος.	„ मेदस् *mēdas*, 'brain,' Lat. *medulla*, 'marrow.'
„ Ναιος as in Ναιαδες = Ναιο + αδες.	„ नद् *nada*, 'a river.'
„ τεθνηως and τεθνεως.	Gr. τεθνηκως, corresponding to Sans. जघ्निवस् *jaghnivas*, of which form the suf. वस् *vas* is modified as κοτ in Greek as already shown (see p. 115). The initial *k* of the Greek suffix κοτ is elided in the forms τεθνηως and τεθνεως. Compare πεφυκως, masc. sing., बभूवस् *babhūvas*, τεφυκυια, बभूवुषी *babhūvuṣī* contracted into εφυως and πεφῦυῖα.
Sans. ऐस् *ēs*, the instr. pl. suf.	Sans. एभिस् *ēbhis*, older suffix used in the Vedas only.

Gr. *οις*, *αις*, dat. plu. suf.	Sans. भ्यस् *bhyas*[1] of which the initial भ *bha* is elided and the following य *ya* is weakened into a mere vowel.
,, *ἱαρος*.	,, वीध्र *vīdhra*, Gr. *καθαρος*, 'pure.'
,, *αιπυς* / ,, *αιπος*	Sans. ऊर्ध्व *ūrdhva*, 'high.'
,, *αιμη*, 'thorn,'	Gr. *ακμη*, 'point,' from *ακη*, 'point.'
,, *πιοτερος* and *πιοτατος*, comp. and sup. degrees of *πιων* which is itself a comp. degree allied to Sans. भूयस् *bhūyas*.	,, भूयस्तर *bhūyastara* and भूयस्तम *bhūyastama*, from भूयस् *bhūyas*, comp. degree of बहु *bahu*, Gr. *παχυς*.
,, *σπεος*,	Lat. *specus*, 'a cave.'

In the above examples, *κ*, *δ*, *bh*, *dh* and *r* are elided.

In the following, final consonants such as *t*, *d*, *n*, *s*, are cut off :—

Gr. *το*, sing. nom. of the neut.	Sans. तद् *tad*, 'that.'
,, *τα*, plu. nom. of *το*.	,, तानि *tāni*, 'they.'
,, *a*, neut. pl. nom. of nouns as in *ξυλα*, 'trees.'	,, आनि *āni*, as in ज्ञानानि *jñānāni*, 'knowledges.'

[1] In Latin it is modified as *bus* and *bi* and occurs in all the declensions except the first in which it occurs very rarely, as *alibi*, *omnibus*, and as *ιφι* and *φι* in Gr. *θυριφι*, 'outside,' *θυρα*, 'door,' and perhaps *ιφι*, 'strongly,' dat. pl. of *ις*, 'strength.'

Gr. *οι* and *αι*, Lat. *æ*, *i*, &c. Sans. आस् *ās*, आसस् *āsas*,[1] pl. nom. suf.

,, *ηκα*,[2] 'small,' Prāk. ,, ईषत् *īṣat*, 'little.'

इसि *isi*, 'little.'

In all the verbal forms which in Sanskrit end in *t* as in the imperfect singular, aorist singular and the like, the final *t* disappears in Greek, as अभवत् *abhavat*, *εφυε*, भू *bhū*, *φυ*, 'to be;' अद्रौषीत् *adrauṣīt*, *ελυσε*, 'was dissolved;'

---

[1] The pl. suf. आसस् *āsas* is used only in the Vedas, and seems to be the original form from which sprang the latter suffix आस् *ās* by the elision of the central स *s*. This suffix आसस् *āsas* may be a reduplicated form of the singular अस् *as*, the lengthening of the initial vowel of the first part being arbitrary. In this case the idea of plurality must arise from the reduplication of the singular suffix अस् *as*. Or the suffix आसस् *āsas* may be a reduplication of the other suf. आस् *ās* which being doubled becomes आसास् *āsās* and then is modified as आसस् *āsas* by shortening the second आ *ā*. In this case we may attribute the idea of plurality to the change of अस् *as* into आस् *ās*. In the Aryan languages very likely there was no idea of number attached to nouns as also to verbs, and the ideas of singularity and plurality must have arisen in nouns after the divergence of the singular form by the modification of the suf. अस् *as*. Both of the theories presuppose that in the Aryan languages the declensional system first arose out of the अ *a* stem and was afterwards applied to the इ *i*, उ *u* and other stems. The plural form of the अ *a* stem was analyzed as, for instance, राम *Rāma* + अस् *as* and the suffix अस् *as* so derived was added to the other stems.

[2] In the Prākṛtic languages as in Greek the final consonants of Sanskrit words are very generally cut off, as ता *tā*, तत् *tat*, 'that'; इसि *isi*, ईषत् *īṣat*, 'little;' ताव *tāva*, तावत् *tāvat*, 'then;' जाव *jāva*, यावत् *yāvat*, 'when.'

अदुद्रुवत् *adudruvat*, ελελυκε, 'was dissolved ;' भवेत् *bhavēt*, φυιη, 'may become.'

It is a characteristic feature of the Greek language to shorten words by eliding consonants between two vowels and often by blending the vowels preceding and following the elided consonants into one, or by eliding consonants coming with other consonants and lengthening the quantity of the preceding vowels, and so on. These are some of the laws according to which the Prākṛtic and Vernacular language have been derived from the parent Sanskrit, and some of the modern vernaculars of Southern Europe from Latin and Greek. While the operation of these laws was checked in Sanskrit by the differentiation of the Prākṛtic dialects from Sanskrit at an early time (p. iii), in Greek it was allowed to have its full force, and, in consequence, has simplified many words and grammatical forms; and the new forms so introduced have replaced the old ones. In this respect the Greek language looks more like a daughter than a sister of Sanskrit. In Sanskrit when such words as गुप्त *gupta*, युक्त *yukta*, लब्ध *labdha*, भवति *bhavati*, पतित *patita*, तानि *tāni*, तावत् *tāvat* and तत् *tat*, were modified as गुत्त *gutta*, जुत्त *jutta*, लद्ध *laddha*, होदि *hōdi*, पडिय *paḍiya*, ताइ *tā-i*, ताव *tāva*, ता *tā*, such forms were generally considered as Prākṛtic and were included in a dialect. The same is the case with many Latin words, which when simplified were generally differentiated as the words of a dialect as the Romance language. Thus when the Latin words *fidelitas, crudelis, magister, dubito, rotundus, traditor, punctus, unctus* and *junctus* were shortened into *fealty, cruel, master, doubt, round, traitor, point, oint* and *joint*, they were not admitted into Latin, though they may have been used contemporaneously with their originals.[1]

[1] There are however instances of words in Latin which have been

80. अतस *atasa* may be modified as अथर *athara* by the change of स *s* into र *r* and then अथरि *athari* and अथरी *atharī* by the change of the final अ *a* into इ *i* and ई *ī*. अथरि *athari* and अथरी *atharī* mean 'light,' or 'ray,' as in the following passage :—

द्वियंपंचजीजनन् संवसाना: स्वसारो अग्निंमानुषीषुविक्षु।

Dviryampañca jījanan saṁvasānāḥ svasārō agniṁ mānuṣīṣu vikṣu

उषर्बुधमथर्यो ३ नदंतं शुक्रंस्वासं परशुंनतिग्मम् ॥ IV. 6, 8.

Uṣarbudhamatharyō nadaṁtaṁ śukraṁ svāsaṁ paraśuṁ natigmam.

'The God of fire whom the ten united fingers (sisters ?) produced among mankind, and who is dawn—awaking like the rays of the sun, bright, eating havis, good faced and sharp like axe.'[1]

Though Sāyana interprets अथर्योन *atharyōna* in the above passage by स्त्रिय इव *striya iva*, I think that the meaning is not right, and take the word अथर्य: *atharyaḥ* to mean 'rays.'

Taking the suffix यु *yu*, the word अथर् *athar* becomes अथर्यु *atharyu*, and this word means 'brilliant,' as in the following passage :—

अग्निंनरोदीधितिभिररण्योर्हस्तच्युतीजनयंतप्रशस्तं ।

Agnimnarōdīdhitibhiraraṇyōrhastacyutījanayantapraśastam

दूरेदृशं गृहपतिमथर्युम् ॥ VII. 1. 1.

Dūrēdṛśaṁgṛhapatimatharyum.

---

modified and are optionally used in the modified forms, such as, *providentia, prudentia, fructus, fruitus,* in which latter *c* is cut off, and also of words of which the original forms have been replaced by the corrupt ones such as, *fruor (frugor), struo (strugo), fluo (flugo,* Sans. पृच् *pṛc*, 'to be wet,' वृष् *vṛṣ*, to pour.')

[1] With अतस *atasa*, and अथर *athara* may be connected the Semitic words, Heb. אַתּוּן *atūn* and Aram. [illegible] *atūn*, 'furnace,' and Heb. אֵשׁ *ēs*, and Arab. آتش *ātis*, 'fire.'

'With the araṇi sticks and by the motion of their hands men produced the god of fire with effulgence, praiseworthy, far-seeing, lord of the house, and brilliant.'

The word also means 'having fire,' that is, a 'priest.'

Similarly is derived अथर्वन् *atharvan* from अथर् *athara* by the addition of the suffix वन् *van*. The original meaning of the word अथर्वन् *atharvan* is, therefore, 'one who has fire,' that is, a priest who keeps fire or officiates at the sacred fire. This is the meaning in which the word is used in the following passage:—

अभिते मधुना पयोथर्वाणो अशिश्रयुः ।

Abhitē madhunā payōtharvāṇō aśiśrayuḥ

देवंदेवायदेवयु ॥ IX. 11. 2.

Dēvaṁdēvāyadēvayu.

'O sōma, with thy sweet juice the priests prepared for Indra a drink which is savoury and goes to the gods.'

With this word अथर्वन् *atharvan* may perhaps be connected the Gr. θεραπων which in the oblique cases assumes the form of θεραποντ. Compare मघवन् *maghavan* which is declined both as मघवाणौ *maghavānau* and मघवन्तौ *maghavantau*, nom. dual, and मघवानः *maghavānaḥ* and मघवंतः *maghavantaḥ*, nom. pl., &c. Though the word θεραπων means an attendant or inferior kind of servant in the later language and has thus degenerated in meaning, yet it is applied in the elder language to persons whose service was free and honorable. This meaning quite agrees with the character of the priest अथर्वन् *atharvan*, who, besides his knowledge of the Yāgās and other Vedic ceremonies, was well versed in the performance of various rites, preventive of evils and promoting prosperity, and with the nature of the Atharva Veda which arose on account of the necessity of superintending the solemnization of ceremonies prescribed in the other Vedas, and the preventing of sacrificial blunders, and, in course of time, included other rites, and formulas relating to them. The priest of a king must be well versed in the Atharva Veda and perform rites which will remove evils and increase prosperity. Thus Vasiṣṭha, who was the priest of Dilīpa, is said to have been अथर्वनिधि *atharvanidhi*, 'a treasure of the Atharva Veda,' that is, well versed in the Atharva Veda.[1] But in Greek the word has diverged from that meaning and was first used for a companion in arms. Thus in Homer we find Eteoneus described as the θεραπων of Menelaos, Meriones, of Idomeneus and Patroclus, of Achilles. In the later language the word is used for an attendant or a servant.

The feminine form of θεραπων is θεραπαινα (θεραπανσα properly), which comes from θεραπων, as if the latter were declined as θεραπονος, θεραπονες, &c., without a *t* as मघवानौ *maghavānau* and मघवानस् *maghavānas*.

81. From अतस *atasa* is to be derived अगस् *agas*, 'light,' and it assumes the form अगस्त्य *agastya* by the termination य *ya*, the letter *t* being added to स *s* for the purpose of strengthening as is seen in विष्टप *viṣṭapa*, 'world' = विस्तप *vistapa* = विसव *visava* = विश्व *viśva*, 'all'; स्वस्ति *svasti* = स्वस् *svas* + इ *i*, स्वस् *svas* meaning

---

[1] त्रय्यांचदंडनीत्यांच कुशलस्स्यात्पुरोहितः

Trayyāñca daṇḍanītyāñca kuśalassyātpurōhitaḥ

अथर्वविहितंजानन् नित्यंशांतिकपौष्टिके ॥ Kamantakiya.

Atharvavihitaṁ jānan nityaṁśāntikapauṣṭikē.

'The priest should be versed in the three Vedas, knowing always the ceremonies as prescribed in the Atharva Veda, expiatory and increasing prosperity.

'happiness.'[1] The sage Agastya is so called on account of the brightness of the star which represents him in heaven, or in reference to his own brightness as गोतम *Gautama,* कण्व *Kaṇva* and अंगिरस् *Aṅgiras*; and this last word will be mentioned hereafter.

The name is applied to a plant called also मुनिद्रुम *munidruma,* 'the tree of a hermit' (Agastya), and producing a bright red or white flower. Compare the Gr. *ακανθος,* Lat. *acanthus,* 'bear's breach,' and Gr. *ακακια*; Lat. *acacia,* all of which are traceable to the same source as अगस्त्य *Agastya.*

82. अतस *atasa* is modified as आकाश *ākāśa* through the abovementioned form अगस् *agas,* and means 'sky' or 'air.' From the latter part of the word is derived the roots काश् *kāś* and कास् *kās,* 'to shine,' and काश *āśa,* 'cough,' so called on account of the repeated breathings which take place in coughing. To आकाश *ākāśa* are traceable the Eng. *ghost,* Ang.-Sax. *gast,*[2] Germ. *geist,* Dutch *geest,* 'a spirit,' and also *gust,* 'a sudden blast of wind,' and perhaps *ghast,* 'fear,' 'astonishment,' as in *aghast, ghastly,* and also the technical word *gas* which was first applied by the Belgium chemist Von Helmont to an aeriform fluid, and which seems to have been taken from the Dutch word *geest.*

83. From अतस *atasa* may be derived अतन *atana* by the change of स *sa* into न *na* (compare अहस् *ahas* and अहन् *ahan* and the law illustrated under अहस् *ahas*), and then Αθηνα by the aspiration of त *ta.* Αθηνά with Αθηνη

---

[1] Vide p. 28 and Note 3.

[2] Mr. Skeat observes, however, that *ghost* and *ghast* are not allied, and derives the latter from a root primarily meaning 'to stick,' as the Lat. *haereo.*

and other forms is the name of the Goddess called in Latin *Minerva*. She was the daughter of Zeus without a mother and is also called Τριτογενεα, that is, daughter of the Ocean. The word Τριτογενεα may be translated into Ṣanskrit as सरस्जन्या *sarasjanyā* exactly and may be applied to the goddess of fortune, that is, *Lakṣmi* who is said to have sprung from the milky ocean (vide p. 125.) Αθηνα is the symbol of wisdom and power and she protects every work of wisdom and power. She guards cities in peace and war and is the goddess of war. The radical meaning of the word is 'brightness' or 'day,' and, as morning restores to men their understanding power which is lost in sleep, the goddess is rightly called Αθηνα. This function is attributed to the Sun-god, and उषस् *Uṣas*, 'Dawn,' who is also known by the name of अहना *ahanā*, a word allied both in meaning and form to Αθηνη and to its Laconic form Ασανα. The name Αθηνη was given to a fortress which was established by Cecrops and called Κεκροπια, and which was subsequently enlarged by Theseus. From the fortress the name was applied to the city of Athens and is used in plural like Θηβαι. The government of Theseus at Athens may be explained by reference to the shining of the sun in the day time, *ahas*. The name Θησευς answers to Sans. दुष्यंत *Duṣyanta*[1] or दुष्मंत *Duṣmanta,* which word means 'bright,' consisting of दुस् *dus*, 'light,' and मन् *man*, suffix indicating possession, and in its form is exactly allied to Διονυσος (p. 124.)

84. अहना *ahanā* is a modification of अतस *atasa* like Αθηνη, and, as already noticed, is closely allied to Αθηνη

[1] The word Θησευς comes from the root θεος which is found in θιασος, and suf. ευς indicating 'possession'; and the word radically means 'heavenly' as the corresponding word दुष्मंत *duṣmanta* does.

both in meaning and form. अहना *ahanā* is the goddess of dawn and she is said to go to every house directly and to be very modest. (p. 61.)

85. From अतस *atasa*, 'light,' may be derived अहस् *ahas* of which अहना *ahanā* is an enlarged form and the final स *sa* of which is changed into न *na* before casal suffixes beginning with a vowel. The same change has taken place in अहना *ahanā* (radically अतस *atasa*). अहस् *ahas* is modified as अह्नी *ahnī*, अहनी *ahanī*, NOM. and ACCUS. dual and अहानि *ahāni*, NOM. and ACCUS. pl., अह्ना *ahnā*, INSTR. sing., अह्ने *ahnē*, DAT. sing., अह्नि *ahni* and अहनि *ahani*, LOC. sing. In compounds the word is contracted as अह्न *ahna*, and अह *aha* by the elision of न *na*, as प्राह्ण *prāhṇa*, 'morning,' अपराह्ण *aparāhṇa*, 'evening,' and पुण्याह *puṇyāha*, 'holy day.' Compare ऊधस् *ūdhas*, 'udder,' which is similarly modified,' as कुंडोध्नी *kuṇḍōdhnī*, 'a cow with a big udder.' p. (43).

The change of *s* into *n* is very important in the Aryan languages; and it will be really interesting to see the law illustrated. Many examples have already been given; as, दिन *dina*, 'day'; *Ζην* and the Doric form *Ζαν*, the stems out of which are derived the casal forms of *Ζευς*, which is declined in some cases as a consonantal stem ending in *ν* (नकारांत *nakārānta*), as *Ζηνος* GEN., *Ζηνι* DAT., and *Ζηνα* ACCUS., and the corresponding Doric forms *Ζανος*, &c.; Lat. *Janus*, *Juno*; Sans. दनु *danu* and दानु *dānu*, Gr. *Δαναος*, Egypt. *tanau*, Sans. तनु *tanu* (p. 139) as in तनूनपात् *tanūnapāt*, दानव *Dānava*; *χθων*, चोणी *kṣōnī*; स्योन *syōna*, and स्यून *syūna*; Sans. महस् *mahas*, 'great,' modified as महत् *mahat* and महा *mahā*, Lat. *magnus*, Gr. *μαγαλ*. It is a law which has thus not only affected the forms of many primitive words, but is also a very powerful element underlying the formations of grammatical inflections. I shall therefore give a few more examples here below:—

Sans. अपस् *apas*, — Sans. अप्नस् *apnas*, 'possession', 'property,' Gr. *οπλον*, 'a tool,' 'instrument,' *οπωρα*, 'fruit time' or 'fruit,' *ομπνη*, 'corn' and 'food.'

„ शिरस् *śiras*, — Gr. *κολονη*, 'a mound,' *κορονις*, 'the tip of a bow.'

„ अस् *as*, mas. sing. suf. — „ *ον*,[1] neut. sing. in which the स् of mas. suf. is changed into *ν*, and which corresponds to अम् *am*, neut. sing. suf.

It is this *ν* which reappears in the neutral plural as ज्ञानानि *jñānāni*, 'knowledges' = ज्ञानम् *jñānam* + इ *i* = ज्ञानन् *jñānan* + इ *i* = ज्ञानान् *jñānān* + इ *i*, by the

[1] The *ν* of the Greek suffix *ον* is changed into *m* in Sanskrit; this change is seen in many other instances, such as इम *ima*, अमु *amu*, अमी *amī* and अमू *amū* (pron.), ईम् *īm*, (adv. part.), सदम् *sadam*, 'always,' तदम् *tadam*, 'then,' इदम् *idam*, 'now,' words mentioned in the above list.

lengthening of the penultimate अ *a*; and in the accus. plural, as रामान् *Rāmān* which is only a modification of रामम् *Rāmam*, originally रामन् *Rāman*, the accus. suf. अम् *am* and the allied Gr. ον being the same as the Gr. ον and Sans. अम् *am* of the neut. sing., the neut. suf. producing the accusative idea. The above ν of neut. plur. suf. is wrongly inserted in the neuter dual and plural forms of consonant and vowel stems; and it is this *n* which is seen, I think, in the plural forms of the third person of verbs, as भवंति *bhavanti*, अभवन् *abhavan* for अभवन्त् *abhavant*, and so on.

In the neuter singular of pronouns such as यद् *yad*, तद् *tad*, and कद् *kad*, 'what,' occurring in Samāsa as कदश्वः *kadaśvah*, 'a mean horse,' अन्यद् *anyad*, इतरद् *itarad*, कतरद् *katarad*, एतद् *ētad*; Lat. *illud* and *istud*, &c., the final *n*, which arises out of the masculine suffix स *sa* as shown above, and indicates neuter singular, is hardened into *t* and *d*. But as the Greek language does not allow the letter *t* to stand at the end of a word, the *t* is cut off as in ὅ, 'what' (rel.), Lat. *quid*; το (demon.), 'this' or 'that;' το, definite article.

As the final द् *d* of यद् *yad*, तद् *tad*, कद् *kad* and एतद् *ētad* are shown to be connected with the म *m* of the neuter suffix through the ν of the corresponding Gr. ον, it is highly ungrammatical to attach the *d* to the stem as is done in Sanskrit. Thus, यत्पुरुष *yatpuruṣa*, तत्पुरुष *tatpuruṣa*, एतत्पुरुष *ētatpuruṣa* and कदुष्ण *kaduṣṇa*, are unscientific and ought to be यपुरुष *yapuruṣa*, तपुरुष *tapuruṣa*, एतपुरुष *ētapuruṣa* and कोष्ण *kōṣṇa*, the last of which is optionally used for कदुष्ण *kaduṣṇa*, and also modified as

कवोष्ण *kavōṣṇa.*[1] Compare यादृश *yādṛśa,* यावत् *yāvat ;* तादृश *tādṛśa,* तावत् *tāvat ;* एतादृश *ētādṛśa,* एतावत् *ētāvat ;* कीदृश *kīdṛśa,* कियत् *kiyat,* that is किवत् *kivat* (properly कावत् *kāvat*) ; in which proper stems are used without the wrong suf. *d.* For the same reason the compound किंपुरुष *kimpuruṣa,*[2] 'what man,' 'a kinnara,' is wrong and ought to be किपुरुष *kipuruṣa,* कपुरुष *kapuruṣa* or कुपुरुष *kupuruṣa ;* for the final म *m* of किम् *kim* is the same as that of ज्ञानम् *jñānam,* and the word must be spelt as कम् *kam* answering to the masc. कस् *kas.* But as the masc. कस् *kas* is changed into किस् *kis,* so the corres-

---

[1] The same remark applies to अन्यद् *anyad* (Lat. *aliud* and Gr. Αλλον) which also retains the suf. अद् *ad* as in अन्यदुत्सुक *anyadutsuka,* 'fond of another,' and अन्यदीय *anyadīya,* 'belonging to another,' when the word is not in the genitive and instrumental cases; and optionally, as in अन्यदर्थस् *anyadarthas* and अन्यार्थस् *anyārthas,* 'another's property.'

[2] The word किंपुरुष *kimpurṣa* is coined owing to a wrong analysis of the word किन्नर *kinnara,* किम् *kim* + नर *nara,* 'bad man.' The word must be derived from केसर *kēsara,* 'mane,' or 'hair,' and means 'hairy,' as do the allied words गंधर्व *gandharva,* 'a kind of celestial beings,' and कण्ठीरव *kaṇṭhīrava,* 'lion,' and Gr. Κενταυρ, 'a kind of monster,' which are to be traced to कदर *kadara,* 'hair,' a modified form of केसर *kēsara* (vide *Śiras Group*). It is this word किन्नर *kinnara* which, having been applied to a musical instrument called किन्नरी *kinnarī* in Sanskrit and modified as सितार् *sitar* in Northern India, has migrated to Europe under various forms as κιθαρ, *guitar, cistern, cithern* and so on.

ponding कम् *kam* is changed into किम् *kim,* though this is against the common usage of the language by which the neuter suffix म् *m* in इ *i* and उ *u* stems is omitted. To resume the list :—

Sans. स्य *sya*, gen. sing. suf. which is a corruption of स्वम् *svan*, 'own.'

" अस् *as*, mas. sing. suf.

Sans. नाम् *nām,* gen. plu. suf. as in रामाणाम् *Rāmāṇām*, 'of Rāmas.'

" आनी *ānī*, the fem. sing. suf. corresponding to अस् *as* masc. sing. suf., = अस् *as* + ई *ī* = अन् *an* + ई *ī* = आन् *ān* + ई *ī* by the lengthening of अ *a*. (Comp. आनि *āni*, the neut. plu. nom. suf., p. 169.)

Similarly derived is the नी *nī* in the following :—

असिक्नी *asiknī*, 'young maid servant,' पलिक्नी *paliknī*, 'old woman,' पत्नी *patnī*, (Gr. ποτνεα and ποτνα and Sans. पत्न *patna* as in सपत्न *sapatna*.) In भट्टिनी *bhaṭṭinī*, 'a king's wife,' which ought to be properly भट्टी *bhaṭṭī* from भर्त्री *bhartrī*, fem. form of भर्तर् *bhartar*, 'lord,' नी *nī* is added by wrong analogy. The same is the case, I think, with बंधकिनी *bandhakinī*, सुभगिनी *subhaginī*, परस्त्रीणी *parastrīṇī*, कुलटिनी *kulaṭinī*, कल्याणिनी *kalyāṇinī*, the proper forms of which are बंधकी *bandhakī*, सुभगा *subhagā*, परस्त्री *parastrī*, कुलटा *kulaṭā*, कल्याणी *kalyāṇī*, and which occur in the words बांधकिनेय *bāndhakinēya,* 'son of a bad woman,' सौभागिनेय *saubhāginēya,* 'son of a good woman,' पारस्त्रैणेय *pārastraiṇēya,* 'son of another's woman,' कौलटिनेय *kaulaṭinēya,* 'whore's son,' and काल्याणिनेय *kālyāṇinēya,* 'the son of a good woman.' In the North Indian vernaculars, the suffixes इनि *ini,* इन *ina,* अन *ana,* अनि *ani,* आणि *āṇi,* ईण *īṇa,* एण *ēṇa,* &c., are used as suffixes to derive from masculine nouns their corresponding feminine forms, and some of them, as अन *ana,* अनी *anī* and आणी *āṇī,* are traceable to the above आनी *ānī* : *e. g.,*

धोबिन *dhōbina,* 'washerwoman'	धोबि *dhōbi,* 'washerman.'
कुम्हारिन *kumhārina,* 'potter's wife.'	कुम्हार *kumhāra,* 'potter.'
पंडिताणी *paṇḍitāṇī,* 'a learned woman.'	पंडित *paṇḍita,* 'pandit.'
चाकराणि *cākarāṇi,* 'a female servant.'	चाकर *cākara,* 'servant.'
कमीनणी *kamīnaṇī,* 'a female menial servant.'	कमीन *kamīna,* 'a male menial servant.'
जटिणि *jaṭiṇi,* 'a Jot's wife.'	जटु *jaṭu,* 'a Jot.'
हिंदिणी *hindiṇī,* 'a Hindu female.'	हिंदु *hindu,* 'a Hindu.'
सुगरीण *sugarīṇa,* 'a skilful woman.'	सुगर *sugara,* 'a skilful man.'
मरेठेण *marēṭhēṇa,* 'a Maratha woman.'	मरेठी *marēṭhī,* 'a Maratha.'

To resume the list :—

Sans. सदस् *sadas,* 'an assembly.'	Gr. εθνος,[1] 'a nation.'

[1] Δ is hardened before *n* as εθνος = εδενος = Sans. सदस्

Sans. अहस् *ahas*, 'brightness.'	Gr. *αχνη*, 'foam.'
,, स *sa*,	Prāk. न *na*, 'he.'
,, एस *ēsa*, 'this,' = इ *i* 'this,' and स *sa*, 'that,'	Sans. एन *ēna*, अन *ana* and इन *ina*, in which स *s* is changed into न *n*, the first part इ *i* being seen in the forms ए *e*, अ *a* and इ *i*.
,, सह *saha* + द्यस् *dyas*, 'with day,' 'whole day,' that is, always, shortened into सद्यस् *sadyas*.	,, सदन् *sadan*, modified as सदम् *sadam* as in सदमित् *sadamit*, 'always.'
,, अद्यस् *adyas*, modified as अद्य *adya*	,, इदन् *idan*, modified as इदम् *idam*, and इदान् *idān*, in इदानीम् *idānīm*.
,, किस् *kis*, 'who,'	,, किन् *kin*, modified as किम् *kim*.
,, इस् *is*, 'this,' the pron. which is	,, इन् *in*,[1] modified as ईम् *īm*, an indeclina-

sadas + अस् *as*. Compare *προχνυ*, Sans. प्रज्ञु *prajñu*, = *προ* + *γονυ*.

[1] The other form इत् *it* contains the usual pronominal suffix त् *t*, and both इत् *it* and ईम् *īm* are used as particles of emphasis as सदमित् *sadamit*, इदानीम् *idānīm* and तदमित् *tadamit* and तदानीम् *tadānīm*.

seen in अयम् *ayam*, 'this,' mas. nom. sing.	able particle used to emphasize.
Sans. तस् *tas*, adv. suf. meaning 'from.'	Gr. *θεν*.
,, ईयस् *īyas* and यस् *yas*, comp. suf. of adjectives in Sanskrit, as in गरीयस् *garīyas* and श्रेयस् *śrēyas*, of which latter the radical word is श्री *śrī*, 'fortune,' 'advantage,' &c.	,, *ιων*, and *ων* in words in which *ι* is cut off, and the final consonant is doubled and sometimes changed, as in *ρασσων* = *ραδιων*, or the preceding vowel is lengthened and the final consonant is simply changed and not doubled as in *μειζων* = *μαγιων*.

86. अहल्या *Ahalyā*, the name of the wife of Gautama, is to be derived from अहस् *ahas*, 'brightness,' the final स *s* of which is changed into ल *l*, as in अतल *atala*, radically अतस *atasa*. By the addition of the suf. य *y* and the change of स *s* into ल *l*,[1] अहस् *ahas* becomes अहल्या *Ahalyā* and means radically 'bright,' 'effulgent,' and, as such, is a suitable counterpart of गौतम *Gautama* which conveys the same radical meaning and has already been explained (p. 62). अहल्या *Ahalyā* was the first woman created according to the Uttara Kanda, and her name is derived thus; हल *hala*, 'ugliness,' हल्य *halya*, 'which is ugly,' and अहल्या *ahalya*, 'who is not ugly,' that is, 'beautiful.'

[1] Vide p. 43.

Brahma created her, and, in spite of Indra's love for her, entrusted her to the care of Gautama who protected her for many years and then restored her to Brahma. He was pleased with the trustworthiness of Gautama and gave her to him as wife. The illicit intercourse of Indra with Ahalyā in the dawn during the absence of Gautama may be explained by reference to a daily phenomenon, viz. the absorption of the natural brightness of the sky in the morning twilight of the east. But Kumārilabhatta says that the story is typical of the sun's carrying away the shades of night and makes the word अहल्या *Ahalyā* mean 'night,' by a forced etymology.[1]

87. Closely allied to अहल्या *Ahalyā* is the Gr. Αχιλλευς or Αχιλευς, Achilles, son of Pelus and Thetis and the bravest of all the Greeks in the Trojan war. He loved Hellen on whose account the Trojan war took place and terminated in her redemption. The name Αχιλλευς radically means 'bright' like अहल्या *Ahalyā* and refers to the sun; and this connection is sufficiently supported by the parentage ascribed to Axilles. He is the son of water both on his father's side and his mother's side, as the name of his mother, Thetis, is a modification of Sans. सिंधु *sindhu* meaning 'ocean' or 'a river,' and his father's name Pelus means 'water,' and is connected with Sans. वार् *vār* and वारि *vāri*, Lat. *mari*, 'water,' Sans. पयस् *payas*, 'water' and 'milk,' पीयूष *pīyūṣa*, 'nectar,' Ved. मयस् *mayas*, 'food,' and Gr. βιος, 'means of living or livelihood,' and forms the root of the word Πελοςγος, a name applied to the

---

[1] अहस् *ahas*, 'day,' ली *lī*, 'to vanish;' अहल्या *ahalyā*, 'vanishing in the day,' that is, the night.—MAX MÜLLER'S *History of Ancient Sanskrit Literature*. p. 529. Vide also Note I, under Αριαδνη, p. 193.

Greeks.[1] In Homer this is the name of a people who were the allies of the Greeks, andwhom Homer places in Thessaly As Thessaly is an inland country lying to the north of Greece which is a peninsula surrounded by water on three sides, the northern Grecians or the southern Thessalians may have been called Pelasgos by the inhabitants of Thessaly; and the name may have subsequently extended to the Greeks themselves. The name of the wife of Achilles, viz. 'Ελλενη has been shown lower down to be a corruption of Sans. अनल *anala*, 'fire.' Ιλιον is a corruption of Sans. दिवम् *divam* and radically means Heaven (p. 60). The Trojan war is, therefore, a war in Heaven and the victorious hero is Achilles (अहस् *ahas*), that is, the sun; and the redemption of Hellen by Achilles must refer to the rising of the morning sun with all his brilliancy of which he is shorn in the preceding evening.

88. The term असुर *asura* must be connected with अतस *atasa* and Gr. αιθρα and αιθηρ and has a very extensive application in the Rig Veda. It means 'bright,' 'strong,' or 'mighty,' &c., and in the passage following the above meaning is clear.

महद्देवानामसुरत्वमेकम् ॥ III. 55.

Mahaddēvānāmasuratvamēkam.

'The power of the deities is great and peculiar.'

इंद्रायह्दियौरसुरोअनंमत ॥ Rig Veda, I. 131. 1.

Indrāyahidyau rasurō anamrata.

'The mighty Heaven bowed to Indra.[2]

---

[1] If so, the γ in Πελασγος may be a change of *y*; and the word may be originally Πελασyος.

[2] Compare the story of the Bhāgavata Purāṇa which says that Kṛṣṇa defeated Vyomāsura (that is, द्यौरसुरस् *Dyaurasuras* in the above passage) on one occasion and on another conquered Indra

The term is applied to Mitra, Varuṇa, Indra and many other Gods; and as such must convey the same meaning. In this meaning it agrees with the Zend *Ahura* which is applied to the highest God in the Parsee religion. But in the later Sanskrit literature, it is applied to the Rākṣasas or giants who are opposed to the deities

When the word thus degenerated, a new word was coined from it to be applied to the deities as an antithesis to it. The deities who were called असुरास् *Asurās* once, became thus सुरास् *Surās* subsequently.

While the word असुर *asura* degenerated[1] in its meaning and was applied to giants and Rākṣasas, it has kept up its ascendancy in its modified form *ahura*, and has been opposed to the word देव *Dēva* which shared the same fate among the Zoroastrians as असुर *asura* among the Hindus; for the motto of the faith of a Zoroastrian is "I cease to be a Dēva worshipper; I profess to be a Zoroastrian worshipper of Ahuramazda, an enemy of the Dēvas, and a devotee to Ahura."[2] It may be interesting to see that many of the other names applied to Rākṣasas in the Hindu Theogony are referrible to the word दिवस् *divas*, 'heaven;' such are the words यातु *yātu*, यातुधान *yātudhāna*, रक्षस् *rakṣas*, राक्षस *rākṣasa*, आसर *āsara*, आशर *āśara*.

---

himself who yielded to him. The peculiarity in the Bhāgavata story is that the term असुर *asura* applied to व्योमन् *vyōman* is used in the sense of an evil spirit, that is a Rākṣasa.

[1] With regard to the degeneration of the word असुर *asura*, compare Sans. दानव *dānava* and Gr. Δαναος, दैत्य *daitya* and τιτυος, and कव *kava* and Pers. *Kava*.

[2] Cox's Introduction to Mythology and Folklore, p. 255.

89. I would derive Sans. उशनस् *Uśanas* from असुर *asura* by the change of the initial अ *a* into उ *u* and of र *r* into न *n* and the addition of the suffix अस् *as*. In the Rig Veda it is the name of a sage and is subsequently applied to the planet Venus, known also by the names of शुक्र *Śukra*, and काव्य *Kāvya* already explained (p. 70). He is the priest of the Daityas just as Bṛhaspati is of the Asuras.

90. असर *asara* is modified as असिर *asira*, and उस्र *usra*, meaning 'a beam' or 'ray of light,' and as अस्र *asra*, meaning 'an arrow.' असिर *asira* is also used in the sense of 'an arrow.' The word उस्र *usra* is applied to a cow and a bull and in that sense is modified as उस्रि *usri* and उस्रिया *usriyā* by the addition of the suffix इय *iya*. उस्रिया *usriyā* is a Vedic word. Compare the words अघ्ना *aghnā*, derived from अहना *ahanā*, गौस् *gaus* from द्यौस् *dyaus*, माहेयी *māhēyī* from महा *mahā*, the last four of which have been mentioned in this Group.

91. From असुर *asura* may be derived असु *asu*, 'life,' 'soul,' and 'knowledge,' and असूया *asūyā*, 'envy,' in which the root is असु *asu*, 'life,' and the suffix या *yā* meaning 'the act of desiring' or 'desire itself' as in अशनाया *aśanāyā*,[1] 'hunger,' formed from अशन *aśana*, 'food,' and या *yā*, meaning radically 'the desiring of food,' that is, 'hunger.'

---

[1] The lengthening of the final vowel in अशन *aśana* and असु *asu* is like that taking place in the dat. case of the अ *a* stem, as रामाय *Rāmāya* from रामस्य *Rāmasya*, the gen. sing. form (vide p. 158). Compare अश्वायति *aśvāyati* which is another form of अश्वस्यति *aśvasyati*, 'he wishes for a horse.'

असुर *asura* is modified as आसर *āsara* and आशर *āśara*; and these words are applied to evil spirits or Rākṣasas like the radical word असुर *asura*.

92. From अगस् *agas* may be derived अग्नि *agni*, 'fire,' and 'the God of fire,' which by the change of the initial *a* into *i* becomes Lat. *ignis*, Gr. αιγλη, 'light of the sun,' 'any light,' and αγλαος, 'splendid,' 'stately.' The root अंज् *añj*, 'to shine,' is to be traced to अग्नि *agni* and has transferred the *n* of अग्नि *agni* to the middle, so that the nasal in अंज् *añj* is to be taken as radical. We have therefore to distribute the conjugational forms like अनक्ति *anakti* as अन् *an* + अ *a* + ज् *j* + ति *ti* by inserting the augment अ *a* between the nasal and the final ज *j* of the root अंज् *añj*. Compare उनत्ति *unatti* (p. xxxv).

93. To the same root may be traced Sans. यक्ष *yakṣa* and Gr. Αιας and Ιασος, in which last the *k* of यक्ष *yakṣa* seems to have been elided. The Yakṣās are a class of celestial beings attendant on Kubēra. In the Greek mythology Ιασος is applied to several persons, such as, the king of Orchomenus and father of Amphion, and son of Argos I. and Evadne, father of Agenor, ruler of Peloponnesus. In the word यक्ष *yakṣa* the initial *y* is an extraneous addition. Compare the following words :—

Sans. वज्र *vajra*, 'thunderbolt.'	Sans. अद्रि *adri*, 'mountain' (p. 203.)
,, वसंत *vasanta*, 'spring season.'	,, अतस *atasa*, 'brightness.'[1]
,, वानर *vānara*, 'monkey,'	Gr. ανηρ, 'man.'
,, वासर *vāsara*, 'day,'	Sans. अतस *atasa*, 'sky.'[2]

[1] Vide p. 181. [2] Vide p. 199.

Sans. यादस् *yādas*, 'water,' ,, यातु *yātu*, 'evil spirit,'	Sans. अतस *atasa*, 'water.'[1]
,, युष्म *yuṣma*, 'you,'	,, उस्म *usma*.[2]
,, यूयम् *yūyam*, 'you.'	,, उवम् *uvam*.[3]
,, युव *yuva*, 'you two,' as in युवाम् *yuvām*, nom. and accus. dual, युवाभ्याम् *yuvābhyām*, instr., dat. and abl. dual, and युवयोः *yuvayōḥ*, gen. and loc. dual.	,, उव *uva*, 'you.'[4]
,, वयम् *vayam*,	,, अवम् *avam*, 'we.'[5]
,, वाष्प *vāṣpa*, 'vapor,'	,, आत्मन् *ātman*,[6] 'clouds.'

The initial *y* of *yakṣa* has been softened into *ia* in the Gr. Ιασος as in Ιον, Sans. यवन *yavana*.

In Gr. Αιας (Αιαντ), Lat. *Ajax*, the central ग *g* of अगस् *agas* is elided and its place occupied by the vowel *i*, and the final स् *s* changed into ν and then into ντ as in वसंत *vasanta*, which I shall explain presently.

94. From अतस *atasa* we may obtain such a form as असन् *asan*, closely allied to the Gr. Αθηνα and Ασανα; and this form, being modified as असंत *asanta*, gives us वसंत *vasanta*, the name of the spring season, in which the ini-

---

[1] Vide pp. 182-3.
[2] Vide p. 133.
[3] Vide p. 133.
[4] Vide p. 133.
[5] Vide pp. 132-3.
[6] Vide p. 103.

tial *v* is an extraneous addition as already shown in the above section. This *v* is retained in the corresponding Latin word *ver* which is a contracted form of वसंत *vasanta*, by the elision of the last two syllables *anta*. The central स *s* is changed into *r* in *ver*. But the Gr. εαρ has elided the central स *s* of वसंत *vasanta*, and its final ρ answers to the final न्त *nt* of the Sanskrit word, which is to be traced to the final स *s* of अतस *atasa*, through an *n*, whereas the ρ of the Greek word stands in the place of the स *s* of अतस *atasa*. With reference to the change of the स *s* of अतस *atasa* into न्त *nt* in वसन्त *vasanta*, compare Gr. απας (απαντ) and Sans. समस्त *samasta*, 'all,' derived from स्वस् *svas*, (p. 15, Note 1), in the former of which the final स *s* of स्वस् *svas* is changed into ντ and in the latter into स्त *st*, and compare also Αιας (Αιαντ) which I have already derived from अगस् *agas* and in which the final स *s* of अगस् *agas* is changed into ντ.

95. From अतस *atasa* can be derived a form आतस् *ātas* which, by the addition of a euphonic *y* at the beginning, becomes यातस् *yātas* (p. 181), and then यादस् *yādas*, by softening the त *t*. यादस् *yādas* means 'water,' 'sperm' and 'the animals of water,' the last of which must be a secondary meaning. The word is also modified as यादु *yādu*, and is used in the general meaning, 'water.' यादुरि *yāduri* and यादुर *yādura* are derivative words originating from यादस् *yādas*, and meaning 'having much seminary fluid' or 'voluptuous.' Perhaps जतु *jatu* and जतुक *jatuka*, 'asafœtida' and 'lac,' may be traced to यादस्

yādas by the change of य *y* into ज *j*.[1] Connected with यादस् *yādas* is यातु *yātu* which means 'water' as in यातुधानः *yātudhānaḥ*, 'residing in water,' that is, a Rākṣasa, and it means also 'mischief' and 'a Rākṣasa.'

96. The word अनल *anala* meaning 'fire' and अनिल *anila* meaning 'wind,' can be easily connected with अतस *atasa*. The Gr. *ανθραξ* is a modification of अनल *anala*, which taking the suffix अक *aka* becomes अनलक *analaka* and then अनरक *anaraka* by the change of ल *l* into र *r*. अनरक *anaraka* is shortened into अन्रक *anraka*, and, with *δ* inserted between न *n* and र *r* as in *ανδρος* = *ανρ* + *ος* = *ανηρ* + *ος*, and the *δ* hardened into *θ*, it assumes the form *ανθραξ*,[2] meaning 'coal. With अनल *anaḻa* may be connected Sans. अलात *alāta*, 'fire-brand,' and Gr. *ελανη*, 'torch,' which are kindred with Ἑλενη explained lower down and in which the two consonants न *n* and ल *l* have been transposed, and न *n* hardened into त *t*. I would mention here Gr. *εσχαρα* and *εσχαρη* which are formed from अतस *atasa* just in the same way as Sans. अक्षर *akṣara* has been, with this difference that the

---

[1] With equal propriety जतु *jatu* and जतुक *jatuka* may be connected with रस *rasa*, 'water,' राक्षा *rākṣā*, and लाक्षा *lākṣā*, 'lac,' Lat. *lac* (*ct*), 'milk,' Gr. *λα* (*κτ*) as in *γαλα* (-*λακτος*), 'milk,' and Sans. अलक्त *alakta*, 'lac,' and other words included in the *Salila Group*.

[2] The termination अक *aka* is often shortened in Greek and Latin as अक् *ak*; e. g., Gr. *δοναξ* (*ak*), 'reed,' *κλιμαξ* (*ak*), 'a ladder,' which ought to be properly *κλιναξ*; Lat. *capax* (*ac*), 'spacious,' *tenax* (*ac*), 'tenacious,' *rapax*, 'rapacious.'

k and *s* are transposed and by the aspiration of *k* becomes σχ.[1] Eσχαρα means 'hearth,' 'an altar for burning offerings.'

97. The names of the Vedic sages अंगिरस् *Aṅgiras* and आंगिरस *Āṅgirasa*, the son of अंगिरस् *Aṅgiras*, in their radical sense convey the idea of brightness as has already been noticed (p. 62), and must be traced to the same root अतस *atasa* through अहस् *ahas*, 'brightness.' As a proper name अंगिरस् *Aṅgiras* was first applied to an author of some Vedic hymns, who was also one of the seven ṛṣis. It was subsequently the name of a Prajāpati. The descendants of अंगिरस् *Aṅgiras* were also called अंगिरस् *Aṅgiras* or आंगिरस *Āṅgirasa*, who were the personification of luminous bodies. The *Aṅgirasas* were also priests who repeated formulas and hymns of the Atharva

---

[1] Compare Gr. εσχατος, 'furthermost' = εξ, 'out,' + τατος = εκτατος = εκσατος, by the change of τ into σ, then = εσκατος by the transposition of κ and ς, and at last, = εσχατος by the aspiration of κ; and Sans. तस्कर *taskara*, which radically means 'skilful,' being a shortened form of दक्षतर *dakṣatara*, the comp. deg. of दक्ष *dakṣa*, and which becomes दक्तर *daktara* by the elision of the ष *ṣa* of दक्ष *dakṣa*, then दक्सर *daksara*, दस्कर *daskara*, and at last तस्कर *taskara*. Or, in the words εσχατος and तस्कर *taskara*, we may suppose that the initial *t* of τατο and तर *tara* is cut off as in Gr. υπατος, 'high,' and Sans. उपम *upama*, in which the initial *t* of the allied suf. तत *tata* and तम *tama* are elided. Thus εσχατος = εξ + τατος = εξατος = εσχατος; and तस्कर *taskara* = दक्षतर *dakṣatara* = दक्षर *dakṣara* = तस्कर *taskara*, (p. 32).

Veda to avert evil effects in sacrifices and other occasions.[1] To अंगिरस् *Aṅgiras* are allied the Gr. *αγγελλος* and *αγγαρος*, the latter of which is a Persian word. They are allied in meaning also, the former word meaning 'a messenger,' 'envoy,' and the latter, 'a mounted courier, such as were kept ready at regular stages throughout Persia for carrying the royal despatches.' These meanings are only secondary, being the modifications of the original idea of brightness, such as have taken place in some words meaning 'speech' or 'to speak,' e. g., Gr. *φημι*, Lat. *for*, Sans. भाष् *bhāṣ* and the like.[2] Just as from अंगार *aṅgāra* meaning 'coal' are contracted the words *col* and *coal*, so from अंगिरस् *aṅgiras* meaning 'bright' are contracted Sans. गिर् *gir*, गिरा *girā*, 'speech,' गॄ *gṝ*, 'to speak,' and Gr. *κλεος* and *κλειω*, *κλεω*, *κληζω*, and *γηρυς*, in the meanings of which there is a transition from 'brightness' to 'speaking.' In Sanskrit गीर् *gīr* means 'speech' and is a name of the Goddess of Speech just as in Greek *κλεος* means 'report' and Κλειω, 'the goddess of report,' that is, 'the Muse of Epic Poetry and History.'

98. Some allied words in the Aryan languages expressive of the idea of hearing, and their derivatives may claim kindredship with the words above mentioned. They are the following; Sans. श्रु *śru* and Gr. *κλυω*, in which *κ* is the original letter and श *ś*, a corruption (pp. 152-3), Ang.-Sax. *hyran*, Eng. *hear*, and Lat. *clueo*, 'to hear,' and 'to be heard or famous.' In Gr. *ακροαομαι*, 'to hearken,'

---

[1] The word is sometimes compounded with अथर्वन् *atharvan* as अथर्वांगिरसस् *atharvāṅgirasas* which term is applied to the same person to whom the two words are applied separately.

[2] Vide p. 74.

'to listen,' the initial *a* is euphonic.[1] The Lat. *client*, 'one who listens,' is a corruption of *clucnt*, the pres. part. adj. of a root *cluo*, of which *clueo* is secondary form. Gr. καλεω, 'to call,' and Sans. कल् *kal*, 'to urge,' 'to induce,' are akin to the root श्रु *śru*. The Lat. *clamo* is a causal form of *cluo* which, taking the suf. *eo*, becomes *claveo* and is shortened into *clavo*, and, by the change of *v*[2] into *m*, assumes the form of *clamo*. The Eng. *loud* and *listen* and Ang.-Sax. *hlud* and *hlistcn* are traceable to a participial form Gr. κλυτος, Sans. श्रुत *śruta*, 'heard.'

99. The Sans. अंगार *aṅgāra*, इंगाल *iṅgāla*, 'coal,' are connected with the above words अंगिरस् *Aṅgiras* and Gr. Αγγελλος; and from इंगाल *iṅgāla* are contracted the Eng. *coal* and the Ang.-Sax. *col*.[3]

100. In Ἑλενη which is a modification of Sans. अनल *anala*, 'fire,' अलात *alāta*, 'fire-brand,' and अरणि *araṇi*, 'a piece of wood from which fire is produced by friction,' I see an example of the aspiration of the initial vowel,

---

[1] The radical κροαομαι is a contraction of κροφαομαι, answering to Sans. श्रावयामहे *śrāvayāmahē*.

[2] Similarly arises the letter *p* in Sanskrit in causal forms. The causal augments வி *vi*, பி *pi* and து *tu* in Tamil and the allied augments చు *cu*, పు *pu*, and సు *su*, in Telugu and Kanarese, are derived from the Sans. य *y*.

[3] Compare Tam. கரி *kari*, 'coal.' The words referring to the black colour, such as Sans. काल *kāla*, Gr. κελαινος, Sans. कलुष *kaluṣa* and कल्मष *kalmaṣa* and कल्माष *kalmāṣa*, 'sin and dirt,' and कश्मल *kaśmala*, मल *mala* and Gr. μελας and Sans. मलिन *malina* which are contracted from कश्मल *kaśmala*, are traceable to the same source. The root κμελας suggested by Buttmann is unnecessary.

an orthographical usage extensively prevailing in Greek and other languages. By eliminating this extraneous element, we have the simple form of the word Ελενη which can be easily connected with Gr. ελανη, 'a torch,' and which is very much allied to Sans. अलात *alāta*, 'firebrand.' In the word there is an allusion to fire; but it is not any kind of fire to which the word refers. From 'Ελενη's parentage we can easily suppose that she represents a flaming torch. For she is the daughter of Τυνδαρεος, Tyndareus, and Leda, the first of which names I would connect with Gr. τινθος and τινθαλιος, 'boiling hot,' Lat. *cinis* (*eris*), 'ashes,' Gr. σπινθηρ and Lat. *scintilla*, 'a spark,' in the last two of which the letters *sp* and *sk* stand in the place of an original *s* which represents the initial *t* of Τυνδαρεος, and also with the Eng. *tind* and *tinder*, Ang.-Sax. *tender* and the allied words, and take it to mean tinder, as the word Ληδα has already been supposed to mean thin cloth. The story of 'Ελενη's birth from Τυνδαρεος and Ληδα refers to the burning firebrand lighted by the fire produced from tinder and flint. According to some she was the daughter of Nemises by Jupiter, and Leda was only her nurse. Even in this version of the story we find an explanation from the fact that a thin cloth itself may serve the purpose of tinder, and in this case, the light produced on the substance may be held as the offspring of Heaven, that is, Jupiter. After the restitution of 'Ελενη, which event took place on the destruction of Troy and the Trojan heroes, she was with Menelaus, and, after his death, married several others. She is said by some to have been transported to Leuce, the land of love, after her death, and there married Achilles; and this part of the story contains a belief that, when put out, the light of fire goes to the sun in whom it is absorbed, a belief like that prevailing among the Hindus, viz., that when the sun rises the light of fire enters him and when he sets in the evening his light is preserved in fire.[1] Having thus established the philological alliance of Ἑλενη and Ελανη by mythological facts, I shall quote now a few instances in which an extraneous aspirate sound is added to the initial vowel of a word. Compare the following :—

Ἑλλας, a city of Thessaly, and also a province of which it was the capital.

Ἑλλην, son of Deucalion whose descendants were called the Ἑλληνες, a word first applied to the inhabitants of the Thessalian Hellas and afterwards used to include all the Greeks as opposed to the Barbaroi. Ἑλλην had three sons named Aeolus, Dorus and Xuthus, the last of whom was the father of Ion. From Aeolus, Dorus and Ion are supposed to have descended the three nations who are called respectively the Aeolians, the Dorians and the Ionians, and are collectively included in the term Greek.

Ἑλλη, daughter of Athamas and Nephele (the clouds and sky) and sister of Phrixus. Being afraid of the cruel treatment of her mother-in-law, Ino, she left her father's house accompanied by her brother Phrixus; or some say, she was drawn away by a golden ram, which Neptune had given her mother, and feeling giddy she fell in the sea and

---

[1] अग्निंवावादित्यस्सायंप्रविशति। तस्मादग्निर्दूरान्नक्तंददृशे। उभेहितेजसीसंपद्येते। उद्यंतंवावादित्यमग्निरनुसमारोहति। तस्माद्धूमएवाग्नेर्दिवाददृशे ॥ Tait. Brah. II. 1, 12-13.

Agnimvāvādityassāyampravisati | tasmādagnirdurānnaktamdadṛśē | ubhēhitējasīsampadyatē | udyantamvāvāditya magniranusamārōha ti | tasmāddhūmaēvāgnērdivādadṛśe.

'In the evening the sun enters fire, therefore fire is seen at a distance in the night. There are indeed two lights. Fire ascends the rising sun, and, therefore, only the smoke of fire is seen in the day time.

was drowned. I see in the name a reference to the sunlit clouds of the morning and connect the name with the Sans. इला *ilā* and Gr. Ιλος, which I have already derived from द्यौस् *dyaus*, 'sky,' and the radical meaning of which therefore must be 'sky' or 'bright.' In the word 'Ελλη, therefore, even the initial vowel is an extraneous addition, and the pure vowel so added was afterwards aspirated.[1]

'Εστια, Ion. 'Ιστιη, the Roman Vesta, daughter of Κρονος and 'Ρεα and the guardian of the hearth and home, connected with अतस *atasa*, 'fire,' and अश्मंतम् *aśmantam*, 'hearth,' and the Arab. آتش *ātiṣ* and Heb. אֵשׁ *eṣ*, (p. 163, Note 1.)

'Ηρα, Ion. 'Ηρη, the Lat. *Juno*, queen of the Gods and sister and wife of Zeus. The word is identical with the Gr. ερα and Sans. इरा *irā*, 'earth.' (p. 35).

'Εσπερος, son of Iapetos, brother to Atlas. He came to Italy, and the country was called 'Εσπερια after him. The word has been lower down connected with Sans. अक्षर *akṣara*, 'heaven.'

'Εκτωρ, 'son of king Priam and Hecuba,' which word has been lower down traced to Sans. अक्षर *akṣara*, 'heaven.'

'Ερση, daughter of Cecrops, king of Athens, beloved by Mercury. The word may be connected with αργος, 'brightness.'

'Εκατη, daughter of Perses and Asteria. She is a personification of the starry sky, and the name may be connected with आकाश *ākāśa*, 'sky.'

Hertha or Herta, a goddess among the Germans, who is supposed to be the same as the Earth.

---

[1] Vide pp. 60 and 61.

The names 'Ελλας, 'Ελλην and 'Ελλη, are identical with 'Ελενη in origin, the double λ in them being accidental.

हसंती *hasantī* or हसनी *hasanī*, 'fire vessel,' which can be traced to a form असन्त *asanta* and through it to अतस *atasa* and is allied to Gr. Ἑστια, Lat. *Vesta* and to the following.

Eng. *hearth*, Germ. *herd* and the allied words which are akin to Lat. *ardeo*, 'to burn,' and in which also the initial *h* is extraneous.

101. From अहस् *ahas* may be derived also Gr. *αγαθος*, 'good,' Sans. सत् *sat*,[1] साधु *sādhu*, 'good,' 'eminent,' चटु *caṭu* and चाटु *cāṭu*, 'agreeable,' as applied to a speech, Eng. *good*, Ang.-Sax. *god*; and perhaps the very word God, on account of his goodness; चारु *cāru*, 'beautiful,' कल *kala*, कल्य *kalya*, 'good' and 'auspicious,' Gr. *καλος*, 'beautiful,' and कल्याण *kalyāṇa*, 'good,' which is a modification of कल्य *kalya*, as the Gr. *καλλονη* is of *καλλος*.

102. Sans. अप्सरस् *apsaras*, meaning 'celestial damsel,' is used in the Vedas in the sense of water-nymph and seems to be traceable to अतस *atasa*, or अतर *atara*, in which त *t* being doubled becomes प्स *ps* as in Gr. *κορυπτω* for *κορυττω*, 'to butt with the head,' from *κορυσ* (*θος*), 'head,' and *πιπτω* for *πιττω*, Sans. पत् *pat*, 'to fall.' The word अपसरस् *apsaras* resembles in its derivation Gr. Νηρεις, a daughter of Νηρευς, a sea-god, who ruled under Ποσειδων.

In Sans. अक्षर *akṣara* a change takes place. Just as the doubled त *t* of अतस *atasa* is replaced by प्स *ps* in अप्सरस् *apsaras*, so is it replaced by क्ष *ks*, and अक्षर *akṣara*

---

[1] This is quite different from the सत् *sat*, 'being' properly असत् *asat*, the pres. part. adj. from अस् *as*, 'to be,' answering to Gr. *εων* or *ων* (for *εσων*) and Lat. *ent* and *sent* (for es*ent*.)

means 'sky,' 'water,' 'supreme being,' 'speech,' 'a syllable,' &c.

103. With अक्षर *akṣara,* which has been derived above, I would connect the Gr. 'Εσπερος and Lat. *vesper,* in which the letters *k* and *s* of अक्षर *akṣara* are transposed and *k* changed into *p* (vide p. 164). In the Latin and Greek words the initial *h* and *v* are extraneous additions as in Lat. *Vesta,* Gr. 'Εστια, which have been derived from Sans. अतस *atasa.* 'Εσπερος was the son of Japetus, brother to Atlas. The peninsula of Italy was called 'Εσπερια from him. 'Εσπερος and 'Εσπερα mean 'evening' and also the 'west.' The Lat. *vesper* similarly refers to evening and the west. *Vesperus* is applied to the planet Venus when it shines in the west, and *Vespera,* to evening.

104. From अहर् *ahar,* meaning 'bright,' may be derived a form अगर् *agar* which, being transposed, produces the words αργος, 'bright,' αργης, 'white,' αργυρος, 'the white metal, that is, 'silver,' = αργ + υρος, in which υρος is a termination indicating possession, corresponding to Sans. उर् *ura,* as in दंतुर *dantura,* 'having teeth,' that is 'having protuberant teeth.' Αργυρος answers to Sans. रजतम् *rajatam* and Lat. *argentem,* of which the latter seems to have been formed from *argos,* 'brightness,' and *ent-um* (= Sans. वंत् *vant* + अम् *am,* वंत् *vant* being a suffix indicating possession); अर्चिस् *arcis,* 'brightness,' 'flame,' अर्क *arka,* 'sun,' 'the plant asclepias,' अर्ह् *arh,* 'to be fit,' अर्च् *arc,* 'to worship,' अर्घ *argha,* 'price,' 'preciousness,' may be referred to the same source αργος.

105. The Sans. आर्य *ārya,* 'respectable,' अर्य *arya,* 'lord,' 'a Vaiśya,' and the Gr. αρειος or αρηιος, are to be connected with the above words, the final consonants of which *k*, *c*, *h*, &c., are softened into *y* in Sans. आर्य *ārya* and अर्य *arya*. In the Gr. *αρειος*, there seems to be a formal convergence of two different words, one derived from Sans. आर्य *ārya*, 'good' and 'respectable,' in which the य *y* of आर्य *ārya* is elided, and the other, meaning 'martial,' 'brave,' and derived from Sans. वृष *vṛṣa*, 'brave,' 'manly,' and allied to Lat. *mars*, *maritus*, 'husband,' *mareo*, 'to marry,' and the Gr. Αρης, *αρσην* and *αρρην*, Ion. *ερσην*, 'male,' opposed to *θηλυς*, just as Sans. पुरुष *puruṣa* is opposed to स्त्री *strī*.[1]

The word *αριστος* seems to be the superl. degree of the adjective अर्य *arya* which loses its final consonant before the suffix *ιστος*. In the corresponding Sanskrit word अरिष्ट *ariṣṭa*,[2] the original suffix इष्ट *iṣṭa* is preserved

[1] Sans. पुरुष *puruṣa* is an epenthetical modification of वृष *vṛṣa*; and स्त्री *strī* and Gr. *θηλυς* seem to be allied.

[2] Just as many words have passed from one meaning to the opposite one (*e. g.* शिति *śiti*, 'white' and 'black,' *q. v.*) so has the word come to mean also what is not good, that is, evil. The word was then wrongly analyzed into अ *a* + रिष्ट *riṣṭa*, अ *a* being supposed as a negative particle; and thus came into existence a new word as रिष्ट *riṣṭa* to which were also attached the opposite meanings, 'good' and 'evil.' Αριστερος, 'left,'=*αριστοτερος*, from *αριστος*, 'evil.'

The Gr. *αριστον* meaning 'morning meal,' may either be connected directly with the above word, or with *ηως* and *εως*, 'dawn,' and *ηρι* which appears to be the dat. case of *ηρ*, an obsolete word allied to the Ang.-Sax. *ære* and Eng. *ere* and *early*, and traceable to Sans. अहस् *ahas*, 'day,' and Gr. *ασava*, 'brightness.'

Αρειων and *αριστος* are substituted for the comp. and superl. degrees of *αγαθος*, which ought to be respectively *αγαθιων* and *αγαθιστος* in analogy of साधीयस् *sādhīyas* and साधिष्ठ *sādhiṣṭha* (vide p. 1).

instead of इष्ठ *istha* found in the superlative forms of other adjectives. If αριστος is to be connected with Sans अरिष्ट *arista*, then it follows that answering to αρειων which is the comparative degree of αρειος, 'good,' there must have existed in Sanskrit a comparative of आर्य *ārya* as अरीयस् *arīyas*.

106. Here I have to mention the word Αριαδνη which I have explained under the suf. δνος (p. 131). It answers to Sans. अर्हतरी *arhatarī* and means radically 'very fit.' I have already referred to her parentage; and the names of her father and mother are allied to the Sans. वृष *vrṣa* meaning 'ox' and have been mentioned in the *Vrṣa Group*, her father's name, Minos, being allied to Sans. महिष *mahiṣa* (properly मेष *mēṣa* and मिस *misa*, *h* being a mere orthographical outgrowth), मैनाक *maināka* and मेनाः *mēnā*, and her mother's name, Pasiphæ, to वृषभ *vrṣabha*. Minos was the son of Zeus and Europa, and as the word Europa is connected with Sans. वृषभ *vrṣabha*, उरभ्र *urabhra*, and Gr. ορευς, and radically means 'a cow,' the legend simply means that a bull was born to Zeus by Europa, and his son married Pasiphæ, a cow, in his turn; and this legendary interpretation is sufficiently borne out by the continuation of the myth, that, by the curse of Ουρανος or Ποσειδων, Pasiphæ fell in love with a bull and brought forth Minotauros who was partly of bovine and human forms.[1] Minos I., the grand-father, was the wise

---

[1] Indra, becoming मेना *mēnā*, fell in love with मेना *mēnā* who was the daughter of वृषणश्व *Vrṣaṇaśva*. This is mentioned in the following passage of the Rig Veda; मेनाभवो वृषणश्वस्य *Mēnābhavō vrṣaṇaśvasya*. (I. 51, 13),—'Thou hast become Mēnā to Vrṣaṇaśva, that is, 'thou hast been living with Vrṣaṇaśva just as Mēnā, his daughter was. The Commentator Sāyana quotes passages from the Śāṭyāyana and Tāṇḍya Brāhmaṇās, which say that

legislator in every city of Greece and was made the supreme and absolute judge in the infernal regions. His equity and justice, the radical connection of his name with Sans. वृष *vṛṣa*, and the fact of his being the king of Creta, the Grecian original forms of which are Κρητα and Κρητη, remind us of the Hindu *Kṛta Yuga*, the first of the four great periods of the world, in which *Vṛṣa*, the bull of Virtue, stood with four legs and reigned supreme (vide the *Vṛṣa Group*). In Κρητη I see a trace of κριτις, 'choice,' or the act of chosing, that is, the human volition, or of Sans. कृत *kṛta* or कृति *kṛti*, 'action;' and the legendary government of Κρητη by Minos and the standing of Virtue of a bovine form on four legs must refer to the virtuous disposition of the people in a good age. The Greek Κρητα in its secondary meaning refers to the locality of the virtuous action and the Sans. कृत *kṛta*, to the age.

Indra was living with Vṛṣaṇaśva and when Mēnā attained her age, Indra married her. I am sure that the above connection of Indra and Mēnā is referred to in the following passage of the Taittirīya Āraṇyaka: वृषणश्वस्यमेने। गौरावस्कंदिन् ॥ *Vṛṣaṇaśvasyamēnē gaurāvaskandin.* There is no doubt that the words वृषणश्व *Vṛṣaṇaśva* and मेना *Mēnā* are the same words used in the Rig Vedic passage quoted. I therefore translate the above passage thus: O bull (गौस् *gaus*) that has covered (अवस्कंदिन् *avaskandin*, 'having covered,' voc. sing. qualifying गौस् *gaus*), and O Mēnā (daughter) of Vṛṣaṇaśva. I do not quote here the interpretations of the Commentators as they will appear in the *Vṛṣa* Group in Part II, to which I refer the readers. The word वृषणश्व *Vṛṣaṇaśva* is formed from वृषन् *vṛṣan* and अश्व *aśva*, 'cow' and 'horse,' respectively and answers to Minotauros in formation and meaning. I have to mention in support of the alliance of वृष *Vṛṣa*, मेना *Mēnā* and *Minos* another legend, that Himavān, the personification of the Mount Himalayas, who married Mēnā, assumed the form of a calf to suckle at the udder of the Goddess of earth in her bovine form.

Αρεαδνη is therefore the offspring of Virtue personified as a bull and is the type of merit or fitness created by the possession of virtue, and a suitable wife of Thesus who is a great hero, representing the sun. But she was at last forsaken and left in the island of Naxos and her fate must be a symbol of neglected merit.

The Vedic name अर्यमन् *aryaman* is traceable to अर्य *arya* and formed by the addition of the suffix मन् *man* to अर्य *arya*. The radical meaning of the word must, therefore, be, 'having the quality of goodness,' or 'very good.' The next meaning is 'friendly' and 'liberal,' in which it is used in the Vedas, besides being the proper name of a deity who is so called on account of his goodness. He is generally invoked with Mitra and Varuṇa in the Rig Veda and in the Yajur Veda he is separately mentioned, and rice cakes (*caru*) are to be offered to him.

अर्यम्णेचरुंनिर्वपेत्सुवर्गकामोसौवाआदित्योर्यमार्यमणमेव स्वेनंभागधेयेनोपधावतिसएवैनंसुवर्गंलोकंगमयत्यर्यम्णेचरुंनिर्वपेद्यःकामयेतदानंकामामेप्रजास्युरित्यसौवाआदित्योर्यमायःखलुवैददातिसोर्यमार्यमणमेवस्वेनंभागधेयेनोपधावति ॥

Aryamṇēcarumnirvapētsuvargakāmōsauvā ādityōryamāryamaṇamēvasvēnabhāgadhēyēnōpadhāvatisa ēvainaṁ suvargaṁ lōkamgamayatyaryamṇēcarumnirvapēdyaḥkāmayētadānakāmāmēprajāsyurityasauva ādityōryamāyaḥkhaluvaidadatisōryamāryamaṇamēvasvēnabhāgadhēyēnōpadhāvati.

The above passage shows that the radical idea of goodness which was attached to अर्यमन् *aryaman* was not lost sight of even when the word was monopolized as a proper name; from proper name it resumes its adjectival character with a slight change in the meaning; for the above passage says that he who gives is *Aryaman* (*sc.* a liberal man) यःखलुवैददातिसोर्यमा *Yahkhaluvaidadātisōryamā.* Even in the Rig Veda he is represented as particularly good as can be seen in the following passage:—

त्वमर्यमाभवसियत्कनीनां नामस्वधावन्गुह्यंबिभर्षि ।

Tvamaryamābhavasiyatkanīnaṁ nāmasvadhāvanguhyambibharṣi.

'Thou art charitable, O giver of food, as thou protectest the secret name of virgin.' Rig Veda V. 3, 2.

But Sāyana takes the word अर्यमन् *aryaman* to mean नियंता *niyaṁtā,* that is 'a restrainer,' and interprets the passage in a different way. But the translation of the passage I have given is in accordance with the meaning given by Haradatta in his commentary on the Taittirīya Mantra Praśna in which also the above passage occurs with slight modification.

107. To the same source *αρyος* may be traced Sans. रजस् *rajas,* 'brightness,'[1] रजनी *rajanī,* 'night,' because of the twilight with which it begins and the light of the moon, रंज् *rañj,* 'to be bright with colours,' रश्मि *raśmi,* 'rays,' राजन् *rājan,* 'king,' and the corresponding Latin and Greek *rex* and *αρχων,* and राज् *rāj,* 'to shine.' The Lat. *rex* is a shortened form of राजन् *rājan* and answers to राट् *rāṭ* (राज् *rāj*). राजन् *rājan* is a derivative noun of agency derived from राज् *rāj,* 'to shine,' by the suffix अन् *an* which answers to the suffix *ον* (*οντ*) of the corresponding

[1] It means also 'region of clouds,' 'atmosphere,' 'air,' 'firmament,' 'any sphere' or 'world' as the heaven and earth, 'dust,' &c.

Greek word *αρχων* (*αρχοντες*). The difference between the declensions of राजन् *rājan*[1] and *αρχων* is exactly like that between अथर्वन् *atharvan* and *θεραπων*, of which the declension of the former is more radical and that of the latter, secondary; and the existence of such a feminine form as *θαραπαινι* leads us to think that in Greek *θαραπων* was originally declined as *θεραπονος*. Even when we naturally have the *οντ* declension, there arises along with it also the *ον* declension as in *πεσσων*, (Sans. पचन् *pacan*), which is modified as *πεπων*. The former *πεσσων* is declined as *πεσσοντος* and the latter *πεπων* as *πεπονος*.

108. With रजस् *rajas* may be connected रजि *raji*, राका *rākā* and राहु *rāhu*. रजि *Raji* is the name of a son of आयुस् *Āyus* and he had five hundred sons who were known for their bravery. In a war which occurred between the Rākṣasas and the Deities he sided with the latter and defeated their enemies and received in return for the service he rendered the sovereignty of Heaven instead of Indra. The word occurs in the Rig Veda where it is taken to mean a damsel betrothed to a person called Pîṭhīnas and in another place, to mean either heaven and earth, or the sun and the moon. Either of the latter meanings is possible

---

[1] The existence of a feminine form as *regina*, 'a queen,' and an abstract form as *regnum* which may be analyzed thus, *regina* = *regin* + *a*, in analogy of Sans. राज्ञी *rājñī*, 'a queen' = राजन् *rājan* + ई *ī*, and *regnum* = *regin* + *um* in analogy of *claustrum* = *clauster* + *um*, seems to warrant the supposition in Latin of a form like *regin* corresponding to Sans. राजन् *rājan*. It looks also possible that the genitive plural of *rex*, *regerum* may be owing to the influence of a form *reginum* = *regin* + *um*, answering to Sans. राज्ञाम् *rājñām* = राजन् *rājan* + आम् *ām*, आम् *ām* being the gen. suf. answering to the Gr. *ων* and Lat. *um*. These three suffixes are contractions of साम् *sām*, नाम् *nām* and *rum*, derived

as the word रजि *raji* is a contraction of रजस् *rajas* which means among other things 'any world,' 'heaven and earth.' राका *Rākā* is a Vedic deity representing the full-moon day, and the name must certainly refer to the radical meaning of the word 'brightness.'[1]

109. राहु *Rāhu* is the personification of the eclipse of the moon. Notwithstanding the radical idea of brightness the word refers to the dimness of the part of the solar and lunar discs which are eclipsed. When ambrosia which was obtained by the Gods and Rākṣasas by churning the milky ocean, was to be divided only among the deities to the exclusion of the Rākṣasas, Rāhu, who was a Rākṣasa, assumed the form of a deity and sat among the deities. The sun and moon detected him and reported his presence to Viṣṇu who struck off his head with his chakra. But as he had already tasted ambrosia, he became immortal, and, incensed at the injury done to him by the sun and the moon, he swore vengeance on them and began to eclipse them every year. The story reminds one of the Teutonic god Logi who was a fire-god and resembled Hephaistos in the ugliness of his person, for he was limping, and his deformed figure provoked the laughter of the

---

from स्वम् *svam* (p. 172). The former are added to consonantal stems and the latter to vowel stems. But the suf. *rum* occurs in the consonantal stems also. But Greek which often elides unsteady consonants between vowels has universally cut off the initial स् *s* of साम् *sām* and has changed the remaining आम् *ām* into *ων*, and this suffix is used in all stems, vowel and consonantal.

[1] सिनीवाली *sinīvālī*, which is the name of the new moon with a visible digit of the moon, seems to have been originally किनीवरी *kinīvarī*, which form may be a modification of कनीवरी *kanīvarī*, from कन् *kan*, 'to shine,' and *vara*, suf.

celestials. He assumed the form of a wolf and swallowed the moon. (Cox's *Introd. to Myth. and Folklore*, p. 172.)

110. The word राक्षस *rākṣasa* and रक्षस् *rakṣas* are to be derived from रजस् *rajas* of which the central ज *ja*, originally ग *ga*, is replaced by क्ष *kṣ*. They meant originally 'bright,' 'strong' and 'powerful,' and the transition from the last meaning to 'wicked' and 'mischievous,' which has taken place in the words being the same as that which has taken place in the word असुर *asura*. In the following passage the word रक्षस् *rakṣas* is used in the sense of strength or of injury or wickedness :—

त्वेषासोअग्नेरमवंतोअर्चयोभीमासोनप्रतीतये ।

Tvēṣāsōagnēramavantō arcayōbhīmāsōnapratītayē

रक्षस्विनस्सदमिद्यातुमावंतोविश्वंसमत्रिणंदह ॥ I. 36. 20.

Rakṣasvinassadamidyātumāvatō viśvaṁsamatriṇaṁdaha.

'The effulgent, strong and formidable rays of Agni are not to be approached. O Agni, always burn the strong or injurious Rākṣasas and all enemies.'

111. The Sans. घस्र *ghasra*, 'day,' is a corruption of अहस् *ahas* which, taking the suffix र *ra*, becomes अहस्र *ahasra*, and घस्र *ghasra* by the change of ह *h* into घ *gh*. All the names of the day have been derived in this Group ; and one of these names, viz., वासर *vāsara* which I have taken as a metathetical modification of the Gr. *σημερον* and *σαμερον*, 'day,' may otherwise be derived from a form असर् *asar* of अतस *atasa* of which अहस् *ahas* is a modification. (p. 180.)

112. Gr. Αιγευς (Ægeus) who was the father of Theseus by *Αιθρα*, represents अहस् *ahas*, 'day,' and the name is allied to अहस् *ahas* and आकाश *ākāśa*, from which can be derived also the Gr. Αχαιος, 'an Achaian.'

113. I have shown that the word अगस्त्य *Agastya* is formed from अगस् *agas*, 'brightness,' or आकाश *ākāśa*, 'sky or brightness,' by the addition of the suffix य *y*, the change of ह *h* into ग *g* and the euphonic addition of the consonant त *t* between स *s* and य *y*. Suppose we add the same termination य *y* to काश *kāśa* contracted from आकाश *ākāśa*, we shall then have काश्य *kāśya* which may be modified as कश्प *kaśpa* by the change of य *y* into प *p*, a process often taking place in Sanskrit; e. g., दापयति *dāpayati*, दाययति *dāyayati*, = दा *dā* + अय् *ay* + अ *a* + ति *ti*, wherein दा *dā*, is the root meaning 'to give,' and अय् *ay*, causal termination corresponding to ι, α, ε, αζ, &c., in Greek. Compare वनीपक *vanīpaka*, वनीयक *vanīyaka*, properly वनायक *vanāyaka*, वन् *van*, 'to want,' वनाया *vanāyā*, 'desire,' 'thought;' मपुष्टक *mapuṣṭaka*, another form of मयुष्टक *mayuṣṭaka*, a kind of mustard : and पौतवम् *pautavam*, another form of यौतव *yautava*, a measure in general. कश्प *kaśpa* is modified as कश्यप *Kaśyapa*, the name given to a Prajāpati, creator, who in the later mythology of the Hindus was the son of Marīci and the husband of the thirteen daughters of Dakṣa, and who was the ancestor of all the deities, giants and other beings and animals. In him we see the personification of the Gr. Κοσμος, 'order or beauty,' with which word कश्यप *Kaśyapa* is closely connected, the *m* of Κοσμος being a modification of *p* in कश्यप *Kaśyapa*. With कश्यप *Kaśyapa* I would connect the Sans. कशिपु *kaśipu*, 'food and clothing,' which meaning must be a secondary one, the primary one being order, beauty, harmony or good living.

114. From अतस् *atas* we may go to आपस् *āpas*, 'water,' and अप् *ap*, a contracted form of it. आपस् *āpas* is mentioned in the Unādi Sūtra and occurs rarely in the classical

Sanskrit, as in आपोशनम् *āpōśanam* = आपस् *āpas* + अशनम् *aśanam*, 'drinking of water.' But the contracted form अप् *ap* of which the nominative plural is आपस् *āpas* and which changes *p* into *t* before the casal terminations beginning with भ *bh* as in अद्भिस् *adbhis*, अद्भ्यस् *adbhyas*, is more frequently used; and the fact of this change of प *p* into त *t* is an evidence in favor of the above conjecture that आपस् *āpas* proceeds from अतस् *atas*. It may, otherwise, be derived from अभ्र *abhra* as अंभस् *ambhas* and अंबु *ambu* have already been derived. The Latin word *ebrius*, 'drunk,' *ebriosus*, 'given to drinking,' and their derivatives, may be traced to Sans. अपस् *apas* or अभ्र *abhra*. Compare अभ्रिय *abhriya*, 'what springs from the clouds,' and अभ्रि *abhri*, 'a spoon for drawing water from ships.' The Gr. *νηφω*,[1] 'not to drink wine,' and *νηφαλιος*, 'drinking no wine,' may be analyzed respectively as *νη* + *αφω* and *νη* + *αφαλιος*. Αφαλιος is an adjective from *αφαλον* which answers to Sans. अंभस् *ambhas* or आपस् *āpas*, 'water,' and represents the final स *s* of the last two words by λ; and this conjecture is warranted by the existence of a verb as *αφυσσω*, 'to draw liquids,' 'to drink,' in which the final σ of the root *αφυσ*, answering to that of Sans. अंभस् *ambhas*, or आपस् *āpas*, 'water,' is doubled as in *κηρυσσω* of which the radical part is *κηρυς*, an enlarged form of Sans. कृत् *kṛt*, 'to speak,' 'to proclaim.'

115. From आपस् *āpas* are to be derived अपस् *apas*, Lat. *opus*, and Gr. *οπωρα* and *οπλον*,[2] अप्नस् *apnas*, 'possession,' 'property,' अप्त *apta*, 'a sacrificial act,' अप्तु *aptu*, soma,' अप्तुर् *aptur*, 'water,' and अप्न *apna*, 'work.' In

[1] Νηφων declined as *νηφονος* bears the same relation to *νηφω* as *πεπων* (*πεπονος*) bears to *πεσσω*. [2] Vide p. 169.

अप्नवान *apnavāna,* 'arm,' so called because it works, the suffix वन् *van* is changed into वान *vāna* as मन् *man* is changed into मान *māna,* as in एधमान *ēdhamāna,* the pres. part. adj. of एध् *ēdh,* 'to grow,' (vide p. 112). अप्नवान *apnavāna* means also 'having progeny.'

116. अतस् *atas* is modified as अतर् *atara* and then अतल *atala,* meaning 'a hell beneath the earth,' or one of the seven nether worlds, which lie immediately under the earth. The Greek story of Atlas bearing up the pillar of the high heaven may be explained by reference to the word अतल *atala,* 'air,' or 'empty space,' which lies under the earth. The right form of the word seems to be Ατα-λος shortened into Ατλος and not Ατλας (gen. Ατλαντος), which latter form was given to the word owing to a wrong derivation assigned to it from τλαω, 'to bear up,' of which it was supposed to be a pres. part. adj. form, the initial A having been treated as a euphonic addition.

117. From अतर् *atara* we can derive अद्रि *adri*[1] used in several meanings of which 'heaven' or 'sky' is the first. It is used in the senses of 'the sun,' 'cloud,' 'thunderbolt,' from which meaning the word passes to those of 'a mountain' and 'a tree.' From अद्रि *adri* may be derived द्रु *dru,* द्रुम *druma,* तरु *taru,* Gr. δενδρον, 'a tree,' दारु *dāru,*

---

[1] अद्रिश्शैलद्रुमार्के (ना) *Adriśśailadrumārkē (nā).*—Mēdini.

Just as अद्रि *adri,* the original meaning of which is 'heaven' or 'sky,' comes to mean 'clouds,' and then 'mountains' and 'stones,' so does उपर *upara* which, originally means 'heaven,' take the meanings of 'cloud,' 'mountain' and 'stone,' in the last three of which it is changed into उपल *upala,* sometimes. अद्रिः ग्रावा . . . उपरः उपलः इति त्रिंशन्मेघनामानि ॥ *adriḥ grāvā . . . . uparaḥ, upalaḥ iti trimśanmēghanāmānī.*—Nirukta, Nighaṇṭu, I. 10.

'a piece of wood,' Gr. δορυ, 'the stem of a tree,' दर्वी *darvī*, 'ladle,' Gr. δρυς, 'the oak tree.' अद्रि *adri* may be modified as वज्र *vajra* by the change of द *d* into ज *j* and the euphonic addition of व *v* to the beginning of the word, while अशनि *aśani*, another word meaning 'thunderbolt,' may be directly referred to अतस *atasa*. From अद्रि *adri* meaning 'high,' may be derived Sans. अग्र *agra*, 'top,' Gr. ακρα, 'a peak,' ακτη, 'a mound.' To अग्र *agra* are allied Gr. ακη and Lat. *acies*, 'a point,' 'edge,' Gr. ακις, 'a point, barb,' ακωκη, 'a point,' Sans. अंकुश *aṅkuśa*, 'a goad,' Gr. ακων (οντος,), 'a javelin,' from which Sans. कुंत *kunta* is contracted, ακονη, 'a whetstone,' of which Sans. शाण *śāṇa*, Lat. *cos* and *cautes* are modifications; and ακμη, 'point,' αιχμι, 'the point of a spear,' in which κ is aspirated; and αιμος, 'a thorn,' in which the κ is elided. अग्र *agra* yields, further, अंकुर *aṅkura* and अंकूर *ankūra*,[1] 'a bud,' because it is pointed, अञ्चल *añcala*, 'tip,' 'border,' and अश्रि *aśri*, 'verge,' अग्रु *agru*, अंगुल *aṅgula*, अंगुलि *aṅguli*, 'fingers,' Lat. *ungula*, 'hoof,' *unguis*, 'nail,' Sans. अंह्रि *aṁhri* and अंघ्रि *aṅghri*, 'leg.' अंगुष्ठ *aṅguṣṭha*[2] which means 'the biggest finger or toe,' is only a modification of अंगुर *aṅgura* of which the final र *r* is changed into ष्ठ *ṣṭh* as in the following :—

गंभीर *gambhīra*,	गंभिष्ठ *gambhiṣṭha*, 'deep.'
गौर *gaura*, 'red,'	कुष्ठ *kuṣṭha*, 'a disease which changes the colour of the skin into red.'

---

[1] अंकुरोंकूरएवच *aṅkurōṅkūraēvaca*,—Dvirūpakōśa.

[2] अंगुष्ठ *aṅguṣṭha* is modified in Marāthi as गोट *goṭa* and then as बोट *boṭa*, 'a finger,' 'a toe.'

आम्र *āmra*, 'sour or mango.'

अम्बष्ठा *ambaṣṭhā*,[1] several plants, such as Clypea Hernandifolia, Oxalis, Cornu-cu-lata, and others which are so called perhaps on account of sour taste.

अंगुर *aṅgura* is changed into अंगर *aṅgura*, then अनगर *anagara* by the insertion of अ *a* between the anusvāra and ग *g*. While अनगर *anagara* is shortened into *ονυξ* (*κος*) in Greek by the elision of the latter part, it is shortened into नख *nakha* and नखर *nakhara*, 'nails,' by the elision of the former part. (Compare अंभस् *ambhas* which becomes अनभस् *anabhas* and then नभस् *nabhas*.) खुर *khura*, 'hoof,' is a further contraction of नखर *nakhara* and is allied to Gr. *Χηλη*.

118. From अद्रि *adri*, 'tree,' can be derived अजिर *ajira*, 'a field,' originally 'a field of trees,' Lat. *ager*, 'a field of trees,' Gr. *αγορα*,[2] 'an assembly,' 'a market-place,' in all of which there is a regular transition of meanings, the original idea being that of tree; secondly, that of a field of trees; thirdly, a habitable ground, and lastly, the inhabitants of a place assembled or any assembly of people. In Gr. *αγων* which is a contraction of *αγορα*, the *r* of *αγορα* is changed into *ν* as in the allied Sans. अंगण *aṅgaṇa* and अंगन *aṅgana*, 'courtyard.' Sans. अगार *agāra*, 'a house,' comes from Gr. *αγορα*. From *αγορα* is derived the root *αγειρω* which is a shortened form of *αγορεω* contracted into *αγορyo* and then modified as *αγειρω* by the elision of *y* and the conversion of the preceding short vowel

---

[1] अंबष्ठ *ambaṣṭha* becomes अंबट *ambaṭa*, meaning 'sour.'

[2] From *αγορα* are to be derived the Tam. அங்காடி *aṅgāḍi*, Mal. അങ്ങാടി *aṅṅāḍi* and Kan. and Tel. ಅಂಗಡಿ *aṅgaḍi*, 'shop.'

o into *ει* the long.[1] Αγορα is shortened into *αγρος* and means 'a country or a rural habitation,' in contrast to a town. Αγορα is modified as *αγγορα* (*ανγορα*),[2] and this form *ανγορα* receiving an epenthetic *α* between *ν* and *γ* becomes *αναγαρα* from which Sans. नगर *nagara*, 'town,' has originated. These evolutions and contractions are very like those that have taken place in the words नभस् *nabhas* and नखर *nakhara* (pp. 136 and 204).

119. Akin to अद्रि *adri* is Sans. अत्रि *Atri*, the name of the author of several hymns of the Rig Veda. The moon is called अत्रिसुत *Atrisuta*, 'son of अत्रि *Atri*,' and is supposed to have sprung from the eye of the sage. But I should think that in this connection अत्रि *Atri* is only a personification of the sky or Heaven. There is no doubt about the alliance of this word to the Gr. Ατρευς. According to the Greek theogony Ατρευς was the son of Pelops and Hippodamia and was the husband of Aerope by whom he had two sons, Menelaus and Agamemnon. These are called Ατρειδαι, just as the descendants of अत्रि *Atri* are called आत्रेय *Atrēya*. Regarding the identity of the formations of these two words compare Ἱπποταδης, Sans. आश्वपतेयस् *Aśvapatēyas* and Ναιας and नादेयस् *Nādēyas* mentioned in pp. 121-22.

120. I may next proceed to Sans. अश्मन् *aśman*, 'stone,' which comes from आत्मन् *ātman* by the change of त *t* into स *s* and then into श *ś*. The transition of the meaning from the 'sky' to a 'stone' is the same as has occurred in many other words originally 'sky' and then applied to a 'mountain,' because, being high, it is connected with the sky, and at last to 'a stone.' Compare उपर *upara*,

---

[1] Vide p. 104.

[2] Vide the Note, p. xii, Table of Alphabets.

उपल *upala* which are derived from उपर् *upara*, 'sky,' and अद्रि *adri*. The Gr. ακμων, 'anvil,' so called on account of its hardness, αδαμας (αδαμαντος), 'the hardest of metals, steel and also diamond,' and मणि *maṇi*, a contracted form of अश्मन् *aśman*, 'a precious stone,' माणिक्य *māṇikya*, 'a ruby,' are to be connected with the Sans. अश्मन् *aśman*. फाणित *phāṇita* which is applied to a kind of crystalized sugar, seems to be a modification of मणि *maṇi*. In स्फटिक *sphaṭika* which contains an initial *s* added to the root to strengthen फ *ph*, the word मणि *maṇi* has undergone the same change as in फाणित *phāṇita*. Perhaps the names of some other gems also may be traced to the word अश्मंन् *aśman*. मरकत *marakata* and मकरत *makarata* and the corresponding Gr. σμαραγδος, Lat. *smaragdus*, 'a precious stone of green colour,' may be derived from अश्मंत *aśmanta* modified as अश्मंतक *aśmantaka* by the addition of the suffix क *ka*, then स्मनतक *smanataka* by the elision of the initial *a* and the insertion of *a* between the letter त *t* and the anusvāra preceding it; and at last स्मरकत *smarataka* by the change of न *n* into र् *r*. From this common form स्मरतक *smarataka* we can derive on the one side Sans. मरतक *marataka* by the elision of the initial स *s* and मरकत *marakata* and मकरत *makarata* by metathesis; and σμαραγδος[1] by the softening of क *k* and त *t* into γ and δ respectively. स्यमंतक *syamantaka*, a precious gem which was worn by Krishna, may be a corruption of अश्मंतक *aśmantaka* modified as समंतक *samantaka* and then स्यमंतक *syamantaka* by the addition of य *y* to स *s*. This gem was given to Satrājit by the God sun whose favour he sought by his piety; and it was

[1] Also μαραγδος and मरक्त *marakta*.

lost and came to the possession of Jambavan who was living in a den. Krishna discovered and recovered it from Jambavan whom he attacked and defeated in a duel. Jambavan knowing that Krishna was Vishnu himself gave him the gem and married his daughter Jambavati to him. Krishna returned the gem to the King Satrājit who presented it to Krishna and asked him to marry his daughter.

सत्राजित्तनयांतन्वींकृष्णायगतकिल्बिषः ॥

Satrājittanayām tanvīm krisṇāyagata kilbiṣah,

स्यमंतकेनमणिनास्वयमुद्यम्यदत्तवान् ॥

Syamamtakēna maṇinā svyamudyamya dattavān.

Bhāgavata, Sk. X, Ch. 16.

King Satrājit who was absolved from sin, having taken up his lean daughter Satyabhāmā with the precious gem syamantaka, presented them to Krishna.

ADDENDA ET CORRIGENDA.

PAGE.	LINE.	
		SCHEME OF TRANSLITERATION.
vi,	18,	for ∘ and *ṁ* read ∘ *ṁ* or *ṅ*, *ñ*, *ṇ*, *n*, and *m*.
		CONTENTS.
viii,		the last out two lines, for δεοτερος read δευτερος.
x,	20,	for Υπεριων read Ὑπερίων ; delete *suparvan*.
xi,	14,	for *dōṣa* read *dōṣā*.
,,	17,	for *diva* read *divā*.
,,	18,	
,,	19,	for *dēvata* read *dēvatā*.
xii,	9,	delete *kṣāmā*.
xiv,	5,	for ιφθμος read ιφθιμος.
xv,	14,	for *fecudus* read *fecundus*.
xvii,	7,	for ήβη read ἥβη.
,,	25,	for *yavan* read *yavana*.
xviii,	5,	ror ζενος read ξενος.
xxi,	28,	for Ατριδης read Ατρειδης.
xxii,	4,	for *formidōlosus* read *formidolōsus*.
xxiv,		last but one line, for γσγγυλος read γογγυλος.
xxv,	0,	for *gavinī* read *gavīni*.
xxvi,	10,	for *atharvyu* read *atharyu*.
,,	31,	for *ahaś* read *ahas*.
xxvii,	10,	for *ahas* read *agas*.
,,	27,	for αγγελλος read αγ,ελος.
xxviii,	19,	for *ḥasanti* read *hasantī*.
,,	24,	for *cātu* read *cāṭu*.
xxix,	9,	for *analogy* read *analysis*.
,,	28,	for *ārya* read *arya*.
xxx,	12,	for Αεγευς read Αιγευς.
xxxi,	4,	for *āṅghri* read *aṅghri*.

INTRODUCTION.

PAGE.	LINE.	
vi,	14,	for मर्त *marta* read मर्त्य *martya*.
xvii,	9,	for ಗೂಡುವಂಗೆ read ಕುರವಂಗೆ.
xxii,	22,	for *καιτη* read *χαιτη*.
xxx,	Note	for *Angellos* read *Angelos*
,,	,,	for Breareōs read Briareōs.
,,	,,	for *Hanvanu* read *Hauvanu*.

THE BOOK.

PAGE.	LINE.	
12,	18,	for δεoτερος read δευτερος.
,,	19,	for δεo read δυo.
15,	8,	for *hkuṣāmud* read *khuṣāmud*.
,,	,,	for *hkuṣ* read *khuṣ*.
,,	9,	for *hkuṣī* read *khuṣī*.
,,	25,	for oπας read ἀπας.
,,	26,	for *form* read *word*.
19,	23,	for *sagnus* read *sanguis*.
21, ,,	3, 4,	delete Sans. सुपर्वन् *suparvan*, 'a deity.'
32,	6,	for *the last Group* read *p.* 184.
36,	8,	for ρυνη read γυνη.
,, ,,	18, 19,	delete *and then* गणिका *gaṇikā*, '*a whore.*'
37,	20,	for νυχ read νυξ.
38,	16,	for विश्वंस्य read विश्वस्यं.
42,	12,	for वियस् *viyas* read वियत् *viyat*.
46,	20,	for Ιλυς read Ιλος.
48,	28,	after '*sky*' insert *vide p.* 167.
51,	6,	for ἥβος and ἥβη read ἥβος and ἥβη.
,,	15,	for Οεδιπους read Οιδιπους.
55,	4,	for *you brought* read *thou broughtst*.
59,	5,	after *Ikṣwākus* insert *out of spite*.
,,	16,	for *its* read *her*.
64,	17,	for Ιαπετον read Ιαπητον.
,,	20,	after *to* insert *deep-eddying Oceanus*.
,,	25,	for *commentators* read *commentator*.
67,	6,	for *development* read *counterpart*.

PAGE.	LINE.	
74,	15,	for 45 read 44.
„	27,	for *fecudus* read *fecundus*.
„	28,	for *foecudus* read *foecundus*.
76,	19,	for भर्त्संयति read भर्त्सयते.
„	20,	for *bhartsayati* read *bhartsayatē*.
81,	19,	for *ἤδις* read *ἤδυς*.
82,	last line,	for *p.* 96 read *pp.* 95 *and* 96.
83,	24,	at the end of the second paragraph *insert* Vide p. 76.
85,	8,	after *divas* insert *or* गभस्ति *gabhasti*.
88,	10,	for *κοττυς* read *κοττος*.
90,	1,	for पेंशंसा read पेशंसा
„	16,	for ते read तं.
94,	15,	after *and* insert शुच् *śuc and*.
98,	1,	for *leik* read *lic*.
„	3,	for *leik* read *lic*.
„	4,	for *leik* read *lic*.
„	8,	for *leik* read *lic*.
„	11,	for *leik* read *lic*.
„	last line,	for *αλγκιος* read *αλιγκιος*.
99,	21,	after *non-radical* insert *Vide pp.* 188, 189.
107,	17,	for *τκτον* read *τεκτον*.
„	22,	for *ετομο* read *ετυμο*.
108,	13,	for त्वना *tvanā* read त्वता *tvatā*.
„	29,	for 119-120 read 121-123.
109,	7,	after *robigon*, q. v., insert *from robus + tvan, by the elision of t and the change of v into g*.
114,	1,	for *ησσων* read *ἥσσων*.
„	2,	for *εσσων* read *ἕσσων*.
118,	30,	for *analogy of such wrong forms* read *wrong analogy of such forms*.
119,	3,	for एध् *ēdh* + ईस् *īs* + अन् *an* read एध् *edh* + इ *i* + यीस् *yīs* + अन् *an*.

PAGE.	LINE.	
120,	23,	for Θητυς read Τηθυς.
121,	24,	for Ατριδης read Ατρειδης.
123,	23,	for लेलिह्वतस् *lēlihvatas* read लिलिह्वांसस् *lilihvāṁsas*.
,,	24,	
124,	6,	for *formidōlosus* read *formidolōsus*.
125,	4,	for Ιππων read ʻΙππων.
128,	26,	for *βοηδιον* read *βοιδιον*.
132,	24,	for त्वत *tvata* read त्वन् *tvan*.
134,	17,	for स्यन *syana* read स्थन *sthana*.
136,	18,	for Ναιδες read Ναιαδες.
,,	20,	for Αδρυάδες read Αδρυαδες.
139,	21,	for (δες) read (οδες).
,,	31,	for Δαναιος read Δαναος.
145,	14,	for *glebus* read *globus*.
153,	20,	for आनि read आनी
155,	7,	for *canabum* read *cannabum*.
,,	26,	for *αιρ* and *αιθρα* read *αηρ* and *αιθηρ*.
159,	24,	for *τεφυκυια* read *πεφυκυια*.
,,	26,	for *εφυως* read *πεφυως*.
,,	27,	for *πεφῠυῖα* read *πεφῠυῖα*.
160,	10,	for *αιμη* read *αιμος*.
163,	18,	for अथर् *athar* read अथर *athara*.
172,	21,	for *ποτνεα* read *ποτνια*.
174,	3,	for एस *ēsa* read एष *ēsa*.
175,	11,	for *ρασσων* and *ραδιων* read *ῥασσων* and *ῥαδιων*.
182,	9,	after *stands* insert *directly*.
185,	2,	for *αγγελλος* read *αγγελος*.
186,	13,	
189,	last line but one,	for *identical* read *differently connected*.
191,	5,	for 164 read 146.
198,	29,	after *of* insert *the day of*.
204,	9,	for *ονυξ* (*κος*) read *ονυξ* (*χος*.)